MARC
for Library Use

Second Edition
Understanding Integrated USMARC

MARC
for Library Use

Second Edition
Understanding Integrated USMARC

Walt Crawford

G.K. HALL & CO.
BOSTON

MARC FOR LIBRARY USE, SECOND EDITION:
UNDERSTANDING INTEGRATED USMARC

WALT CRAWFORD

Copyright 1989
by Walt Crawford

Published by G.K. Hall & Co.
70 Lincoln Street
Boston, Massachusetts 02111

Printed on acid-free paper and
bound in the United States of America.

Library of Congress Cataloging-in-Publication Data

Crawford, Walt.
    MARC for library use.

    (Professional librarian series)
    Bibliography: p.
    Includes index.
    1. MARC System--United States--Format. 2. Libraries
--United States--Automation. I. Title. II. Series.
Z699.4.M2C72 1989   025.3'028'5   88-34724
ISBN 0-8161-1887-6
ISBN 0-8161-1889-2 (pbk.)

Contents

List of Figures   vii

List of Tables   x

Preface to the Second Edition   xiii

1   Introduction   1

2   USMARC Format for Bibliographic Data   21

3   The Structure of USMARC   31

4   Subfields and Indicators   45

5   Books   57

6   Serials   67

7   Maps   77

8   Scores   87

9   Sound Recordings   97

10   Visual Materials   111

11   Computer Files   123

12   Archival and Manuscripts Control   133

13   Authorities   147

14   Holdings   161

15   Linking in USMARC   171

16	Nonroman Text in USMARC	187
17	USMARC: A Brief History	203
18	Format Integration	221
19	Extending USMARC	243
20	MARC-Compatible Systems and Formats	263
21	Partially Compatible Formats and Systems	277
22	Library Use for USMARC	291

Appendix A: *USMARC: Underlying Principles*	307
Glossary	327
Selected Bibliography	343
Index	349
About the Author	359

List of Figures

Figure 1.1:   Catalog Card Replica 10
Figure 1.2:   Bibliographic Record, Tagged Display 11
Figure 1.3:   Compact Bibliographic Display 18
Figure 1.4:   Partial Bibliographic Display 18
Figure 1.5:   Labeled Display 19

Figure 2.1:   Page from *MFBD* 26
Figure 2.2:   Page from *UFBD* 27

Figure 3.1:   USMARC Record in Transmission Format 44

Figure 5.1:   Monographic Record, Formatted Display 61
Figure 5.2:   Monographic Record, Partial Tagged Display . . . 61
Figure 5.3:   Monographic Record, Bibliographic Display 63
Figure 5.4:   Monographic Record, Partial Tagged Display . . . 63
Figure 5.5:   Microform Record, Bibliographic Display 63
Figure 5.6:   Long Contents Note 65

Figure 6.1:   Serials Record, Bibliographic Display. 71
Figure 6.2:   Serials Record, Tagged Display. 72
Figure 6.3:   Serials Record, Bibliographic Display 73
Figure 6.4:   Serials Record, Partial Tagged Display 74
Figure 6.5:   Partial Serials Record, Bibliographic Display 76
Figure 6.6:   Serials Record, Selected Tags 76

Figure 7.1:   Map of Grenada (1) 81
Figure 7.2:   Map of Grenada (2) 82
Figure 7.3:   Map of Grenada (3) 82
Figure 7.4:   Map of Grenada (4) 82
Figure 7.5:   Map of Grenada (1), Tagged Record (Partial) . . . 83
Figure 7.6:   Map of Grenada (2), Partial Tagged Display . . . 84

Figure 7.7:   Map of Grenada (3), Partial Tagged Display 85
Figure 7.8:   Map of Grenada (Miss.), Partial Tagged Display . . 85

Figure 8.1:   Miniature Score, Bibliographic Display 91
Figure 8.2:   Miniature Score, Tagged Display 91
Figure 8.3:   Vocal Score, Bibliographic Display 93
Figure 8.4:   Vocal Score, Tagged Display 93
Figure 8.5:   Collection, Bibliographic Display 94
Figure 8.6:   Collection, Tagged Display 95

Figure 9.1:   *Graceland* (CD), Bibliographic Display 103
Figure 9.2:   *Graceland* (CD), Partial Tagged Display 103
Figure 9.3:   *Graceland* (LP), Bibliographic Display 104
Figure 9.4:   *Graceland* (LP), Partial Tagged Display 104
Figure 9.5:   Stravinsky, Bibliographic Display 107
Figure 9.6:   Stravinsky, Tagged Display (Part 1) 108
Figure 9.7:   Stravinsky, Tagged Display (Part 2) 109
Figure 9.8:   Spoken Word, Bibliographic Display 109
Figure 9.9:   Spoken Word, Tagged Display 110

Figure 10.1:   *Citizen Kane*, Bibliographic Display 116
Figure 10.2:   *Citizen Kane*, Tagged Display (Part 1) 116
Figure 10.3:   *Citizen Kane*, Tagged Display (Part 2) 117
Figure 10.4:   *Citizen Dull*, Bibliographic Display 118
Figure 10.5:   *Citizen Dull*, Partial Tagged Display 118
Figure 10.6:   Photograph, Bibliographic Display 119
Figure 10.7:   Photograph, Partial Tagged Display 120
Figure 10.8:   Poster, Bibliographic Display 121
Figure 10.9:   Poster, Partial Tagged Display 121

Figure 11.1:   Data File, Bibliographic Display 129
Figure 11.2:   Data File, Partial Tagged Display 130
Figure 11.3:   Software, Bibliographic Display 131
Figure 11.4:   Software, Tagged Display 131

Figure 12.1:   Weideman Papers, Bibliographic Display 141
Figure 12.2:   Weideman Papers, Partial Tagged Display 142
Figure 12.3:   Jamestown Railroad, Bibliographic Display . . .143
Figure 12.4:   Jamestown Railroad, Tagged Display 143
Figure 12.5:   Erie Canal Company, Bibliographic Display . . .144
Figure 12.6:   Erie Canal Company, Tagged Display 145

Figure 13.1:   Name Authority Record, Example 1 155

Figure 13.2:   Subject Authority Record, Example 1:
                Untraced Reference 155
Figure 13.3:   Subject Authority Record, Example 2 155
Figure 13.4:   Subject Authority Record, Example 3 156
Figure 13.5:   Subject Authority Record, Example 4 156
Figure 13.6:   Name Authority Record, Example 2 156
Figure 13.7:   Name Authority Record, Example 3 157

Figure 14.1:   Field 843, Examples 165
Figure 14.2:   Field 852, Examples 165
Figure 14.3:   Fields 853-865, Examples 166

Figure 15.1:   MARC 541 and 583 Fields 175
Figure 15.2:   Grouped Display of 15.1 Contents 175
Figure 15.3:   Serial Article Analytic, Bibliographic Display . . .182
Figure 15.4:   Serial Article Analytic, Tagged Display 182
Figure 15.5:   Romney Papers, Partial Bibliographic Display . . .183
Figure 15.6:   Romney Papers, Partial Tagged Display 183
Figure 15.7:   M.L. King Papers, Bibliographic Display 184
Figure 15.8:   M.L. King Papers, Partial Tagged Display 184

Figure 16.1:   Schematic Representation of CJK Record 189
Figure 16.2:   RLIN Editing Screen for CJK (1) 191
Figure 16.3:   Tagged CJK Record (1) 192
Figure 16.4:   Long CJK Display for CJK (1) 193
Figure 16.5:   Long Roman Display for CJK (1) 194
Figure 16.6:   Tagged CJK Record (2) 196
Figure 16.7:   Long Display, CJK (2) 197
Figure 16.8:   Tagged Hebrew Record 198
Figure 16.9:   Long Display, Hebrew Record 199
Figure 16.10:   Tagged Cyrillic/Hebrew/Yiddish Record 200
Figure 16.11:   Long Display, Cyrillic/Hebrew/Yiddish 201

Figure 19.1:   Bilingual Record, Online Form 258
Figure 19.2:   Bilingual Record, LCF Form 258

Figure 20.1:   Structural Transform 273

List of Tables

Table 2.1:	Bibliographic Fields Subject to Authority Control	. 23
Table 2.2:	Common Variable Control Fields	24
Table 2.3:	Common 0xx Variable Fields	24
Table 2.4:	Common Bibliographic Fields: 2xx-8xx	25

Table 3.1:	MARC Leader as defined by Z39.2-1985	32
Table 3.2:	MARC Directory Structure as Defined by Z39.2-1985	33

Table 4.1:	Field 533 Indicators and Subfields	45
Table 4.2:	Field 651 Indicators and Subfields	46
Table 4.3:	Nonfiling Characters Indicators	47
Table 4.4:	Notes and Added Entries Control	48
Table 4.5:	Display Constant Control	48
Table 4.6:	Source of Information or Authority File	49
Table 4.7:	Type of Contents Indicators	49
Table 4.8:	Field 100, Subfields and Examples	52
Table 4.9:	Other Subfields for Personal Name Fields	53
Table 4.10:	Fields 111 and 130	54
Table 4.11:	Consistently Defined Subfields	55

Table 5.1:	Specific 008-006 Codes for Monographs	58
Table 5.2:	Books: Commonly Used Fields, 010-490	59
Table 5.3:	Books: Commonly Used Fields, 500-886	60

Table 6.1:	Serials-specific 008 and 006 Values	68
Table 6.2:	Serials: Commonly Used Fields, 010-035	68
Table 6.3:	Serials: Commonly Used Fields, 040-515	69
Table 6.4:	Serials: Commonly Used Fields, 520-880	70

Table 7.1:	Maps-specific 008 and 006 Values	78
Table 7.2:	Maps: Commonly Used Fields, 007-250	78

Table 7.3:   Maps: Commonly Used Fields, 255-830 79
Table 7.4:   Field 034 80
Table 7.5:   Field 255 80

Table 8.1:   Specific 008-006 Codes for Music 87
Table 8.2:   Scores: Commonly Used Fields, 010-048 88
Table 8.3:   Scores: Commonly Used Fields, 050-830 89

Table 9.1:   Recordings: Commonly Used Fields, 007-490 . . . 98
Table 9.2:   Recordings: Commonly Used Fields, 500-830 . . . 99
Table 9.3:   Field 007 for Sound Recordings 102

Table 10.1:   Specific 008-006 Codes for Visual Materials 112
Table 10.2:   Visual Materials: Commonly Used Fields, 007-521 .113
Table 10.3:   Visual Materials: Commonly Used Fields, 600-840 .114

Table 11.1:   Specific 008-006 Codes for Computer Files 125
Table 11.2:   Computer Files: Commonly Used Fields, 020-565 . .126
Table 11.3:   Computer Files: Commonly Used Fields, 567-830 . .127

Table 12.1:   AMC: Commonly Used Fields, 007-584 139
Table 12.2:   AMC: Commonly Used Fields, 600-851 140

Table 13.1:   Authorities Format, 001-008 151
Table 13.2:   Authorities Format, Fields 010-083 152
Table 13.3:   Authorities Format, Fields 100-551 153
Table 13.4:   Authorities Format, Fields 640-682 154

Table 14.1:   Holdings Format, Fields 001-035 163
Table 14.2:   Holdings Format, Fields 583-868 164
Table 14.3:   Subfields for Field 853 167

Table 15.1:   Linking Techniques Noted Elsewhere 172
Table 15.2:   Linking Techniques Discussed Below 173
Table 15.3:   Field 773 Subfields 181

Table 17.1:   MARC Use in 1972 211

Table 18.1:   Common Elements of Field 008 232
Table 18.2:   Fields Extended Across Formats (1) 233
Table 18.3:   Fields Extended Across Formats (2) 234
Table 18.4:   Fields Extended Across Formats (3) 235
Table 18.5:   Fields Extended Across Formats (4) 236
Table 18.6:   Fields Made Obsolete 237
Table 18.7:   Content Designation Deleted from USMARC . . .238

Table 19.1:   OCLC Field 049, Subfields and Example 245
Table 19.2:   OCLC Extended Fields 019, 090-099 246
Table 19.3:   OCLC Extensions, Fields 590-949 247
Table 19.4:   OCLC Extensions for National Libraries 249
Table 19.5:   RLIN Field 930 251
Table 19.6:   RLIN Call Number and Holdings Fields 252
Table 19.7:   RLIN Acquisitions Fields 254
Table 19.8:   Utlas Field 090 256
Table 19.9:   Other Utlas Fields for Local Data 257
Table 19.10:   Utlas PRECIS Fields 257
Table 19.11:   Utlas Bilingual Fields (1) 259
Table 19.12:   Utlas Bilingual Fields (2) 260
Table 19.13:   Utlas "Unknown" Fields 261
Table 19.14:   Miscellaneous Utlas Extensions 261

Preface to the Second Edition

MARC *for Library Use* was born out of desperation. As manager of Product Batch and as an RLG liaison to MARBI, I found myself trying to explain fine points of the MARC formats—over the phone—to people who lacked a basic understanding of the formats. After two years of that, I set out to locate a book that I could recommend to these people. A search of the RLIN database showed nothing that seemed likely to fill the need; extended checks of publishers' catalogs and discussion with MARBI colleagues confirmed my sense that no such book existed.

That being the case, the only solution was to convince somebody to write one. Somewhere along the way that turned into a joint venture: a book on MARC itself and on programming techniques for MARC. I would write the section on programming techniques if someone else wrote the section on the formats. All of the people I approached with this idea had the good sense to turn down the work involved in such a book. Finally, I started in on the first section myself. That section turned into the entire book.

Knowledge Industry Publications took a chance on a book with an uncertain market. Friends, colleagues, and editors helped me to refine a very rough first draft into something publishable. And here we are, five years later.

Format Integration and the Second Edition

MARC for Library Use served my primary purpose of providing a basic introduction to MARC. The book also had a secondary political motivation—to promote the idea of format integration. I thought format integration would serve the library community well. RLG staff began preparing proposals for integration in 1984, and we have helped to refine the proposals in the intervening years.

Shortly after G.K. Hall purchased the Professional Librarian series, the series editor asked whether the time was ripe for a revised edition of *MARC for Library Use*. I responded that the most likely basis for such a revision would be the integration of the MARC formats. In the meantime my position at RLG changed and, after serving as a voting member of MARBI for two years, I declined reappointment for the 1987-1989 term. As a result, and because of other ALA commitments, I was absent from the two MARBI sessions (Midwinter 1988 and Annual 1988) that completed work on format integration. To some extent, I have moved from active participant to interested observer. I trust that the slightly more disinterested view of MARC that may result will continue to serve readers well.

UNIMARC and other non-U.S. MARC Formats

A number of readers and critics suggested that this edition should cover UNIMARC and other MARC formats such as UKMARC. It is certainly the case that MARC has more international implications now than in the past and that use of MARC formats worldwide will continue to grow.

After some analysis and investigation, I came to the conclusion that a worthwhile treatment of MARC formats beyond USMARC would require a book at least as large as this one. Ideally, such a treatment should be prepared by an author with experience in using such formats. Since I lack the latter, and since even a sketchy treatment would add substantially to the length of this book, I decided not to pursue the matter. My apologies to those who expected or hoped to see non-U.S. MARC formats included in *MARC for Library Use*.

Acknowledgments

The following acknowledgments from the first edition should be repeated here:

My wife, Linda Driver, has tolerated my rantings about MARC ever since we've been married; she's a professional librarian, which helps. Her advice on various library matters is, as always, invaluable; her support for my efforts was critical to their completion.

Many people looked at various drafts, and a few put forth extraordinary effort. Glee Harrah Cady, assistant director for Applications Development at RLG (and my boss), was an early supporter and a tough editor; her suggestions in October 1983 kept the first manuscript from foundering, and her editing and advice have helped the book in ways too numerous to mention. Henriette Avram and others at the Library of Congress provided detailed, careful comments on the manuscript, putting their considerable skills and substantial time into their review. John Attig at Pennsylvania State University provided detailed, insightful comments in his detailed review of the manuscript. Kathleen Bales at RLG provided her insights from teaching library school courses, checked my examples for cataloging accuracy, and helped to develop the final organization of the book.

John Wescoat, Alan Tucker, and Ed Glazier of RLG all provided important early reviews; Charles Stewart and Joan Aliprand of RLG also gave me helpful review comments, as did Richard Greene of OCLC and Gwen Miles Culp of Washington Library Network. Those two, along with Gary McCone of the Library of Congress, and Jack Cain at Utlas, also helped by providing current figures for their institutions.

Acknowledgments for the Second Edition

My special thanks to those who reviewed *MARC for Library Use* in the library literature. I have studied the reviews in preparation for this edition. While I may not have taken all of the advice, and while this edition will surely not satisfy all the wishes of all the reviewers, I did learn from your insights.

Kathleen Bales, Ed Glazier, and Lennie Stovel reviewed the rough draft of this edition and provided insightful comments. Karen Smith Yoshimura and John Eilts helped me locate appropriate examples of Chinese, Hebrew, and Cyrillic cataloging and arranged to produce the printouts used for the figures in chapter 16. Syd Jones of Utlas provided information on Utlas MARC extensions for chapter 19. Finally, Carol Chin at G.K. Hall was both helpful and patient. This is the first time I've revised a published book. At least at the outset, it seemed more threatening than writing one from scratch.

1

Introduction

$\mathbf{M}$any librarians create and use MARC records without ever understanding the nature of MARC itself. While no such understanding is needed for cataloging, librarians need to know more about MARC as library uses of computers expand. A thorough understanding of MARC will help when dealing with vendors of services, when considering online catalogs and other automated systems, and when considering possible local development.

MARC is the single most important factor in the growth of library automation in the United States and other countries. USMARC forms the basis for storing bibliographic information in a consistent form, sharing that information, and manipulating it by computer. This book is designed to show what MARC (specifically USMARC) is, how it works, and how it is changing. The book is also designed to help in dealing with library automation as it relates to USMARC.

This book does *not* attempt to provide a complete technical overview of USMARC or rules for cataloging using the USMARC format. USMARC content designation is thoroughly documented in the *USMARC Format for Bibliographic Data Including Guidelines for Content Designation* (henceforth *UFBD*); in *USMARC Format for Authority Data* and *USMARC Format for Holdings Data*; and in field guides issued by shared cataloging services such as OCLC, RLIN, WLN, and Utlas. Library Cataloging information is available from many sources, including *AACR2* and a variety of manuals and guides interpreting the rules.

What Are MARC and USMARC?

MARC is an acronym derived from **MA**chine-**R**eadable **C**ataloging. Within the United States the terms MARC, LC MARC, and USMARC are generally interchangeable, but the terms do have slightly different meanings:

- *MARC* is a generic term applied to the universe of MARC formats, including UKMARC, CAN/MARC, InterMARC, and so on;
- *LC MARC* refers to the set of options and content designation called "MARC II;"
- *USMARC* is a new name for LC MARC, introduced in the *Underlying Principles* document in 1983.[1]

There is no sharp distinction in content between LC MARC and USMARC. The terms USMARC or MARC are also applied to MARC extensions—formats such as OCLC MARC and RLIN MARC that include data in addition to USMARC data elements.

Informally, MARC and USMARC also identify a range of standards and services:

- the MARC Editorial Office of the Library of Congress and the MARC Distribution Services;
- *USMARC Format for Bibliographic Data Including Guidelines for Content Designation* and *USMARC Format for Authority Data,* standard sets of names for the elements (fields and subfields) of MARC records, used at LC, by users of the major bibliographic

---

1   *The USMARC Formats: Underlying Principles* was first published in *LC Information Bulletin* (May 9, 1983).

services (OCLC, RLIN, Utlas, and WLN) and by MARC subscribers;

- the structure that supports USMARC and other MARC formats
  and provides a standard method of organizing data for communication and storage;[2]
- tens of millions of bibliographic records for books, films, maps,
  serials, sound recordings, computer files, archival material,
  scores, and other materials, and several million authority records, created by LC and thousands of other libraries.

MARC is a set of standards for identifying, storing and communicating cataloging information. MARC tags are standard ways to
identify elements of a bibliographic record such as title, edition and
subject so that those elements can be manipulated by computers and
used by others. MARC structure is a standard way to communicate
bibliographic information between users and between computers.
By establishing a common vocabulary and representation, MARC
makes shared cataloging easier, more powerful, and more flexible.

Bibliographic Formats

USMARC for bibliographic data is a bibliographic format. Although it is by far the most commonly used bibliographic format for
computer processing within the United States, it is by no means the
only current or possible bibliographic format.

A bibliographic format is simply a predefined way of recording
bibliographic information. A bibliographic format could be as simple
as the one below.

---

2   The formal record structure underlying MARC is technically not MARC; it is
established as ANSI Z39.2. For the purposes of this book, the choices made for
USMARC within ANSI Z39.2 are called the MARC structure.

Author:	[25 characters]
Title:	[51 characters]
Date:	[4 characters]

This format could be used to store rather minimal bibliographic information on a punched card to produce simple lists; formats no more complicated were widely used in the 1960s.

The format above substantially restricts not only the *quantity* of information that can be entered, but also the *types* of information. It restricts bibliographic description to an author, a title, and a date.

A more sophisticated microcomputer database might have variable-length fields for an author, a title, a publisher, a date, and a subject. This would also be a bibliographic format, one that makes several important statements about the data to be recorded: there is only one author, there is only one subject, and notes and physical description are of no importance.

Every bibliographic format reflects a view of significant bibliographic data; USMARC is no exception. In the case of USMARC the view emphasizes detailed description of a single entity, with relatively less emphasis on links to other bibliographic entities. A different bibliographic format might, for example, stress relatively complete and accessible entries for chapters, journal articles, and collections, emphasizing links and relationships with less emphasis on the individual work.

USMARC offers a sophisticated, complex bibliographic format that has done much to spread library automation in the United States. It is not the only useful bibliographic format, and indeed it is not the preferable bibliographic format for every application. It is, however, the most important format currently in use.

What Good Is MARC?

Assignment of MARC tags and subfield codes adds some cost to original cataloging. Assignment of coded values can be a significant added cost. Why bother?

Tags and subfield codes provide a context for cataloging. They provide a consistent shorthand notation, telling a computer how to deal with the cataloging and enabling other catalogers to use it more easily. Additionally, tags and subfields make possible computer-based systems that provide more access and flexibility than card catalogs.

MARC records communicate bibliographic information with more precision and flexibility than printed catalog cards. The Library of Congress uses MARC to communicate its prepublication and final cataloging to thousands of other libraries. Thousands of libraries use MARC to share original cataloging. The shared cataloging services have permanently changed the course of library cataloging. Without USMARC these services could not have developed and flourished as they have, nor could users treat records from the services consistently.

MARC also provides the flexibility needed for individual libraries. Libraries can add information to MARC records, define fields for local use, and rearrange existing information without retyping catalog cards and risking transcription error. USMARC provides the vocabulary and structure to produce catalog cards and control online catalog access from a single set of information. MARC increases choices for access and display while retaining the economies of shared cataloging.

Changing Nature of the Formats

The USMARC formats are more than twenty years old and are continually evolving. MARC and MARC II have long been known as LC MARC, since the Library of Congress (LC) publishes the MARC formats and takes primary responsibility for their development and maintenance. LC MARC was originally developed so that LC could distribute its cataloging in machine-readable form, and had a number of areas suited only to LC's needs.

The times have changed. The Library of Congress is the largest single creator of cataloging in the United States, but is no longer the only major source of cataloging data. A deliberate effort, supported by the Library of Congress, has diminished the LC bias of MARC and moved to the format now known as USMARC.

USMARC for bibliographic data is evolving to support new forms of material and new forms of control. The format has been separated from the cataloging code; USMARC supports *AACR2* cataloging but does not restrict cataloging to one set of rules. USMARC now provides for control of archival materials, and a USMARC format for holdings information has been created and is being implemented. USMARC has expanded to provide for cataloging of computer files and to provide better support for visual materials such as prints, photographs, paintings, and sculpture.

Last, but certainly not least, the seven USMARC formats for bibliographic data are being integrated into a single format. Within the single bibliographic format fields may be used as appropriate for a given item, not based strictly on their existence within the MARC format for a given form of material. Chapter 18 describes the history and effect of format integration, probably the largest development in USMARC for the latter half of the 1980s.

Changing Uses of the Formats

LC MARC was initially a vehicle to distribute records from a single source. Since then MARC has become a vehicle to communicate records between systems, to store and manipulate records within national bibliographic services and local libraries, and to communicate records from other libraries to the Library of Congress.

The use of MARC for communications is fundamental to any professionally designed library automation system, but MARC became more than a communications format shortly after it was designed. Libraries have used MARC formats in batch processing for at least fifteen years. MARC has proven to be efficient, flexible, and highly maintainable for such use. Computers are getting cheaper and more powerful; their uses in libraries are growing and changing. More libraries will use MARC as a processing format in commercial and local systems. As libraries link and combine commercial systems and add local extensions, the commonality of MARC will be fundamental to the complex new systems.

Organization

While this book is designed primarily to be read from beginning to end, you may wish to concentrate on particular chapters for special needs:

- Structural aspects of USMARC and related formats, first introduced in the remainder of this chapter, are examined in chapters 2-4, chapters 13-16, and chapters 18-21.
- Historical considerations make up chapters 17 and 18, with some historical notes in other chapters.
- Most complete examples of USMARC bibliographic records are in this chapter and in chapters 5-12, 15, and 16.
- Format extensions, non-MARC formats, and questions of compatibility appear in chapters 13-14 and 19-21.

Definitions

Most special terms in this book are defined as they appear, but a few terms are so basic that they need to be defined now.

Content designation: The codes and conventions that identify data elements and support their manipulation. For MARC these are tags, indicators, and subfield codes.

Fields: Groups of one or more data elements defined and manipulated as a unit, such as the 245 (Title) and 001 (Record number). Each field is identified by a tag.

Indicators: Two characters at the beginning of each field except for control fields. Indicators provide additional information about the field.

Subfields: Data elements within fields. Each subfield is identified by a *subfield code,* which is composed of a delimiter—shown as "‡" in this book—and a single character.

Tags: Labels for fields. For example "245" is the tag for the Title field.

Shared cataloging services: Term used in this book to refer to OCLC, RLIN, Utlas, and WLN. These four agencies are sometimes called "bibliographic utilities" or "online networks."

MARBI: An ALA interdivisional committee: the American Library Association Resources & Technical Services Division / Library & Information Technology Association / Reference & Adult Services Division Committee on Representation in Machine Readable Form of Bibliographic Information.

USMARC advisory group: A group composed of MARBI, liaisons from LC, the National Library of Medicine, the National Agricultural Library, the National Library of Canada, the shared cataloging services, RTSD's Committee on Cataloging: Description and Access (CC: DA), the Music Library Association, the Society of American Archivists (SAA), and other interested parties. The USMARC advisory group advises the Library of Congress on additions and changes to the USMARC formats.

Examples and Figures

Several USMARC records are used in this book to illustrate use of the MARC formats. With certain exceptions these records were derived from actual cataloging records available on RLIN. Records used reflect a variety of cataloging sources and practices: some are pre-*AACR2*, some use other cataloging conventions, and several are non-LC cataloging.

Please note that the records appearing in figures illustrate actual use of USMARC, and are *not* intended to show correct or desirable cataloging practice. These records may include cataloging errors and should not be used as examples of correct practice.

Two forms of record display are commonly used in figures: a traditional formatted display similar to that used for catalog cards and some online catalogs, and a tagged display showing each US-MARC tag, subfield, and indicator. Four special characters are used in some cases for clarity:

"_" is an explicit blank or space.

"‡" is the subfield delimiter.

"¶" is the field terminator, as used in OCLC.

"§" is the record terminator.

The subfield delimiter "‡" is used consistently throughout figures and text, usually followed by a code, as in ‡*a* ("Subfield a"). The explicit blank "_" is used only where presence or absence of a blank is ambiguous. The field terminator "¶" is used throughout tagged displays. The record terminator "§" is used rarely except here and in chapter 3. The subfield delimiter, field terminator, and record terminator are fully explained in chapter 3.

USMARC documentation uses the convention that positions within a record or field begin at 0, not 1: for example, the first position of the leader is Leader/0, and the sixth is Leader/5. That convention is used throughout this book.

In those figures where both labels and MARC data appear, the labels appear in *italics* and MARC data appears in upright type. Within text MARC data from examples appears in *italics*.

From Catalog Card to USMARC

Crawford, Walt.
   Bibliographic displays in the online catalog / by Walt Crawford, with Lennie Stovel and Kathleen Bales. -- White Plains, NY : Knowledge Industry Publications, c1986.
   vi, 359 p. : 28 cm. -- (Professional librarian series)
   Includes index.
   ISBN 0-86729-198-2 (soft) : $30.00
   1. Catalogs, On-line. 2. On-line bibliographic searching. 3. Information display systems--Library applications. 4. Information display systems--Formatting. 5. Machine-readable bibliographic data. I. Stovel, Lennie. II. Bales, Kathleen. III. Title. IV. Series.

Figure 1.1: Catalog Card Replica

The traditional means of storing bibliographic information is a catalog card. Figure 1.1 is a replica of a catalog card. The library catalog card is a remarkable medium, providing a large amount of information in a small amount of space. As designers of online catalogs have found, it is difficult to replace all the functions of a card catalog. Two strengths of catalog cards are their standard structure and the flexibility of that structure. For example the tracings paragraph has a known meaning for librarians and sophisticated users, but one book may have no tracings at all while another may have dozens.

```
Ldr        00971nam__2200277_a_4500
001        RLINCRLG86-B27¶
005        19880728165537.0¶
008        861014s1986___nyu_____00110_eng__¶
010    __  ‡a___86015348_¶
020    __  ‡a0867291982 (soft) :‡c$30.00¶
040    __  ‡dCStRLIN¶
050    00  ‡aZ699.3‡b.C69 1986¶
082    00  ‡a025.3/028/5‡219¶
100    10  ‡aCrawford, Walt.¶
245    10  ‡aBibliographic displays in the online catalog /‡cby Walt Crawford,
with Lennie Stovel and Kathleen Bales.¶
260    0_  ‡aWhite Plains, NY :‡bKnowledge Industry Publications,‡cc1986.¶
300    __  ‡avi, 359 p. :‡c 28 cm.¶
440    _0  ‡aProfessional librarian series¶
500    __  ‡aIncludes index.¶
650    _0  ‡aCatalogs, On-line.¶
650    _0  ‡aOn-line bibliographic searching.¶
650    _0  ‡aInformation display systems‡xLibrary applications.¶
650    _0  ‡aInformation display systems‡xFormatting.¶
650    _0  ‡aMachine-readable bibliographic data.¶
700    10  ‡aStovel, Lennie.¶
700    10  ‡aBales, Kathleen.§
```

Figure 1.2: Bibliographic Record, Tagged Display

A computer-based cataloging record should carry at least as much information as a catalog card; otherwise it is a step backward. MARC II was designed to provide the extreme flexibility required for cataloging without losing reasonable computer efficiency. A MARC record contains all the information on a catalog card, and some additional information as well. Figure 1.2 is a tagged display for the USMARC record used to produce Figure 1.1.

Tagged displays show the content designation of USMARC and include some of the structural elements of USMARC (indicators, subfields, and fields). Other structural elements of USMARC do not usually appear as such in online usage, but are vital to communication and some forms of processing; these elements include the directory and portions of the leader, discussed in chapter 3. You may never see a complete leader or a directory online, but those elements make USMARC processing efficient and flexible.

USMARC Bibliographic Example, Element by Element

T he discussion that follows examines each element of the record (except for the leader, discussed in chapter 3) as it appears in the tagged display of Figure 1.2. All quoted passages that follow are from *UFBD*.

Variable Control Fields

Fields with tags beginning *00* contain data that may be required to process the bibliographic record. These fields do not include indicators or subfield codes. Data elements begin in a fixed location relative to the beginning of the field. This record includes three variable control fields: 001, 005, and 008.

---

001 Control number
RLINCRLG86-B27¶

Field 001 is mandatory in all MARC records and must be unique within the system that originates the record. Field 001 does not have a fixed length or fixed pattern.

---

005 Date and Time of Latest Transaction
19880728165537.0¶

The latest transaction took place on July 28, 1988 (*19880728*) at 4:55 p.m. (and 37.0 seconds) (*165537.0*). The contents follow ANSI standards: X3.30 for calendar date, X3.43 for local time.

Eventually all communicated MARC records should include field 005. It allows a receiving agency to do two things unambiguously:

- Determine whether a received record is, in fact, a more current version than the record already in place
- If a tape or transmitted file contains more than one copy of a record, determine which copy is the latest.

The former capability is critical for shared authorities work and useful for bibliographic work. The latter is important for those receiving transaction tapes from shared cataloging services or sending tapes to those services: any institution receiving tapes with the expectation of updating a database will find field 005 important. All systems known to provide field 005 generate the field automatically.

Field 008: Fixed Length Data Elements

Field 008 has different meanings depending on the type of material. For monographs field 008 contains nineteen different codes. These are described below in the order in which they appear in the field.

```
008/00: Date entered on file:  821119
008/06: Type of date/Publication status:  s
008/07: Date 1:  1982
008/11: Date 2: ____
008/15: Place of publication, production or execution:    nyu
```

The record first appeared on November 19, 1982. The date in Date 1 is a single known or probable date. The book was published in New York. These five elements appear in *all* bibliographic 008 fields regardless of material type.

```
008/18: Illustrations: ____
008/22: Target audience: _
008/23: Form of item: _
008/24: Nature of contents: ____
008/28: Government publication: _
```

There are no illustrations. (Although the book in question is almost entirely tables and figures, it does not have illustrations as defined in *AACR2* Rule 2.5C.) There is no stated target audience and the book is not a reproduction or other special form. Up to four codes can be used to specify certain types of material used frequently for reference purposes; none of the codes applied to this book. The book is not a government publication.

> *008/29: Conference publication:* 0
> *008/30: Festschrift:* 0
> *008/31: Index:* 1
> *008/32: Main entry in body of entry:* 1
> *008/33: Fiction:* 0
> *008/34: Biography* _

This book is not a conference publication or festschrift. It does include an index to its own contents, and the main entry also appears in the body of the entry. The work is nonfiction and does not contain biographical material.

> *008/35: Language:* eng
> *008/38: Modified record:* _
> *008/39: Cataloging source:* _

The predominant language of the book is English. The MARC record contains the same information that would be found in manual cataloging copy; it has not been modified to fit into MARC. The book was cataloged by the Library of Congress. These three elements also appear in all 008 fields for bibliographic records.

Variable Data Fields

All of the remaining fields in the record contain indicators and subfield codes.

> *010 LC Control Number*
> _‡a___86015348_¶

Subfield ‡a contains the current LC control number (LCCN). The two indicators are always blank. This number could be displayed as *86-15348*.

> 020 *International Standard Book Number (ISBN)*
> __‡a0867291982 (soft):‡c$30.00¶

The two indicators for field 020 are always blank. The field can contain three subfields: ‡a, *International Standard Book Number* (and binding information); ‡c, *Terms of availability*; and ‡z, *Cancelled or invalid ISBN*.[3] ISBNs are stored without hyphens; for most (but not all) ISBNs hyphens can be supplied on printed products by computer algorithm. In this case the data would appear on a catalog card as *ISBN 0-86729-198-2.*

> 040 *Cataloging Source*
> __‡dCStRLIN¶

As with field 020, the two indicators for field 040 are not defined and are always blank. Field 040 can contain five subfields: ‡a, *Original cataloging agency*; ‡b, *Language of cataloging*; ‡c, *Transcribing agency*; ‡d, *Modifying agency*; and ‡e, *Descriptive conventions.*

This record was cataloged and transcribed by the Library of Congress and modified either by RLG catalogers or through computer processing when it was loaded into RLIN (*CStRLIN*).

> 050 *Library of Congress Call Number*
> 00‡aZ699.3‡b.C69 1986¶

The first indicator says whether LC has the item (*0* indicates that the item is in LC); the second indicator says whether the call number was actually assigned by LC (*0*) or by some other agency (*4*).

Subfield ‡a contains the class number *Z699.3*; ‡b contains the item number *.C69 1986.*

---

3   Like almost every other USMARC field, field 020 can also contain ‡6, *Linkage.* This subfield—currently used only for nonroman cataloging—is generally not mentioned in discussions of fields. See chapter 16 for its use.

---

082 Dewey Decimal Call Number
00‡a025.3/028/5‡219¶

The first indicator states the type of edition used; *0* stands for the full edition. The second indicator has the same values as for 050.

Subfield ‡a contains the *Dewey number*. Subfield ‡2 states the source of the number, in this case the edition of Dewey (edition 19).

---

100 Main Entry—Personal Name
10‡aCrawford, Walt.¶

Field 100 begins the main portion of the bibliographic description. Indicator 1 is *1*: the name includes a single surname. This information is useful in sorting entries and in preparing index entries. Indicator 2 is *0*: main entry/subject relationship is irrelevant. A system would not be expected to generate a subject entry from the contents of field 100. Subfield ‡a is the *Personal name*. The field has many other subfields.

---

245 Title Statement
10‡aBibliographic displays in the online catalog /‡cby Walt Crawford, with Lennie Stovel and Kathleen Bales.¶

Indicator 1 is *1*: a title added entry should be generated from this field. Indicator 2 is *0*: there are no nonfiling characters at the beginning of the first subfield. Subfield ‡a is the title or title proper; ‡c is the statement of responsibility. Because of the first indicator, this field generates the tracing shown as "III. Title" in Figure 1.1 and would also generate an added entry under the title (in cases where added entries are generated).

---

260 Publication, Distribution, etc. (Imprint)
0_‡aWhite Plains, NY :‡bKnowledge Industry Publications,‡cc1986.¶

Indicator 1 is *0*: the name of the publisher, distributor, etc., is present. The second indicator is undefined. Subfields ‡a, ‡b, and ‡c give the *Place, name,* and *date* of publication, distribution, etc., respectively. The *c* preceding *1986* indicates that it is a copyright date.

```
300  Physical Description
__‡avi, 359 p. :‡c28 cm.¶
```

Neither indicator is defined. Subfield ‡a gives *Extent,* ‡c *Dimensions.*

```
440  Series Statement/Added Entry—Title
_0‡aProfessional librarian series¶
```

This field contains a series statement consisting of a series title in catalog-entry form. The field may be used to generate a series tracing identical to the data in this field; in this case, the tracing *IV. Series.* and the added entry *Professional librarian series.*

The first indicator is undefined; the second gives the number of nonfiling characters. Subfield ‡a contains the series *title.*

```
500  General Note
__‡aIncludes index.¶
```

The indicators are undefined. This field may contain any information for which a specialized note has not been defined. Theoretically this particular note *Includes index* could be generated for display from field 008/31, *Index;* in practice, such automatic generation rarely takes place.

```
650  Subject Added Entry—Topical Term
```

The Library of Congress assigned five subject headings for this book. Indicator 1 specifies the level of the subject heading. No information on level was provided in this record. Indicator 2 specifies the source of the subject heading. In these cases *0* identifies a Library of

Congress subject heading (LCSH). Subfield ‡a contains the *Topical term or geographic name used as entry element*. Subfield ‡x in three of the headings contains a *General subdivision*. Subject headings may also have *Chronological subdivisions* (‡y) and *Geographic subdivisions* (‡z).

---

700 *Added Entry—Personal Name*

Field 700 has the same first indicator meaning and subfield structure as field 100; in this record the same first indicator and subfield appear in both 700 fields.

Formatted Displays from USMARC Records

Figure 1.1 shows the most common form of formatted display—a complete main entry display. When bibliographic data is stored in USMARC form, displays can be varied to meet different needs. Three examples of possible formatted displays are shown in Figures 1.3 through 1.5.

Crawford, Walt. BIBLIOGRAPHIC DISPLAYS IN THE ONLINE CATALOG. 1986.

Figure 1.3: Compact Bibliographic Display

Crawford, Walt.
  Bibliographic displays in the online catalog / by Walt Crawford, with Lennie Stovel and Kathleen Bales. -- White Plains, NY : Knowledge Industry Publications, c1986.
  vi, 359 p. : 28 cm. -- (Professional librarian series)

Z699.3.C69 1986

Figure 1.4: Partial Bibliographic Display

TITLE:	Bibliographic displays in the online catalog / by Walt Crawford, with Lennie Stovel and Kathleen Bales
PUBLISHED:	White Plains, N.Y. : Knowledge Industry Publications, c1986.
MATERIAL:	vi, 359 p. : 28 cm.
NAMES:	Crawford, Walt.
	Stovel, Lennie.
	Bales, Kathleen
SUBJECTS:	Catalogs, On-line.
	On-line bibliographic searching.
	Information display systems—Library applications.
	Information display systems—Formatting.
	Machine-readable bibliographic data.
SERIES:	Professional librarian series

Figure 1.5: Labeled Display

2

USMARC Format for Bibliographic Data

MARC II designers originally had in mind a single format for all bibliographic material.[1] The work required to build such a comprehensive set of content designation, however, would have delayed the appearance of the format considerably. As has often been the case, pragmatism prevailed over elegance. When MARC was first developed it appeared as a format for books.[2] Later, a somewhat similar format was developed for serials. Other formats were added, until by 1976 (with publication of the MARC music format) there were six MARC formats for bibliographic information.

In 1980 the separate format publications were replaced by the *MARC Formats for Bibliographic Data*, generally called *MFBD* in this book.[3] The Library of Congress replaced *MFBD* with *UFBD*, the *USMARC Format for Bibliographic Data Including Guidelines for Content Designation*, in 1988. As the 1980s come to a close, *UFBD* will docu-

---

1   Henriette D. Avram, *MARC, Its History and Implications* (Washington, D.C.: Library of Congress, 1975).

2   Library of Congress, Automated Systems Office, *Books: A MARC Format* (Washington, D.C.: Library of Congress, 1970).

3   Library of Congress, Automated Systems Office, *MARC Formats for Bibliographic Data* (Washington, D.C.: Library of Congress, 1980).

ment the integration of the bibliographic formats into a unified whole.

Chapter 18 discusses the history and significance of format integration, and includes tables of fields now common to all bibliographic formats that were previously available in some subset of the formats. This chapter notes the core of fields and codes that has for some years been common to all bibliographic formats.

The Common Core of Bibliographic Fields

A bibliographic record has common characteristics, no matter what the record describes.

- There will always be a *title* or *identifying name*. An entry for an author is the same sort of entry no matter what the material. Some items don't have any author entries, and some have many. Sometimes it is reasonable to call one of the author entries a main entry, and sometimes it isn't. (Whether an author becomes a main entry depends in part on the cataloging rules followed in creating the record.)
- Most nonfiction items have *subjects*: they are about someone or something. Subjects can be people, corporations, conferences, or topics; they can also be titles or geographic names. Some items aren't "about" anything, and some are "about" quite a number of things.
- Catalogers may need to make *notes* about any sort of item being cataloged. Any item may have restrictions on use, might require a citation or summary, or might simply need some general notes.
- Most items are *published, produced, or released* at a specific location and time by a specific person or agency.
- All bibliographic items need to be *described physically*.

These attributes are common to everything that can be cataloged, and they form the basic descriptive language of cataloging and of USMARC. They are the core bibliographic data elements, common to all bibliographic formats.

100	Main entry—personal name
110	Main entry—corporate name
111	Main entry—meeting name
130	Main entry—uniform title
400	Series statement/added entry—personal name
410	Series statement/added entry—corporate name
411	Series statement/added entry—meeting name
600	Subject added entry—personal name
610	Subject added entry—corporate name
611	Subject added entry—meeting name
630	Subject added entry—uniform title
650	Subject added entry—topical term
651	Subject added entry—geographic name
700	Added entry—personal name
710	Added entry—corporate name
711	Added entry—meeting name
730	Added entry—uniform title
800	Series added entry—personal name
810	Series added entry—corporate name
811	Series added entry—meeting name
830	Series added entry—uniform title

Table 2.1: Bibliographic Fields Subject to Authority Control

Table 2.1 lists the commonly defined fields subject to authority control. These fields are all suitable for use as access points and make up the bulk of fields specifically intended as access points. (Prior to format integration, fields 400-411 were not defined for archival and manuscripts control.)

Table 2.2 shows the control fields common to all formats. Fields 001 and 005 specifically identify a particular version of a single USMARC record. Field 008 has commonly defined elements at the beginning and end of the field; each type of material or type of treatment defines different elements for the central positions, 008/18 through 008/34. (Chapters 5 through 12, on the individual types of material and treatment, include specifications for that portion of 008 or the equivalent field 006.)

001 . . . . .Control number
005 . . . . .Date and time of latest transaction
007 . . . . .Physical description fixed field
008 . . . .**Fixed length data elements:**
008/00-05 . . . . . . .Date entered on file
008/06 . . . . .Type of date/Publication status
008/07-10 . . . . . . .Date 1
008/11-14 . . . . . . .Date 2
008/15-17 . . . . . . .Place of publication, production or execution
008/35-37 . . . . . . .Language
008/38 . . . . .Modified record
008/39 . . . . .Cataloging source

Table 2.2: Common Variable Control Fields

010	LC control number (LCCN)
035	System control number
040	Cataloging source
041	Language code
045	Time period of content
052	Geographic classification code
060	National Library of Medicine call number
066	Character sets present
070	National Agricultural Library call number
072	Subject category code

Table 2.3: Common 0xx Variable Fields

The common 0xx fields (i.e., fields 001-099) shown in Table 2.3 contain additional background information for a bibliographic record, much of it not available on a printed card. Field 035 makes it possible to trace a record as it moves from system to system. Other

0xx fields contain call numbers, show who has cataloged the item and transcribed that cataloging into USMARC, and provide codes that can serve as special access points or to qualify other access points.

240	Uniform title
242	Translation of title by cataloging agency
245	Title statement
250	Edition statement
260	Publication, distribution, etc. (Imprint)
300	Physical description
440	Series statement/added entry—title
490	Series statement
500	General note
506	Restrictions on access note
520	Summary, abstract, annotation, scope, etc. note
580	Linking entry complexity note
773	Host item entry
880	Alternate graphic representation

Table 2.4: Common Bibliographic Fields: 2xx-8xx

Table 2.4 shows the commonly defined bibliographic fields that are not normally considered subject to authority control. These fields include several of the most commonly used: title, imprint, physical description, untraced series, and general note.

USMARC and *UFBD*

T he *USMARC Format for Bibliographic Data* combines many varieties of information into a single publication, making it the primary reference for content designation for the USMARC bibliographic format. Most of the information in this and the following chapters is derived from *UFBD*—or its predecessor, the *MARC Formats for Bibliographic*

MARC Formats for Bibliographic Data

007/04 KIND OF SOUND	REPEAT-ABILITY	FORMATS				
007/04 KIND OF SOUND	NR	VM		MU		
WHEN 007-00 = SOUND RECORDING (S)		VM		MU		
a Acoustic		VM		MU		
f Monaural (digital)		VM		MU		
g Quadraphonic (digital)		VM		MU		
j Stereophonic (digital)		VM		MU		
k Other (digital)		VM		MU		
m Monaural (electric)		VM		MU		
q Quadraphonic (electric)		VM		MU		
s Stereophonic (electric)		VM		MU		
o Other (electric)		VM		MU		
u Unknown		VM		MU		
z Other kind of sound		VM		MU		

DESCRIPTION

This character position is used to specify the kind of sound on a sound recording when 007/00 contains "s." — VM MU

The kind of sound produced using an acoustical horn and diaphragm to transmit the sound pulses varies considerably from the kind of sound produced using electrical recording techniques, and all analog recordings have sound characterisitcs which differ from the sound characteristics of digital recordings. — VM MU

A one-character alphabetic code indicates that the sound recording is either an analog recording (acoustically or electrically recorded) or digitally recorded and specifies the kind of sound (monaural, quadraphonic, stereophonic, or other) for both analog and digital recordings. — VM MU

Acoustic – A term used to describe sound recorded usually on disc or cylinder, using an acoustical horn and diaphragm to transmit the sound pulses. Acoustical recording was used until 1927/29 when electric microphones and amplifiers became generally available. Acoustical recordings are almost always monaural. — VM MU

Monaural (electric) – A disc or tape recording, recorded using electric microphones and amplifiers, which has all the sound information stored and reproduced on one channel. — VM MU

Quadraphonic (electric) – A disc or tape recording, recorded using electric microphones and amplifiers, in which four separate channels are used to convey the sound informatiion to the listener. — VM MU

MARC Formats for Bibliographic Data

007/04 KIND OF SOUND (Continued)	FORMATS				

DESCRIPTION (Continued)

Stereophonic (electric) – A disc or tape recording, recorded using electric microphones and amplifiers, which has two individual channels or tracks, each with separate information, and from which the sound is reproduced from two or more speakers. — VM MU

Other (electric) – A disc or tape recording, recorded using electric microphones and amplifiers, which has more than four separate channels or tracks. — VM MU

Monaural (digital) – A disc or tape recording, digitally recorded for analog reproduction, which has all the sound information stored and reproduced on one channel. — VM MU

Quadraphonic (digital) – A disc or tape recording, digitally recorded for analog reproduction, in which four separate channels are used to convey the sound information to the listener. — VM MU

Stereophonic (digital) – A disc or tape recording, digitally recorded for analog reproduction, which has two individual channels or tracks, each with separate information, and from which the sound is reproduced from two or more speakers. — VM MU

Other (digital) – A disc or tape recording, digitally recorded for analog reproduction, which has more than four separate channels or tracks. — VM MU

Other kind of sound – For items which cannot be coded by any of the above categories, e.g., discs or tapes which are digitally recorded for digital reproduction. — VM MU

On AACR2 records, information that the sound recording is monaural (electric), quadraphonic, or stereophonic can be found in subfield "b" of field 300 (Physical Description (AACR2)). — MU

Figure 2.1: Page from *MFBD*

007/13
(Sound recording)

Format/NLR
BK AM CF MP MU VM SE

007/13   Capture and storage technique   *M   M*

Codes

a	Acoustical capture, direct storage	*A*	*A*
b	Direct storage, not acoustical	*A*	*A*
d	Digital storage	*A*	*A*
e	Analog electrical storage	*A*	*A*
u	Unknown	*A*	*A*
z	Other capture and storage technique	*A*	*A*

CHARACTER POSITION DEFINITION AND SCOPE

A one-character alphabetic code indicates how the sound was originally captured and stored. Re-releases of recordings should be coded for the original capture and storage technique, even though such re-releases may have been enhanced using another technique.

GUIDELINES FOR APPLYING CONTENT DESIGNATORS

■ **CODES**

a – Acoustic
Code a indicates acoustical capture and direct storage of sound: usually a disc or cylinder recording, captured using an acoustical horn and diaphragm and stored directly on a master surface. Most acoustical recordings date from before 1927/29 when electrical recording equipment became available.

b – Direct storage, not acoustical
Code b indicates direct storage that is not acoustical: disc recordings captured using electrical equipment and stored directly on a master surface. All recordings made with microphones and other electrical equipment prior to the availability of magnetic recording techniques in the late 1940s used direct storage. Commercial recordings marked "direct to disc" or some equivalent phrase also use this technique.

d – Digital storage
Code d indicates digital storage: sound recordings which were captured electrically and stored using digital techniques. Such recordings are normally identified as "digitally recorded" or some similar phrase on the label or package. "Digital remaster" or "digital mixing" does not imply original digital storage. *Note:* Digital storage and digital playback should not be confused. The need for digital playback should be recorded in 007/12 (Special playback characteristics).

Figure 2.2: Page from *UFBD*

Data—but represents only a tiny portion of the information available there.

MFBD represented a landmark effort for its day, combining database implementation by RLG with textual input and editing by the Library of Congress. The resulting publication was limited to a single typeface, and was formatted in "landscape mode"—with the text running parallel to the long side of an 8.5 by 11 inch sheet— in order to leave room for the ever-present columns denoting which format or formats given information referred to. Figure 2.1 is a reduced copy of a page from *MFBD*, reproduced at 60 percent of the original size.

The *USMARC Format for Bibliographic Data*, no longer produced using RLG facilities, offers somewhat more information presented in a far more legible and easy-to-use format. While any field will be valid in any format, *UFBD* provides guidance as to which fields are *expected* and *typical* for each format. Figure 2.2 is a reduced copy of a page from *UFBD*, also reproduced at 60 percent of the original size. The two pages provide similar information. The old page is for 007/04 for sound recordings. In between the two editions, the content of the original 007/04 has been split into two values, the new 007/04 and 007/13 (Capture and Storage Technique). The new page is for 007/13, which includes much more explanatory material than the new 007/04.

Note the simple but effective use of typography and white space in the sample from *UFBD*. Although the text may be illegible or barely legible at the reductions used for these tables, the improvement should be evident.

Coded Values

Roughly one-third of the main text of *UFBD* concerns the leader and fields 006, 007, 008, and 009. Each coded value is explained in detail: values defined for the code, how each value is used and, frequently, instructions on assigning values, together with notes on LC practice. This portion of *UFBD* and *MFBD* grew considerably in the early 1980s as LC and others worked through each code to make its values distinct, explicit, and assignable. A relatively simple example of *UFBD* explanation and guidelines for content designation for a coded value follows, taken from the material for field 007, position 11, for sound recordings: "Kind of Cutting" (code values: "h": Hill-and-dale cutting, "l": Lateral or combined cutting, "n": Not applicable, "u": Unknown):

A one-character alphabetic code indicates the kind of cutting of the grooves used on a disc. The primary use of this element is to identify discs which contain only hill-and-dale information.

h - Hill-and-dale cutting: Code h indicates a vertical cutting, with no lateral information intended for reproduction. All cylinders and some early discs have this cutting.

l - Lateral or combined cutting: Code l indicates a cutting containing lateral information intended for reproduction. Such discs may also have vertical components intended for reproduction. Most contemporary discs (i.e., all quadraphonic discs and nearly all stereophonic discs) contain both vertical and lateral information and are coded l. Monophonic discs are normally lateral only.

n - Not applicable: Code n indicates that the item is not a disc or a cylinder. Compact audio discs are coded n as they are pitted rather than cut.

u - Unknown: Code u indicates that the kind of cutting is unknown.

Some descriptions are shorter; many are much longer. The intent is to make coded values useful and clear enough so that non-specialists can assign values correctly.

Descriptions and LC Practice Notes

Most of the text of *UFBD* is descriptions of fields, LC practice notes, and examples. Field definition and scope statements give uses for fields, relate fields to other fields, cite *AACR2* practice where appropriate, and sometimes include historical notes. LC practice appears in many cases. Besides serving as the master reference for USMARC bibliographic formats, *UFBD* is the data dictionary for LC MARC distribution services.

Many fields include guidelines for applying content designation, detailing practice for each indicator and subfield code. Examples appear below most paragraphs. Some fields include references to related fields or documents outside *UFBD*; some fields include history of the field and its elements.

Appendices and Related Publications

Several appendices and related publications enhance the value of *UFBD*. Appendices include national level record and minimal level record requirements; 007 listings by character position and names; 008 listings by character position and names; full record examples; an alphabetical listing of ambiguous names; initial definite and indefinite articles; changes in *UFBD*; and a keyword index. Supporting publications include the *USMARC Code List for Countries*; *USMARC Code List for Geographic Areas*; *USMARC Code List for Languages*; *USMARC Code List for Relators, Sources, Description Conventions*; and the *USMARC Specifications for Record Structure, Character Sets, Tapes*.

3

The Structure of USMARC

When you build a MARC record you label the data using tags, indicators, and subfield codes. When a bibliographic service writes a record to tape, it adds several other structural elements to provide the fundamental structure of a USMARC record. The fundamental structure of MARC is established in national and international standards. USMARC is a specific implementation of these standards, taking specific choices from a range of possibilities.

ANSI Z39.2-1985: What It Says, What It Means

The American National Standards Institute (ANSI) is the accrediting body for standards organizations in the United States. All ANSI standards are voluntary. ANSI-accredited agencies are formed in various areas where there are enough organizations interested in standards to make an agency workable and worthwhile. The National Information Standards Organization (NISO) is the accredited standards agency for libraries, information science, and publishing. Effectively, NISO is the "library technical standards organization" in the United States. NISO was formerly ANSI Committee Z39, and most NISO standards carry numbers preceded by Z39.

ANSI Z39.2-1985 is the *American National Standard for Bibliographic Information Interchange*. Standard Z39.2 was first promulgated in 1971, and has always been the basis for the structure of MARC records. It "specifies the requirements for a generalized interchange format which will accommodate describing all forms of material susceptible of bibliographic description, as well as related data such as authority records."[1] The standard "does not specify the content of the bibliographic description and does not, in general, assign meaning to tags, indicators, or data-element identifiers." Z39.2-1985 specifies an overall schema for a record.

Offset	Usage
0-4	Record Length
5	Status
6	Type of Record
7	Bibliographic Level
8-9	Reserved for Future Use
10	Indicator Count
11	Identifier Length
12-16	Base Address
17-19	Implementation Defined Positions
20-23	Entry Map

Table 3.1: MARC Leader as defined by Z39.2-1985

Each MARC record must begin with a leader twenty-four characters long, as shown in Table 3.1. All numeric elements (record length, indicator count, identifier length, base address, and entry map) must be character numerics (characters "0"-"9"). The entry map, which describes the structure of directory entries, has four single-digit positions:

---

1   All cited material in this chapter is from Z39.2.

Position 20: Length of length-of-field
Position 21: Length of starting character position
Position 22: Length of implementation-defined portion
Position 23: Reserved

The directory contains "at least one entry" for each variable field and begins at position 24, immediately following the entry map. The first portion of a directory entry is always a three-character tag. That portion of the directory entry is not specified in the entry map. Each directory entry consists of up to four portions, all but the tag being defined by the entry map. The directory identifies each field in the record by a three-character tag, shows where the field begins, and gives the length of the field. The structure of a directory entry, in its most general terms, is shown in Table 3.2.

Part 1 . . . . .Tag
Part 2 . . . . .Length of Field
Part 3 . . . . .Starting Character Position
Part 4 . . . . .Implementation Defined Portion

Table 3.2: MARC Directory Structure as Defined by Z39.2-1985

The standard allows a very wide range of implementations. A format need not have any indicators or subfields to be a Z39.2 format (i.e., positions 10 and 11 of the leader could both be "0"). A format could also have eight indicators per field and subfield codes which were six characters long—with positions 10 and 11 being "86"—and still be a Z39.2 format.

An implementation could even *theoretically* have different directory structures for different records, since the leader in each record defines that record's directory. In practice such an implementation would be quite difficult to use, as the associated data dictionaries and parsing rules would be extremely complex.

ANSI Z39.2-1985 provides a basic structure for records. A properly designed computer program can check that the first five characters of a record are all numeric and that positions 10-16 and 20-23 are all numeric. Given that, and the assumption that the record is a Z39.2 record, the program can read the directory and locate fields within the record. The program can even locate and identify subfields. This can all be done without knowing anything about the producer of the record, the conventions followed, or even what sort of MARC format is being processed. The leader provides enough information to allow a program to break a record and its fields into component parts, but not enough information to make any logical sense of those component parts.

USMARC: An Implementation of ANSI Z39.2

USMARC is a specific implementation of ANSI Z39.2, making specific choices from the options provided in the standard. The descriptions that follow include choices made for USMARC within ANSI Z39.2.

The Leader

USMARC defines all three of the implementation defined positions—positions 17-19—and has fixed values for five leader positions. The indicator count and identifier length are always 2. Position 17 is encoding level, position 18 is descriptive cataloging form, position 19 is the linked-record code. The entry map is always *4500*: four-character length of field, five-character length of starting position, no implementation-defined portion. The final digit is undefined and reserved for later use. A typical leader appears below, with its elements explained.

Leader	00971nam__2200277_a_4500

00-04   *Logical record length* 00971
This record is 971 characters long.

The first five characters of a MARC record contain five numeric characters. These five characters make up a right-justified and zero-filled number which gives the total length of the record, *including the logical record length itself.*

---

05 *Record status* n
This record is new (has not been modified).

The record status is added by the agency that prepares a US-MARC record for transmission, to be used by the agency that receives the record. Common values for record status are *n* (new), *c* (changed), and *d* (deleted). LC has also used *a* (increase in encoding level) and *p* (increase in encoding level from prepublication record).

For bibliographic records there is really only one specifically useful value for record status: if it is *d*, the record is deleted and should be removed from any current files. Value *c* can be used only to distinguish new records from changes if the receiving agency is certain that it has all records ever created by the generating agency. In practice most agencies treat *c* and *n* identically, adding the record if an older version does not exist in the database, replacing it if it does.

Legend

The legend occupies four character positions, 06-09. USMARC defines only the first two of those four positions, positions 06 and 07. Positions 08 and 09 are always blank in USMARC records. The legend identifies and describes the record, implying the general content and the meaning of content designators. Within the integrated USMARC format the legend specifically identifies the meaning of positions 18-34 of field 008.

---

06 *Type of record* a
Language material (including microforms)

This code (type of record) can be used to distinguish bibliographic records from other USMARC formats and, in most cases, to distinguish the type of material being described. Authorities records have value *z*; the holdings format uses values *x* and *y*. In those cases where archival and manuscripts control information is of greater concern than the form of the item or collection itself, value *b* is used. In all other cases the code specifies the *primary* type of material. For example *c* signifies "Music, printed or microform" and *k* represents "Two-dimensional nonprojectable graphic representations" such as charts, drawings, and photoprints.

> *07 Bibliographic level* m
> *Monograph or Item*

"Bibliographic level" is defined only for the bibliographic format. The two most common values are *m* (monograph) and *s* (serial). With the inclusion of analytics and archival control, four more values are useful: *a* (component part, monographic), *b* (component part, serial), *c* (collection), and *d* (subunit). Collections are groups of materials treated together for cataloging and control; subunits are components of a collection.

> *10 Indicator count* 2
> *Each variable data field begins with two indicator positions.*

Although Z39.2 allows 0 to 9 indicators per field, USMARC has always specified two. As a result position 10 of the leader is always 2.

> *11 Subfield code count* 2
> *Subfields are identified by two-character codes, of which the first character is the delimiter ǂ*

USMARC always uses two-character subfield codes: the delimiter ǂ followed by a single-character identifier. As a result position 11 of a USMARC leader is always 2.

12-16 *Base address of data* 00277
The first character of field 001 is 277 positions past the first character of the record.

Like the logical record length, the base address is a five-character right-justified zero-filled number. This number shows the offset (distance from the first character) at which the first data character is found. This address is important because starting character positions in directory entries are given as offsets from this base. The starting character position for field 001 is always *00000*, by Z39.2 definition. In order to find a specific field a program must add the base address to the starting character position.

The base address serves two valuable purposes. First, it is more efficient to have directory searching end at a given position (the base address minus one) than to test for the field terminator at each entry. Second, the base address allows low-overhead modification of MARC records. Suppose that you have an incoming USMARC record to which you need to add one local field. Adding the field makes the directory twelve characters longer. Without the base address all the starting positions would be different and you would need to rebuild the entire directory, even if the new field was at the end of the record. Because MARC uses a base address, all you need do is add an item to the directory, add the field at the end of the record, and increment the base address by twelve: the rest of the directory is still valid.

The leader is always twenty-four characters long, and the directory in USMARC records is always a sequence of twelve-character entries, ending with a field terminator. This record has twenty-one directory entries (twenty-one fields). Thus the base address is *24 + (12 * 21) + 1*, or *24 + 252 + 1*, which equals *277*.

The number of fields in a record is always equal to the base address, minus twenty-five, divided by twelve.

> 17 Encoding level _
> Full level: the information used is derived from an inspection of the physi-
> cal material.

This single character identifies the degree of completeness of the record. Blank is "full." Normally a blank in any coded position means nothing, that is, that no information has been provided. The use of blank for "full" is a historical anomaly. Initially, the values in this position reflected preliminary stages of Library of Congress catalog-ing, and only full records were distributed. Now cataloging-in-pub-lication records are distributed (as are other partial records).

> 18 Descriptive cataloging form a
> Record is cataloged according to the provisions of AACR2 and AACR2-
> based cataloging manuals approved by LC.

This single alphabetic character indicates the form of descriptive cataloging used in the record. As currently defined it can specify either form of descriptive cataloging or form of punctuation. Blank means that no information is given: you *cannot* assume either *AACR2* or ISBD form. Value *i* means "full ISBD" without regard to the cata-loging rules. Descriptive cataloging form is not defined for authori-ties or holdings: the position is left blank.

> 19 Linked record code _
> Related record not required.

Position 19 of the leader was defined in 1982 as part of the solution to coding analytics in USMARC. Two values are possible: blank and *r*. If a record is coded *r*, a related record is required in order to process the record fully. All records prior to 1984 and most records since then, including most analytics, have a blank in Leader/19. Most catalogers doing analytics would put a brief citation in the "In" field, field 773.

Value *r* is used in cases where the cataloger feels that the most up-to-date complete bibliographic record for the host item (the book or serial) is required, and codes only a record control number to identify the host. In the latter case no system could present a complete display or printed reference to the record at hand without fetching the related record, to provide the "In" value. The linked record code allows system designers to check for such a situation at the beginning of the record.

> 20-23 *Entry Map*
> 4500
> *The length-of-field portion of a directory entry is four digits long; the starting-character-position portion is five digits long. There is no implementation-defined portion.*

The entry map defines the structure of directory entries. All USMARC records currently have an entry map of *4500*. The final zero—Leader/23—is a placeholder, currently undefined but reserved for possible future use.

The Directory

A MARC directory consists of a series of entries, one for each field in the record, showing the tag of the field, its length, and its starting position relative to the first field in the record. The leader allows a program to recognize a record and establish basic processing aspects. The directory allows a program to locate data in a record quickly and easily.

Variable control fields (fields 001-009) are always represented at the beginning of the directory and are always in ascending order. The first directory entry is always for field 001. If the next tag is 005 (as it always is in a complete USMARC record), you can be sure that there are no 002, 003, or 004 fields.

After the variable control fields the tags are sequenced by first character. A record can have a 600 field followed by a 651 followed by a 650 followed by a 600. This allows a cataloger to define the order of fields within a range as desired. A proper USMARC record will *never* have a 710 followed by a 651, since the first characters would then be out of order.

From a programming viewpoint, first-digit sequencing provides valuable information. If you're processing subject entries and you see a tag beginning with 7, 8, or 9, you're through with subjects (6xx). But if you're looking for personal names as subjects (600) and you see a 610, you're not necessarily through; the tag after the 610 might very well be a 600.

Fields need not be stored in the same order as the directory. Except for control fields, any field can start anywhere in the record. This flexibility helps minimize the cost of maintenance. Suppose that you get a USMARC record and want to add hyphens to the 020 (ISBN). The easiest way to do that is to move the new 020 to the end of the record. All you need to do is change the 020 directory entry and the record length; the rest of the directory and the rest of the record are fine. If you insert the expanded 020 where the old one was, all fields following the 020 will have different starting character positions, and most of the directory must be rebuilt. In this case the record contains both an old unhyphenated ISBN and a new hyphenated one, but the old unhyphenated 020 is not mentioned in the directory. Proper MARC handling programs always take the starting character position and length of each field from the directory; thus the "garbage" in the record is effectively invisible.

It is also legitimate, though rare, for two different fields to have precisely the same content. A system could carry the text once and have two directory entries (with different tags) pointing to the same text.

Uses for the Directory

The directory does represent avoidable overhead, since each tag could be stored at the beginning of its field. If you're processing an entire record, field-by-field, this would be roughly as efficient and save nine characters per field. But when computers process US-

MARC they are not always working with every field and may not look at fields in a particular order. If you're preparing a quick finding list you may want to deal only with fields 100-111, 245, and 090 (or 090-099). You don't care what's in any of the other fields—and you don't want to have to process them to get to the fields you need.

The processing required to find fields from the directory is simple and efficient in most computers. For applications that look at many fields, it can be made even more efficient: pointers to each *range* of tags (1xx, 2xx, etc.) can reduce processing time even further. Processing an extremely long text string to find individual elements is considerably less efficient in most computers, and somewhat more difficult to design.

The directory also lends stability to existing programs: if a program is looking for fields 245 and 260, it doesn't matter if three more fields between 245 and 260 have been defined since the program was implemented. Since the program is not looking for any intermediate fields, it will run equally well using records that contain them, thanks to the directory.

Variable Fields

The directory and most of the leader represent processing overhead. Bibliographic information, coded and textual, is divided into fields. Some USMARC fields consist of nothing but a series of codes, but most are subdivided into indicators and subfields.

Variable Control Fields

Variable control fields have tags beginning with *00*. They differ from other fields in that they do not have indicators or subfields. A given control field has either a single data element or a series of data elements identified by relative character position. Control fields are sometimes called *fixed-length fields*, but this name is incorrect and misleading. While control fields may contain fixed-length data elements, control fields are not inherently fixed-length.

Only one control field is mandatory in USMARC: field 001, the control number. This field is variable-length, and processing systems that have assumed a fixed length have had problems. While the LC card number that appears in 001 fields for MARC distribution tapes is fixed-length up to the end of the number itself, suffixes and revision dates can follow that number. Other control fields generally serve either to identify a record or version of a record, or to provide coded values that can be used to select or process records. Field 005 contains a date/time stamp. Field 008 contains a number of coded values including country of publication, language, and frequency and regularity (for serials). The contents of the 008 are defined by the contents of the legend. Field 007 contains other coded data elements; these fields have several different versions, which are defined by the first character of the field itself. Field 006 contains coded values for aspects of a record (such as enclosed materials) that cannot be treated in the 008; as with field 007, the first character of the field defines the remaining characters.

Variable Data Fields and Tags

Fields with tags that don't begin with *00* are variable data fields. If you use USMARC directly or indirectly you probably use tags; they represent the most common method for identifying data for entry or maintenance. Each bibliographic service provides its own documents listing and describing the available tags, including those added to USMARC by the service. The *USMARC Format for Bibliographic Data* includes all nationally defined bibliographic tags, indicators, and subfields.

Tags are the level of content designation used to define independent elements of a record. Because tags are stored in fixed-length directory elements, they can be retrieved quickly and easily in computer processing, allowing flexible processing of the contents of a record. In most cases a variable data field is independently useful within the context of the bibliographic record. The remaining two levels of content designation, indicators and subfields, depend on the context of the variable field within which they are contained. Indicators and subfields are discussed further in chapter 4.

Delimiters

All MARC formats use delimiters to separate elements. A delimiter is a character with a unique meaning, used to mark a location within a record. USMARC uses three types of delimiters, known as the subfield delimiter, the field terminator, and the record terminator. The subfield delimiter is part of the subfield code, and is essential in processing USMARC. It is defined as ASCII 1/15, or hexadecimal 1F. This book (and most USMARC documentation) uses the double dagger ‡ to indicate the subfield delimiter. The subfield delimiter is sometimes shown as $ when no double dagger is available in a character set.

The field terminator appears at the end of the directory and at the end of each field. It is defined as ASCII 1/14, or hexadecimal 1E. The field terminator is redundant information, as the length of field is given in the directory. Some processing programs use the field terminator as a convenient way of knowing that the end of field has been reached. In text processing this is sometimes easier than using the length of field. There is no common graphic representation for the field terminator; this book sometimes uses ¶ (as does OCLC).

The record terminator is always the last character in the logical record, and is coded as ASCII 1/13, or hexadecimal 1D. One easy test of the validity of a USMARC transmission is to take the logical record length and look at the character at that character position. If it is not a record terminator, something is wrong with the record. When used in this book the record terminator appears as §.

USMARC: Transmission Form

When a USMARC record is communicated on tape or disk or over an electronic link, it is written as a long string of characters. That string is difficult for a person to interpret, but easy for a computer to process. Figure 3.1 shows the record that appeared in chapter 1 in a simulation of the actual transmission form. The long character string is broken down into fifty-character pieces for convenience. You should never have to read a record in the format of Figure 3.1; it wasn't designed for people. This format allows a computer to deal with the flexibility of USMARC without losing efficiency.

Offset	Text
0	00972nam__2200277_a_45000010015000000050017000 1500
50	800410003201000160007302000350008904000120012400500
100	02200136082002000015810000200017824501090019826 0006
150	50030730000260037244000340039850000200043265000230
200	04526500037004756500055005126500045005676500041006
250	12700002000653700002200673¶RLINCRLG86-B27¶19880728
300	165537.0¶861014s1986____nyu_____00110_eng__¶
350	__‡a___86015348¶__‡a0-86729-198-2_(soft)_:‡c$30.00
400	¶__‡dCStRLIN¶00‡aZ699.3‡b.C69_1986¶00‡a025.3/028/5
450	‡219¶10‡aCrawford,_Walt.¶10‡aBibliographic_display
500	s_in_the_online_catalog_/‡cby_Walt_Crawford,_with_
550	Lennie_Stovel_and_Kathleen_Bales.¶0_‡aWhite_Plains
600	,_NY_:‡bKnowledge_Industry_Publications,‡cc1986.¶_
650	_‡avi,_359_p._:‡c_28_cm.¶_0‡aProfessional_libraria
700	n_series¶__‡aIncludes_index.¶_0‡aCatalogs,_On-line
750	.¶_0‡aOn-line_bibliographic_searching.¶_0‡aInforma
800	tion_display_systems‡xLibrary_applications.¶_0‡aIn
850	formation_display_systems‡xFormatting.¶_0‡aMachine-
900	readable_bibliographic_data.¶10‡aStovel,_Lennie.¶
950	10‡aBales,_Kathleen.¶§

Figure 3.1: USMARC Record in Transmission Format

4

Subfields and Indicators

Tags convey meaning independently of a particular record or even a particular type of material. The bibliographic tag 533 *always* means "Reproduction Note" and 651 *always* means "Subject Added Entry - Geographic Name."

The two lowest levels of content designation convey meaning only within the context of a particular field. It is generally meaningless to refer to "‡b" or any other subfield in isolation, although a reference to "651 ‡b" (Geographic name following place entry element. *Obsolete.*) makes perfectly good sense.

533/I1 . . . . .Undefined
533/I2 . . . . .Undefined
533/‡a . . . . .Type of reproduction
533/‡b . . . . .Place of reproduction
533/‡c . . . . .Agency responsible for reproduction
533/‡d . . . . .Date of reproduction
533/‡e . . . . .Physical description of reproduction
533/‡f . . . . .Series statement for reproduction
533/‡3 . . . . .Materials specified
533/‡6 . . . . .Linkage

Table 4.1: Field 533 Indicators and Subfields

Tables 4.1 and 4.2 show the indicators and subfields for fields 533 and 651. Quick inspection shows that there are only three common definitions: neither field has a defined first indicator, ‡3 means *Materials specified*, and ‡6 supplies *Linkage* in both fields. Actually ‡3, ‡6, and some other numeric subfields represent exceptions to the general rule that indicators and subfields do not have independent meanings.

651/I1	.Undefined
651/I2	.Subject heading list or system/thesaurus
651/‡a	.Geographic name or place element
651/‡b	.Geographic name following entry element (obs.)
651/‡x	.General subdivision
651/‡y	.Chronological subdivision
651/‡z	.Geographic subdivision
651/‡2	.Source of heading or term
651/‡3	.Materials specified
651/‡6	.Linkage

Table 4.2: Field 651 Indicators and Subfields

Indicators

Each USMARC variable data field begins with two indicators. Indicators serve a number of functions in USMARC fields. Some indicators expand on the tag, defining the field contents more narrowly: for instance, the second indicator for field 780 (Preceding Entry) specifies the type of preceding entry. Other indicators say something about the source of the data or specify text to precede the field when it is displayed or printed. Indicators can give the length of an initial article to aid in sorting, or can control access to or display of a field's data.

Indicators, like subfields, follow patterns. The USMARC bibliographic format shows five common uses for indicators and a handful of miscellaneous uses.

Nonfiling Characters

Table 4.3 shows fields for which a nonfiling characters indicator is defined.[1] In each field where defined, the nonfiling characters indicator is a number from 0 to 9 showing how many characters of the first subfield should be ignored in sorting.

First Indicator: *130, 630, 730, 740*
Second Indicator: *222, 240, 242, 243, 245, 440, 830*

Table 4.3: Nonfiling Characters Indicators

245 03‡a*Le Bureau =*‡b*La Oficina = Das Buro.*‡h*[Filmstrip]*¶
FILE AS: Bureau

The example above shows a typical use of the nonfiling characters indicator. Nonfiling characters indicators are an example of the limited sorting support provided in USMARC; no such indication is available for the title subfield of author/title fields such as 700.

Notes and Added Entries Control

The indicators shown in Table 4.4, next page, can be used to suppress unwanted notes and to generate needed added entries. The letter following each tag shows the pattern of indicators used. Note that pattern D, used in the second indicator of field 245 and the first indicator of fields 760-787, uses a reverse logic to the other three patterns. Unlike the others, in which *0* means "Do nothing," Pattern D uses *0* to mean "Print or display a note."[2]

---

1 Excluding obsolete fields, as do most tables in this chapter.

2 Pattern C is the exact opposite of Pattern D, one of the rare flat contradictions in USMARC. Unfortunately, both Pattern C and Pattern D exist in hundreds of thousands of records; the contradiction could not reasonably be eliminated as part of format integration.

First Indicator: *210/A, 240/C, 242/B, 243/C, 245/B, 246/A,247/B, 760/D, 765/D, 767/D,770/D, 772/D, 773/D, 775/D, 776/D, 777/D, 780/D, 785/D, 787/D*
Second Indicator: *028/A, 247/D*

Pattern A:	0 = No note, no added entry	
	1 = Both note and added entry	
	2 = Note but no added entry	
	3 = Added entry but no note	
Pattern B:	0 = No added entry	
	1 = Added entry	
Pattern C:	0 = Not printed or displayed	
	1 = Printed and displayed	
Pattern D:	0 = Note	
	1 = No note	

Table 4.4: Notes and Added Entries Control

Display Constant Control

Display constants are text strings used to precede fields or subfields when they are displayed or printed, but not stored as part of the fields or subfields. "ISSN ", "Issued with: ", and "Continued by: " are some of the many suggested display constants defined for USMARC.

First indicator: *028, 505, 510, 511, 520, 555, 565*
First indicator/special: *516, 521, 522, 524, 556, 567, 581*
Second indicator: *246, 780, 785*

Table 4.5: Display Constant Control

Indicators are frequently associated with suggested display constants. Table 4.5 shows cases in which display constants may be controlled by indicators. In the cases of fields 028, 246, 780, and 785, the indicators serve more than one purpose: they also serve to further qualify the information within the field, and are mentioned again later in this section. The second group in Table 4.5 consists of indicators with only two values: *blank* for "No information provided" and *8* for "No display constant generated." The *UFBD* definitions for these fields include display constants, but catalogers may choose to suppress the constants if they are inappropriate for the particular material. In general value *8* can be used with any 5xx field for which display constants may be generated in order to suppress the display constant.

Source of Information/Thesaurus

First Indicator: *086*
Second Indicator: *050, 060, 072, 082, 600, 610,*
611, 630, 650, 651, 655, 656, 657

Table 4.6: Source of Information or Authority File

The indicators noted in Table 4.6 are used in the fields that were originally used only by national libraries. For call number fields the indicator shows whether the call number was assigned by the national library or by some other agency; for subject fields the indicator can show a specific subject authority file or list, refer to a code in subfield ‡2 as the source, or show that the source is not specified. (Value *7* consistently means "Source found in ‡2.")

Further Qualification of Field Contents

Type of Number	*024/1, 028/1*
Type of Date	*033/1, 045/1*
Type of Scale	*034/1*
Type of Edition	*082/1*
Type of Personal Name	*100/1, 400/1, 600/1, 700/1, 800/1*
Type of Corporate Name	*110/1, 410/1, 610/1, 710/1, 810/1*
Type of Meeting Name	*111/1, 411/1, 611/1, 711/1, 811/1*
Type of Title	*246/2*
Type of Contents Note	*505/1*
Type of Participant	*511/1*
Type of Added Entry	*700/2, 710/2, 711/2, 730/2, 740/2*
Type of Relationship	*780/1, 785/1*

Table 4.7: Type of Contents Indicators

Many indicators say more about the contents of the field, serving to qualify the tag, as shown in Table 4.7. The first indicator in fields 100, 400, 600, 700, and 800 specifies whether a personal name appears as a forename only (0), includes a single surname (1), multiple surnames (2), or as a name of family only (3). This information can be useful in sorting and retrieval, as can similar indicators in conference and corporate name fields. Some further qualifications affect display constants, such as the eight possible values for field 780 (Preceding entry) and nine possible values for field 785 (Succeeding entry).

Miscellaneous Indicators

The five categories just discussed cover most defined indicator positions. Remaining indicators provide a variety of special information, from "Level of international interest" (field 022, first indicator) to "Existence of pronoun referring to main entry" (fields 400, 410, 411, Indicator 2). Most other indicator positions are undefined and contain blanks.

Subfields

Subfields represent the lowest level of content designation in US-MARC. A subfield code always identifies the data that immediately follows the code, terminated either by the next subfield code or by a field terminator. A simple field may have only a subfield ‡a (for instance, field 501: "With" Note). A field with a complex set of data elements may have many more; for example, field 600 (Subject Added Entry—Personal Name) has twenty-six defined subfields. Subfields generally help to interpret their contents, and can allow those contents to be manipulated for special purposes.

The contents of a subfield can be interpreted only within the context of the field. The combination of a field and subfield gives specific significance to data, but the data may not be independently useful. Consider a 110 field *20‡aBell and Howell.‡bMicro Photo Divi-*

sion¶. The tag says that this is a Main Entry—Corporate Name; the indicators say that it is a Name (direct order) and that the relationship between the main entry and subjects is irrelevant. Within the context of a 110, subfield ‡b identifies a subordinate unit in a hierarchy. But "Micro Photo Division" is meaningless in and of itself: the subfield and its contents are dependent on the remainder of the field for context.

Subfield codes allow hierarchical indexing and authority control. Subfield codes allow selective display under certain conditions. They also serve many other purposes. Because text processing is required, subfields are generally more difficult to process than fields; however, subfields involve less overhead. They are appropriate where a data element is not independent, but does need to be identifiable.

Basic Aspects of USMARC Subfields

Casual acquaintance with USMARC may lead to some misconceptions about subfields and their use, although *UFBD* is quite explicit about such matters. The points that follow need to be understood clearly:

- While most USMARC fields do begin with ‡a, it is incorrect to assume that ‡a will always be the first subfield or even that every field will contain ‡a. (Field 040 is the clearest exception: records originally cataloged by LC may not contain ‡a.)

- There is *no* requirement or assumption that subfields will appear either in alphabetic order or in the order given in *UFBD*. The order of subfields within an actual field depends on cataloging rules and practice, not on an arbitrary order imposed as part of USMARC. (There are cases in which USMARC does prescribe that certain subfields appear in a certain order. In each such case, the prescription is clearly stated in *UFBD*.)

- Except for the numeric subfields ‡2, ‡3, ‡4, ‡5, ‡6, and ‡7 (and, as of this writing, ‡w), subfield codes *do not have independent meaning* without the context of the field. For example while ‡x) is "ISSN" in a number of fields, it is "General subdivision" in subject added entries.

- Consistently defined subfields are *not* universally applicable, with the (possible) exception of ‡6, the linkage subfield.
- As with tags, subfields support a wider variety of possible cataloging practice than that defined by *AACR2*. While US-MARC supports *AACR2* cataloging, it is not limited to that support.

Many USMARC fields, including most notes, use only a nonrepeatable subfield ‡a, having the same name as the field itself. Where multiple subfields are used, they sometimes follow patterns.

100	**Main entry - personal name**
‡a	Personal name
‡b	Numeration
‡c	Titles and other words associated with name
‡d	Dates associated with name
‡e	Relator term
‡f	Date of a work
‡g	Miscellaneous information
‡k	Form subheading
‡l	Language of a work
‡n	Number of part/section of a work
‡p	Name of part/section of a work
‡q	Fuller form of name
‡t	Title of a work
‡u	Affiliation
‡4	Relator code
‡6	Linkage
100	*00‡aFriedrich‡bII,‡cder Grosse, King of Prussia,‡d1712-1786.¶*
100	*01‡aFrancesco d'Assisi,‡cSaint.‡kLegend.‡pVita Thomae Celanensis .‡pTractatus secundus.‡lEnglish.¶*

Table 4.8: Field 100, Subfields and Examples

The subfields for field 100, as listed in Table 4.8, form the pattern for *all* personal name fields and appear, with those meanings, in fields

400, 600, 700, and 800 (and in the equivalent fields in the authority format). The other four fields include additional subfields, as defined in Table 4.9.

Additional Subfields for 600, 700 & 800
‡h   Medium
‡m   Medium of performance for music
‡o   Arranged statement for music
‡r   Key for music
‡s   Version

Additional Subfield for 400 & 800
‡v   Volume/sequential designation

Additional Subfield for 400 & 700
‡x   ISSN

Additional Subfield for 600 & 700
‡3   Materials specified

Additional Subfields for 600
‡x   General subject subdivision
‡y   Chronological subdivision
‡z   Geographic subdivision
‡2   Source of heading or term

Additional Subfield for 700
‡5   Institution to which field applies.

Table 4.9: Other Subfields for Personal Name Fields

With few exceptions the added fields are equivalent for other forms of entry. Thus, for example, field 110 (Main Entry—Corporate Name) carries nearly the same definitions for ‡a, ‡e, ‡f, ‡k, ‡l, ‡n, ‡p, ‡t, ‡u, and ‡4 as field 100, but defines ‡b, *Each subordinate unit in hierarchy*; ‡c, *Place*; and ‡d, *Date (of conference or meeting)* differently than field 100, and there is no ‡q. The 410, 610, 710, and 810 fields bear the same subfield relationships to field 110 as 400, 600, 700, and 800 bear to field 100. Examples of field 110 follow.

110
10‡aUnited States.‡tConstitution.‡n1st-10th amendments.¶
20‡aDemocratic Party (Tex.).‡bState Convention‡d(1857 :‡cWaco)¶

Similar patterns appear for the x11 Conference or Meeting fields (111, 411, 611, 711, and 811) and for the x30 Uniform Title fields (130, 630, 730, and 830). Table 4.10 shows changes in subfielding between 110, 111 and 130 and examples of the latter two fields.

111	**Main entry—conference or meeting**
	Subfields defined differently than 110:
‡b	Number (of conference or meeting) (obsolete)
‡e	Subordinate unit
	Additional subfield in 111:
‡q	Name of meeting following jurisdiction name element
	20‡aOlympic Games‡d(1976 :‡cMontreal, Quebec).
	‡eOrganizing Committee.‡eArts and Culture Program¶
130	**Main entry—uniform title heading**
	Subfields defined differently than 110:
‡a	Uniform title
‡d	Date of treaty signing
‡g ‡h ‡m ‡o ‡r ‡s:	Defined as for field 600
	Subfields *not* defined in 130:
‡b ‡c ‡q ‡u ‡4	
	00‡aConcertos,‡mviolin, string orchestra,‡rD major.¶

Table 4.10: Fields 111 and 130

As noted earlier, subject fields for names and uniform titles follow subfield patterns that are similar to name and uniform title entries, always using five common subfields ‡x, ‡y, ‡z, ‡2, and ‡3. The other subject entry and "index term" fields also use these subfields and a small number of other subfields. (The exception, field 653 *Index Term —Uncontrolled*, contains only ‡a.)

The linking fields 760-787—discussed in chapter 15—are the only other major cluster of fields with common subfield definitions. There are some subfields, however, that are defined consistently whenever they are defined.

Consistently Defined Subfields

Subfield	Meaning
‡2	Source
‡3	Materials specified
‡4	Relator code
‡5	Institution to which field applies
‡6	Linkage subfield
‡7	Control subfield
‡w	Control number

Table 4.11: Consistently Defined Subfields

Some of the subfields in Table 4.11 add coded information to the field beyond the coded information carried in the indicators. Others relate the field to a portion of the material described in the record, to a particular institution's copy of an item, to another field in the same record, or to another bibliographic record.

> 650 with ‡2 subfield:
> 17‡aacoustic measurement‡2test¶
> Topical subject heading taken from "test," the *Thesaurus of Scientific and Engineering Terms* (Washington: United States Dept. of Defense)

Subfield ‡2 carries coded values for the sources of information in cases where the source should be a controlled list or authoritative agency, such as subject headings, genre headings, or government document numbers. The Library of Congress publishes tables of codes to identify agencies and controlled lists, as they do for relators, countries, and languages. For example, Hennepin County's list of additional subject headings can be used with ‡2*henn*.

> 546 with ‡3 subfield: __‡3John P. Harrington field notebooks‡aApache ‡bphonetic alphabet¶
> The language note refers only to a portion of the material, specifically the John P. Harrington field notebooks.

Subfield ‡3 carries free-text information specifying some part of the material described in a bibliographic record.

> 700 with ‡4 subfield: 11‡aWeber, Lucas.‡4egr¶
> Lucas Weber engraved this item.

Relator subfields specify the relationship of a given field to the item as a whole. LC publishes a list of codes to be used for relator subfields.

> 500 with ‡5 subfield: __‡aPlates 4, 5, and 9 are wanting.‡5DLC¶
> This note applies to the copy held by LC.

Subfield ‡5 makes it possible to record information that applies only to a particular copy but that is meaningful for record distribution. (Local notes would go in field 590.)

> 773 with ‡7 and ‡w subfields:
> 0_‡7p1am‡aSpray, Irene Mary (Bliss).‡tPapers of the Palliser expedition, 1857-1860‡dToronto, Champlain Society, 1968‡w(DLC)__77574016 ¶
> The name in ‡a is a personal name, single surname; the host record is a printed monograph and has record number __77574016 .

Subfield ‡7, used only with linking entries, makes it possible to record the type of author name given in ‡a, the form of that name and the bibliographic level and type of the record to which this entry links. Subfield ‡w gives the actual record number of the linking entry and the NUC code for the system in which the record appears.

5

Books

Libraries are, at heart and by etymology, places of books. Libraries began with books or their equivalent, and libraries are still thought of primarily as places to find books. The first MARC bibliographic format was a format for books, and several times more USMARC records describe books (printed monographs including microforms) than describe all other materials combined.

The integrated USMARC format defines field 006 to contain those portions of field 008 with different definitions for different types of material (i.e., positions 008/18 through 008/34). These positions are mapped into 006/01 through 006/17. The first character of an 006 indicates the significance of the remainder of the field. Field 006 makes it possible to carry coded information for aspects of an item that are not properly covered by its type of material.

Within the integrated USMARC format, records for books may be recognized by the legend *am*—"Language material, monographic." Table 5.1 shows the elements of field 008 that are defined specifically for books, together with their positions in field 006 (when 006 position 0 is *a*).

008 006	Code
18-21 01-04	Illustration
22 05	Target audience
23 06	Form of item
24-27 07-10	Nature of contents
28 11	Government publication
29 12	Conference publication
30 13	Festschrift
31 14	Index
32 15	Obsolete
33 16	Fiction
34 17	Biography

Table 5.1: Specific 008-006 Codes for Monographs

Any nonserial that is basically textual should be coded with legend *am*, using 006 fields for other material forms contained within or with the item. Therefore the 006 field just defined should rarely be used. The word "basically" leaves considerable latitude, however; some items that are not basically monographs may have substantial text components. For example many contemporary microcomputer software packages come with manuals hundreds of pages long; some come with several books, one or more of which are independently available as monographs. Are such packages books with software attached or software with documentation? That is a cataloging decision, not one that should be made as part of USMARC itself; by defining a monographic 006, the integrated format leaves the decision open.

Commonly Used Fields in Monographs

MARC for monographs predates other bibliographic MARC formats and most MARC records are for monographs. Thus it is hardly surprising that the commonly used fields for books are, by and large, the core fields—the fields included in chapter 2 as being commonly applicable for all material.

About the Occurrence Tables

Tables 5.2 and 5.3, and comparable tables in later chapters, show fields that occur more than once per hundred records in large samples of current MARC use. Each sample represents six weeks of activity (new cataloging and maintenance) on RLIN. One six-week sample was taken in mid-1986. The second sample was taken in August 1988. Except as noted, occurrences represent the average of the two samples. Each sample included more than 600,000 records. Fields 001, 005, 008, and 245 appear exactly once in each bibliographic record and are omitted here and in comparable tables in later chapters.

Tag	Occ	Description
010	60.8	LC Control Number
015	3.8	National Bibliography Number
020	65.5	ISBN
035	8.5	System Control Number
040	72.8	Cataloging Source
041	6.3	Language Code
043	33.9	Geographic Area Code
050	56.1	LC Call Number
060	2.1	NLM Call Number
066	3.1	Character Sets Present
082	47.3	Dewey Decimal Call Number
100	73.3	Main Entry—Personal Name
110	4.7	Main Entry—Corporate Name
111	1.7	Main Entry—Meeting Name
240	3.8	Uniform Title
250	16.8	Edition Statement
260	99.7	Publication, Distribution, etc. (Imprint)
263	4.7	Projected Publication Date
300	95.6	Physical Description
440	15.5	Series Statement/Added Entry—Title
490	16.4	Series Statement

Table 5.2: Books: Commonly Used Fields, 010-490

Tag	Occ	Description
500	64.3	General Note
502	1.6	Dissertation Note
504	49.1	Bibliography, etc. Note
505	4.4	Formatted Contents Note
520	1.5	Summary, Abstract, Annotation, etc.
533	2.0	Reproduction Note
600	16.3	Subject Added Entry—Personal Name
610	5.5	Subject Added Entry—Corporate Name
630	1.0	Subject Added Entry—Uniform Title
650	128.5	Subject Added Entry—Topical Term
651	23.3	Subject Added Entry—Geographic Name
700	47.2	Added Entry—Personal Name
710	16.4	Added Entry—Corporate Name
730	1.0	Added Entry—Uniform Title
740	9.5	Added Entry—Uncontrolled Related/Analytical Title
810	1.0	Series Added Entry—Corporate Name
830	4.9	Series Added Entry—Uniform Title
880	14.1	Alternate Graphic Representation
886	*2.6	Foreign MARC Information Field

* 1988 sample only: did not appear in 1986 sample.

Table 5.3: Books: Commonly Used Fields, 500-886

Catalogers using USMARC would rarely if ever assign field 066, field 880, or field 886. Field 880 is used to store nonroman fields, and is discussed further in chapter 16. This tag is typically assigned indirectly when the catalog assigns almost any other tag and creates a nonroman field. Field 066 is created when field 880 is used. The Library of Congress uses field 886 to store fields from other MARC formats that don't have a direct USMARC equivalent so that the data in these fields can be distributed.

We may expect to see use of a somewhat wider range of fields following full implementation of the integrated USMARC format, but books catalogers have typically used a fairly narrow set of notes fields and relatively straightforward tagging in general. As with all other forms of material, the addition of dozens of new tags does not *require* catalogers to use them; it simply makes it *possible and legitimate* to use them, as needs require.

A Few Examples

Records for books can be short and simple or long and fairly complex. The rest of this chapter shows a few such records.

MARC Users' Group Seminar (1983)
  Databases for books, their uses for selling, acquiring and cataloguing : proceedings of the MARC Users' Group Seminar, 3 May 1983. London : The Library Association, 1983.
  58 p. ; 30 cm. (LA conference proceedings series in library automation ; 4)
  1. MARC System--Great Britain--Congresses. 2. Libraries--Great Britain--Automation. I. Library Association. II. Title. III. Series.

Figure 5.1: Monographic Record, Formatted Display

020		‡a0853656568¶
035		‡a(NAIU)Geac00637960¶
035		‡a(OCoLC)ocm10718924¶
040		‡aNAIU‡cNAIU‡dCStRLIN¶
043		‡ae-uk---¶
111	20	‡aMARC Users' Group Seminar‡d(1983)¶
245	10	‡aDatabases for books, their uses for selling, acquiring and cataloguing :‡bproceedings of the MARC Users' Group Seminar, 3 May 1983.¶
260	0	‡aLondon :‡bThe Library Association,‡c1983.¶
300		‡a58 p. ;‡c30 cm.¶
440	0	‡aLA conference proceedings series in library automation ;‡v4¶
650	0	‡aMARC System‡zGreat Britain‡xCongresses.¶
650	0	‡aLibraries‡zGreat Britain‡zAutomation.¶
710	20	‡aLibrary Association.¶

Figure 5.2: Monographic Record, Partial Tagged Display

---

035 System Control Number
__‡a(NAIU)Geac00637960¶
__‡a(OCoLC)ocm10718924¶

The system from which this record was downloaded is *at least* the third system on which the record has existed. Each 035 includes an NUC code identifying the institution and a control number that should be unique to that institution. In this case the first 035 appears to be a number assigned to a record on SUNY Albany's Geac system; the second is an OCLC control number. These numbers would become useful if, for example, tapes including this record went to either SUNY Albany or OCLC. Either institution could use the 035 number to determine

- that the record has been (and, presumably, should still be) on its own system;
- the specific record number that should match the record.

That information should simplify processing for the record. If the system maintains an 005 equivalent internally, it can take the 005 value in the record and determine whether this represents a possible update. The 035 is particularly useful if, for some reason, the record has been modified in such a way that normal searching techniques will not clearly identify the matching record on the other system.

---

043 Geographic Area Code
__‡ae-uk---¶

The record concerns Europe (*e*), specifically the United Kingdom (*uk*). Codes for geographic areas appear in a related LC publication.

---

111 Main Entry—Conference or Meeting
20‡aMARC Users' Group Seminar‡d(1983)¶

The indicators say that this is a direct-order name and that the main entry/subject relationship is irrelevant. Subfield ‡d contains the

Date of the conference or meeting. The first indicator in field 710 carries the same meaning as in field 111.

Somerson, Paul
 PC magazine DOS power tools : techniques, tricks and utilities / Paul Somerson. -- [New York, N.Y. : Bantam] c1988.
 xx, 1275 p. : ill. ; 24 cm. + 1 disc (5 1/4 in.)
 Includes index.
 ISBN 0553345265 (pbk.) : $39.95
 1. Operating systems (Computers). 2. PC DOS (Computer operating system). I.Title.

Figure 5.3: Monographic Record, Bibliographic Display

Figure 5.3 shows another relatively simple USMARC record in formatted version, with a portion of the tagged version shown in Figure 5.4. This record includes a computer file, but gives no indication of what is on that computer file or even what system it is designed to run on.

020   ‡a0553345265 (pbk.) :‡c$39.95¶
100   10   ‡aSomerson, Paul¶
245   10   ‡aPC magazine DOS power tools :‡btechniques, tricks and utilities /‡cPaul Somerson.¶
260   0   ‡a[New York, N.Y. :‡bBantam]‡cc1988.¶
300   ‡axx, 1275 p. :‡bill. ;‡c24 cm. + 1 disc (5 1/4 in.)
500   ‡aIncludes index.¶
650   0   ‡aOperating systems (Computers).¶
650   0   ‡aPC DOS (Computer operating system).¶

Figure 5.4: Monographic Record, Partial Tagged Display

Bevan, Alan.
 Report of a pilot ...*(text omitted)*...1976.
 Microfiche. Boston Spa, West Yorkshire : British Library, Lending Division, 1976. 1 microfiche ; 11 x 15 cm.

Figure 5.5: Microform Record, Bibliographic Display

This example shows coding and fields for a microform publication. Figure 5.5 shows part of the bibliographic display; three fields worth noting are discussed below.

---

007 Physical Description Fixed Field
herbmb020buuu¶

Field 007 contains physical description codes not carried in field 008; like field 006, it is defined by its first character, "Category of material," in this case *h* for Microform. Given that first character, the rest of the codes can be interpreted as follows:

---

e: Specific material designation: *Microfiche*
r: Original vs. Reproduction: *Reproduction*
b: Polarity: *Negative*
m: Dimensions (Microform): *4x6 in. or 11x15cm*
b020: Reduction Ratio: *Normal, 20:1*
b: Color (Microforms): *Monochrome*
u: Emulsion on Film: *Unknown*
u: Generation: *Unknown*
u: Base of Film: *Unknown*

---

533 Reproduction Note
__‡aMicrofiche.‡bBoston Spa, West Yorkshire :‡cBritish Library, Lending Division,‡d1976.‡e1 microfiche ; 11 x 15 cm.¶

Subfield ‡a specifies *Type of reproduction*; ‡b is *Place of reproduction*; ‡c the *Agency responsible for reproduction*; and ‡d the *Date of reproduction*. Subfield ‡e gives the *Physical description*. Other available subfields include ‡f, *Series statement for reproduction*, and ‡3, *Materials specified*.

Finally Figure 5.6 shows part of the bibliographic display for a record which, although simple from a tagging viewpoint, is difficult from the viewpoint of display or card-printing. The tags represented in the display are, in order, 245, 260, 300, 440, 504, and 505 (tracings are omitted). The 505, although abbreviated, is so long that it would not fit on a single screen of a well-formatted display or on a single catalog card (in most cases). The display constant *Contents:* is provided by the system, not included in the field.

New analytical techniques for trace constituents of metallic and metal-bearing ores : a symposium / sponsored by ASTM Committee E-3 on Chemical Analysis of Metals, American Society for Testing and Materials, Chicago, Ill., 24 June 1980 ; Adelina Javier-Son, editor. -- Philadelphia, Pa. (1916 Race St., Philadelphia 19103) : ASTM, c1981.

135 p. : ill. ; 23 cm. -- (ASTM special technical publication ; 747)

Includes bibliographical references and index.

Contents: Trace constituent analysis for metallic systems / Adelina Javier-Son -- Progression of analytical technology for trace constituents in metal-bearing systems / Margaret McMahon -- Analysis of low-alloy steel using a sequential atomic absorption spectrophotometer equipped with an autosampler / A.A. Klein -- Determination of aluminum, barium, calcium, lead, magnesium, and silver ferrous alloys by atomic emission and absorption spectrometry / T.C. Rains -- A comparison of the capabilities of atomic absorption and inductively coupled plasma spectroscopy for the analysis of metallurgical samples / G.F. Wallace -- Background correction used with a high-resolution spectrometer for plasma emission spectrochemical analysis / A.T. Zander -- Multielement d-c plasma emission spectrometric analysis of steels and irons / James Belliveau, Hank Griffin, and Arnold Savolainen -- Quantitative measurement of trace impurities in 99.95 percent palladium by d-c plasma emission spectrometry / M.A. Worthington -- Spectrochemical determination of impurities in uranium following solvent extraction using tributyl phosphate in methyl isobutyl ketone / J.G. Chang and R.L. Graff -- Isotope dilution spark source mass spectrometric determination of sulfur in selected NBS iron-base alloys / P.J. Paulsen ... et al.

Figure 5.6: Long Contents Note

6

Serials

Serials are the dominant format in most scientific fields and are an area of great concern to many librarians. The MARC serials format was in use for many years and was the basis for one of the library field's most successful cooperative programs, CONSER. At least one university library is estimated to hold more than one quarter of a million different serial titles, and the RLIN database included more than 2.3 million serial records as of January 1988.[1]

Seriality distinguishes serials, but the serials format was designed primarily for printed language materials. One major impetus for format integration was the need to provide more complete information for serials in other formats, such as serial maps and videocassettes.

Table 6.1 shows the portion of field 008 specifically defined when the legend is *as*, and the equivalent 006, which would begin with *s*.

---

1   January 4, 1988: 2,378,894 records representing roughly 1.6 million titles and title variations.

008	006	Code
18	01	Frequency
19	02	Regularity
20	03	ISDS center
21	04	Type of serial
22	05	Form of original item
23	06	Form of item
24	07	Nature of entire work
25-27	08-10	Nature of contents
28	11	Government publication
29	12	Conference publication
30-32	13-15	Undefined (obsolete)
33	16	Original alphabet of title
34	17	Successive/latest entry

Table 6.1: Serials-specific 008 and 006 Values

Commonly Used Fields in Serials

MARC for serials had more special fields defined than any other format. Serials frequently involve a complex of information not needed for nonserial publications, such as where a serial is indexed, its predecessors, its successor, its frequency, and so on.

The RLIN samples of current serials work show an astonishing sixty fields (excluding control fields and local fields) used more than once in every hundred records. Tables 6.2, 6.3, and 6.4 show those fields. *Italicized* fields are common only in serials, or occur at least twice as frequently as across all bibliographic formats.

Tag	Occ	Description
010	50.0	LC Control Number
022	*43.9*	*ISSN*
030	*7.1*	*CODEN Designation*
032	*1.0*	*Postal Registration Number*
035	11.2	System Control Number

Table 6.2: Serials: Commonly Used Fields, 010-035

Tag	Occ	Description
040	86.1	Cataloging Source
041	4.0	Language Code
042	*40.4*	*Authentication Code*
043	32.5	Geographic Area Code
050	34.7	LC Call Number
060	*5.8*	*NLM Call Number*
070	*1.1*	*NAL Call Number*
074	*1.7*	*GPO Item Number*
082	26.2	Dewey Decimal Call Number
086	*2.8*	*Government Document Class. Number*
110	18.9	Main Entry—Corporate Name
111	1.4	Main Entry—Meeting Name
130	*5.6*	*Main Entry—Uniform Title*
210	*17.3*	*Abbreviated Title*
212	*4.7*	*Variant Access Title*
222	*31.3*	*Key Title*
246	*29.1*	*Varying Form of Title*
247	*7.8*	*Former Title or Title Variations*
260	96.0	Publication, Distribution, etc. (Imprint)
265	*22.5*	*Source for Acquisition/Subscription Address*
300	77.5	Physical Description
310	*26.6*	*Current Publication Frequency*
321	*7.4*	*Former Publication Frequency*
350	*8.9*	*Price*
362	*74.4*	*Dates of Publication and/or Volume Designation*
440	1.7	Series Statement/Added Entry—Title
490	3.8	Series Statement
500	52.7	General Note
504	1.3	Bibliography, etc. Note
510	*43.0*	*Citation/References Note*
515	*14.7*	*Numbering Peculiarities Note*

Table 6.3: Serials: Commonly Used Fields, 040-515

Tag	Occ	Description
520	2.2	Summary, Abstract, Annotation, etc.
530	*1.8*	*Additional Physical Form Available*
533	2.5	Reproduction Note
546	*7.7*	*Language Note*
550	*16.7*	*Issuing Body Note*
555	*4.9*	*Cumulative Index/Finding Aids Note*
570	*4.9*	*Editor Note*
580	*9.3*	*Linking Entry Complexity Note*
610	5.8	Subject Added Entry—Corporate Name
650	113.8	Subject Added Entry—Topical Term
651	19.2	Subject Added Entry—Geographic Name
700	8.0	Added Entry—Personal Name
710	*63.0*	*Added Entry—Corporate Name*
730	*3.1*	*Added Entry—Uniform Title*
760	4.4	*Main Series Entry*
770	1.7	*Supplement/Special Issue Entry*
772	1.5	*Parent Record Entry*
780	27.1	*Preceding Entry*
785	13.2	*Succeeding Entry*
787	2.6	*Nonspecific Relationship Entry*
830	1.7	Series Added Entry—Uniform Title
880	2.3	Alternate Graphic Representation

Table 6.4: Serials: Commonly Used Fields, 520-880

Fields of special importance or frequent use for serials include the following:

- serials-specific control fields—022, 030, 032, and 042;
- additional title fields, of which 246 will be most important for the integrated format;
- frequency and publication date fields—310, 321 and 362;

- special notes—515, 550, 555, 570, 580— and field 510 used for indexing;
- linking fields 760-787, particularly 780 and 785.

Some of the fields in Tables 6.2-6.4 have been made obsolete as part of format integration; in each case, suitable alternative fields are identified. (See chapter 18 for details.) The obsolete fields will continue to appear in records for some time to come. A comparison of the 1986 and 1988 samples suggests fairly dramatic increases in use of some specific notes and linking entries. The CONSER project to add indexing information has certainly played a part in this change.

A Few Examples

Serials records tend toward complexity, even without detailed holdings information. Complexity can take different forms for different records. Figures 6.1 and 6.2 show one type of complexity, when several journals merge to form one (this record is for one of the original journals).

American medical digest.
Vol. I (1882)-v. 8, no. 6 (1889).
-- New York.
  8 v.

Monthly.
Summary: Issued in monthly parts. A digest of current medical literature, abstracts and reviews, in three parts: medicine, surgery, diseases of women and children and obstetrics.
  Merged with Medical register (Philadelphia 1887-1889), Philadelphia medical times and Polyclinic (Philadelphia) to form Times and register.
  Absorbed by: Times and register 1889-1895 Related Rec. ID: (CStL)88-S380

Figure 6.1: Serials Record, Bibliographic Display

```
008        880803d18821889nyumr_____0____0eng_d
035        ‡a(DNLM)SR0028593(s)¶
040        ‡aMnMULS‡cMnMULS‡dOCoLC‡dNSDP‡dMnU-B‡dCSt-L¶
245    00  ‡aAmerican medical digest.¶
260    01  ‡aNew York.¶
300        ‡a8 v.¶
362    0   ‡aVol. I (1882)-v. 8, no. 6 (1889).¶
520        ‡aIssued in monthly parts. A digest of current medical literature,
abstracts and reviews, in three parts: medicine, surgery, diseases of
women and children and obstetrics.¶
580        ‡aMerged with Medical register (Philadelphia 1887-1889),
Philadelphia medical times and Polyclinic (Philadelphia) to form Times
and register.¶
785    04  ‡tTimes and register‡g1889-1895‡w(CStL)88-S380¶
785    17  ‡tMedical register (Philadelphia 1887)‡g1887-1889‡w(CStL)88-S378¶
785    17  ‡tPhiladelphia medical times‡g1871-1889¶
785    17  ‡tPolyclinic (Philadelphia)‡g1883-1889‡w(CStL)88-S379¶
```

Figure 6.2: Serials Record, Tagged Display

008/07 Beginning Date of Publication: 1882
008/11 Ending Date of Publication: 1889

The serial was published from 1882 to 1889.

008/19 Regularity: r

The serial was regular—that is, always published monthly, with
no planned extra or missing issues.

008/34 Successive/Latest Entry Indicator: 0

The cataloging follows successive-entry rather than latest-entry
practice.

> 580   *Linking Entry Complexity Note*
> __‡aMerged with Medical register (Philadelphia 1887-1889),
> Philadelphia medical times and Polyclinic (Philadelphia) to form
> Times and register.¶

In many cases the equivalent note can be generated directly from a combination of two 785 fields, each with indicators 07. A properly programmed system, seeing two such fields in a row, will create a note "Merged with *first serial* to form *second serial.*" That doesn't work in this case because *three* serials merged to form a fourth. The solution is to change the first indicators in the 785 fields to 1 (don't display a note) and create a 580 field.

Note that the bibliographic display shows three pieces of information that don't appear textually in the tagged display. The note *Monthly.* is generated from the frequency code because the record lacks a 310 (Current Frequency) field. The display constants *Summary:* and *Absorbed by:* are generated based on indicator values in the 520 and first 785 fields, respectively.

> Library and Information Technology Association (U.S.)
>   LITA newsletter.
> No. 1 (winter 1980)-
> -- Chicago : The Association, 1980-
>   v. : ill. ; 28 cm.
>   3 no. a year
>   Two no. a year
>   Quarterly
>   L.I.T.A. newsletter
>   Newsletter
>   Title from caption.
>   ISSN 0196-1799 = LITA newsletter
>   1. Libraries--Automation--Periodicals. 2. Library science--Technological innovations--Periodicals. 3. Library science--Data processing--Periodicals. I. Library and Information Technology Association (U.S.). Newsletter. II. Title. III. Title: L.I.T.A. newsletter.

Figure 6.3: Serials Record, Bibliographic Display

Figures 6.3 and 6.4 show portions of a record for a relatively simple periodical, illustrating some of the remarkable variety of titles (now simplified slightly through format integration). This newsletter, which has always been called *LITA Newsletter* on its banner, masthead, and running caption, was cataloged with *six* title fields, two of them identical. Note also the two previous publication frequencies.

```
022   0    ‡a0196-1799¶
110   20   ‡aLibrary and Information Technology Association (U.S.)¶
210   0    ‡aLITA newsl.¶
212   0    ‡aLibrary and Information Technology Association newsletter¶
222   00   ‡aLITA newsletter¶
245   10   ‡aLITA newsletter.¶
246   10   ‡aL.I.T.A. newsletter¶
246   00   ‡aNewsletter¶
260   00   ‡aChicago :‡bThe Association,‡c1980-¶
265        ‡aALA, Library and Information Technology Asso., 50 E. Huron St.,
Chicago, IL 60611¶
310        ‡aQuarterly¶
321        ‡a3 no. a year¶
321        ‡aTwo no. a year¶
362   0    ‡aNo. 1 (winter 1980)-¶
500        ‡aTitle from caption.¶
710 21 ‡aLibrary and Information Technology Association (U.S.).
‡tNewsletter.¶
```

Figure 6.4: Serials Record, Partial Tagged Display

```
210 Abbreviated Title
0_‡aLITA newsl.¶
```

An abbreviated title assigned by the International Serials Data System in accordance with ISO 4-1972, based on the key title.

```
212 Variant Access Title (Obsolete)
0_‡aLibrary and Information Technology Association newsletter¶
```

"This field is used to record a variant form of access to the title when the title contains an initialism, abbreviation...[etc.]"

```
222  Key Title
00‡aLITA newsletter¶
```

The key title assigned by the National Serials Data Program. Note the constructed note in the bibliographic display consisting of the ISSN (from field 022) and this title.

```
246  Varying Form of Title
10‡aL.I.T.A. newsletter¶
```

The first indicator says to make a title added entry; the second that this is some "other" title either on the piece or called for by the rules.

```
246
00‡aNewsletter¶
```

This varying title does not receive a title added entry. The field is somewhat mysterious; I can only assume that it was created as an access point for the ‡t subfield in the 710 field, or because the *LITA Newsletter* itself occasionally uses *Newsletter* as a shortened form within text when the context is absolutely clear. While this particular varying title has no real use for access, in many cases, seemingly odd variations can provide access that might otherwise be lost.

The final example in this chapter, the most recent of three records for *Library Journal*, shows some of the results of CONSER's work. CONSER participants have succeeded in adding huge numbers of 510 fields, making indexing coverage much more apparent. Most notes in this example include indicator-based display constants and the subfield-based display constant *ISSN*.

Library journal.
v. 101, no. 9- May 1, 1976-
[New York, Bowker]
  v. ill. 29 cm.
  Semimonthly (monthly July-Aug.) , May 1, 1976-
  Semimonthly (monthly Jan., July, Aug. & Dec.) , Feb. 15, 1985-
  Indexed in its entirety by: Education index ISSN 0013-1385
  Indexed in its entirety by: Library literature ISSN 0024-2373
  Indexed in its entirety by: Magazine index 1977-
  Indexed selectively by: ABI/INFORM 1976-Oct. 1977
  Indexed selectively by: Annual bibliography of English language and lit-
erature ISSN 0066-3786
  Indexed selectively by: Art and archaeology technical abstracts ISSN 0004-
2994
  ...*ten indexing notes removed*...
  Indexed selectively by: Reference sources ISSN 0163-3546
  Continues: LJ, Library journal ISSN 0360-3113 Related Rec. ID:
(OCoLC)2171727

Figure 6.5: Partial Serials Record, Bibliographic Display

310 ‡aSemimonthly (monthly Jan., July, Aug. & Dec.)‡b, Feb. 15, 1985-¶
510 1 ‡aEducation index‡x0013-1385¶
510 1 ‡aLibrary literature‡x0024-2373¶
510 1 ‡aMagazine index‡b1977-¶
510 2 ‡aABI/INFORM‡b1976-Oct. 1977¶
510 2 ‡aAnnual bibliography of English language and literature‡x0066-
3786¶
780 00 ‡tLJ, Library journal‡x0360-3113‡w(OCoLC)2171727¶

Figure 6.6: Serials Record, Selected Tags

7

Maps

Maps—or, more properly, cartographic materials—include all materials that represent all or part of the earth or any celestial body. Map cataloging involves a wide range of materials including atlases, globes, navigational and celestial charts, aerial and satellite photographs with cartographic purposes, and even maps of imaginary places.

Map cataloging adds a special vocabulary to that required for books and serials, with emphasis on scale, projection, coordinates and other information needed to specify the area covered by the map and how it is covered. Many maps and atlases are published as serials, although the frequency of publication is not always clear.

Indeed, "not always clear" may be one of the biggest problems in cataloging maps. Much of the information required for proper description (e.g., title, date, author) may be missing or ambiguous on a typical printed map and on most other cartographic materials.

Table 7.1 shows the positions defined specifically for maps within field 008 when the legend begins with e (Maps, printed or microform) or f (Maps, manuscript), and the corresponding positions in field 006, which would begin with either of those two characters.

008	006	Code
18-21	01-04	Relief
22-23	05-06	Projection
24	07	Prime meridian
25	08	Cartographic material type
28	11	Government publication
31	14	Index
33-34	16-17	Special format characteristics
(Other positions undefined or obsolete)		

Table 7.1: Maps-specific 008 and 006 Values

Commonly Used Fields in Maps

Tables 7.2 and 7.3 show the thirty-three commonly used MARC fields in two samples of maps records. Fields in italics occur at least twice as often in records for maps as across the average of all formats.

Tag	Occ	Description
007	14.8	*Physical Description Fixed Field*
010	19.3	LC Control Number
017	1.0	*Copyright Registration Number*
020	7.3	ISBN
034	48.0	*Coded Cartographic Mathematical Data*
035	2.0	System Control Number
040	53.0	Cataloging Source
041	7.1	Language Code
045	7.7	*Time Period of Content*
050	19.0	LC Call Number
052	60.6	*Geographical Classification Code*
074	5.2	*GPO Item Number*
086	5.9	*Government Document Classification Number*
100	14.7	Main Entry—Personal Name
110	57.8	*Main Entry—Corporate Name*
250	14.0	Edition Statement

Table 7.2: Maps: Commonly Used Fields, 007-250

Tag	Occ	Description
255	72.5	*Geographic Mathematical Data*
260	99.4	Publication, Distribution, etc. (Imprint)
265	7.2	*Source for Acquisition/Sub. Address*
300	92.1	*Physical Description*
440	9.1	*Series Statement/Added Entry—Title*
490	12.2	*Series Statement*
500	185.4	*General Note*
504	4.3	Bibliography, etc. Note
505	3.9	Formatted Contents Note
507	6.1	*Scale Note for Graphic Material*
610	1.2	Subject Added Entry—Corporate Name
650	41.8	Subject Added Entry—Topical Term
651	59.6	*Subject Added Entry—Geographic Name*
700	22.9	Added Entry—Personal Name
710	36.7	Added Entry—Corporate Name
740	21.3	*Added Entry—Uncontrolled Related/Analytical Title*
830	4.3	Series Added Entry—Uniform Title

Table 7.3: Maps: Commonly Used Fields, 255-830

Personal name main entries are, not surprisingly, less common for maps than for books—but far more common than for serials. Other tags used less frequently or more frequently than for books also make sense given the nature of the material; the very high occurrence of general notes reflects the need to provide comments to explain the maps. Three fields are fairly distinctly associated with maps: 034, 255, and 507. Field 507 is used only for maps cataloged according to pre-*AACR2* rules and provides a scale note.

Field 034 is used to record a coded equivalent of field 255. It is repeatable, since a single record may involve more than one set of scales. Used fully, the field stores a good indication of what area is actually covered by the map, although the indication is not precise.

034	Coded Mathematical Data
Ind. 1	Type of scale
‡a	Category of scale
‡b	Constant ratio linear horizontal scale
‡c	Constant ratio linear vertical scale
‡d	Coordinates - westernmost longitude
‡e	Coordinates - easternmost longitude
‡f	Coordinates - northernmost latitude
‡g	Coordinates - southernmost latitude
‡h	Angular scale
‡j	Declination - northern limit
‡k	Declination - southern limit
‡m	Right ascension - eastern limit
‡n	Right ascension - western limit
‡p	Equinox

1_‡aa‡b253440‡dE0790000‡dE0860000‡fN0200000‡gN0120000¶

Table 7.4: Field 034

In the example above the flat map (or maps, or map[s] within an atlas) has a single scale, given as a linear scale, 1:253440 horizontal (one inch equals four miles). The map covers the area E 79°—E 86°/N 20°—N 12°, which would be the southeast portion of India and part of the Bay of Bengal and Indian Ocean.

255	Mathematical Data Area
Inds.	Undefined
‡a	Statement of scale
‡b	Statement of projection
‡c	Statement of coordinates
‡d	Statement of zone
‡e	Statement of equinox

Table 7.5: Field 255

This field provides much the same information as field 034, but in textual form. Field 034 could be used directly for retrieval (e.g., as

part of a geographic retrieval system); field 255 follows proper cataloging practice for description.[1]

---

255 *Mathematical Data Area*
__‡aScale 1:250,000 ;‡bTransverse Mercator proj. Everest
spheroid‡c(W 74°50'--W 74°40'/N 45°05'--N 45°00').¶
__‡aScale 1:59,403,960. "Along meridians only, 1 inch = 936 statute
miles."¶

Examples

Grenada. Where is it—and what maps can we find? Figures 7.1
through 7.4 show the bibliographic displays for part of the result of
such a search.

Great Britain. Ordnance Survey.
　　Grenada, island of spice, scale 1:50,000. -- Ed. 4-O.S.D. 1985, ed. 4 partially
rev. by OSD 1985 with addition of Point Salines International Airport. Scale
1:50,000 ; Transverse Mercator proj. (W 61°49'--W 61°35'/N 12°15'--N 11°58'). --
Southampton, England : Govt. of the United Kingdom (Ordnance Survey)
for the Govt. of Grenada ; St. George's, Grenada : Lands and Surveys Dept.,
Office of the Prime Minister, c1985.
　　1 map : col. ; on sheet 70 x 80 cm., folded to 18 x 14 cm.
　　Relief shown by contours, shading, gradient tints, and spot heights.
　　Panel title.
　　"Grid:-British West Indies."
　　Standard map series designation: Series E703.
　　Includes text, indexed insets of "South-west peninsula" and "St. George's,"
parish boundary diagram, and location map.
　　I. Title. II. Title: Series E703. III. Series: D.O.S. (Series) ; 442.

Figure 7.1: Map of Grenada (1)

1　　As specified in *AACR2 for Cartographic Materials: A Manual of Interpretation*,
prepared by the Anglo-American Cataloguing Committee for Cartographic
Materials.

United Nations. Physical Planning Office.
  Grenada: Electric transmission. July 1972. [New York, 1972]
  map on sheet 73 x 47 cm.
  Scale ca. 1:50,000.
  Photocopy.
  "Dwg. no. G. 2415."
    1. Electric power distribution--West Indies--Grenada--Maps. 2. Grenada,
West Indies--Maps.

Figure 7.2: Map of Grenada (2)

[United States. Central Intelligence Agency]
  Grenada. [Washington : Central Intelligence Agency, 1976]
  1 map : col. ; 22 x 17 cm.
  Scale 1:300,000.
  "502472 1-76 (541646)."
  "Transverse Mercator projection."
    1. Grenada, West Indies--Maps.

Figure 7.3: Map of Grenada (3)

Grenada County Chamber of Commerce.
  Maps, city of Grenada, Grenada Lake, and Grenada County. [Grenada,
Miss., 1967?]
    map 55 x 43 cm. fold. to 22 x 10 cm.
    Scale not given.
    Folded title: Grenada--it's all go!
    Includes indexes and maps of Grenada/Grenada Lake region and Grenada
County.
    Text, municipal information, location map, and illus. on verso.
    1. Grenada, Miss.--Maps.

Figure 7.4: Map of Grenada (4)

Without pausing to muse on the idea of a seagoing invasion of
Grenada, Mississippi, we go on to show portions of the MARC
records that created these bibliographic displays.

```
007        aj|canzn¶
008        860513s1985____enkabcgbh_a__f__0___eng__
034    1   ‡aa‡b50000‡dW0614900‡eW0613500‡fN0121500‡gN0115800¶
050    0   ‡aG5130 1985 ‡b.G7¶
052        ‡a5130¶
052        ‡a5134‡bS3¶
110    1   ‡aGreat Britain.‡bOrdnance Survey.¶
245    10  ‡aGrenada, island of spice, scale 1:50,000.¶
250    ‡aEd. 4-O.S.D. 1985, ed. 4 partially rev. by OSD 1985 with addition of
Point Salines International Airport.¶
255        ‡aScale 1:50,000 ;‡bTransverse Mercator proj.‡c(W 61°49'--W 61°35'/N
12°15'--N 11°58').¶
260    0   ‡aSouthampton, England :‡bGovt. of the United
Kingdom (Ordnance Survey) for the Govt. of Grenada ;‡aSt. George's,
Grenada :‡bLands and Surveys Dept., Office of the Prime Minis-
ter,‡cc1985.¶
265        ‡aDirector General, Ordnance Survey, Romsy Rd.,
Southampton, England, SO9 4DH¶
300        ‡a1 map :‡bcol. ;‡con sheet 70 x 80 cm., folded to 18 x 14 cm.¶
500        ‡aRelief shown by contours, shading, gradient tints, and spot heights.¶
500        ‡aPanel title.¶
500        ‡a"Grid:-British West Indies."¶
500        ‡aStandard map series designation: Series E703.¶
500        ‡aIncludes text, indexed insets of "South-west peninsula" and "St.
George's," parish boundary diagram, and location map.¶
740    01  ‡aSeries E703.¶
830    0   ‡aD.O.S. (Series) ;‡v442.¶
```

Figure 7.5: Map of Grenada (1), Tagged Record (Partial)

The relief codes *abcg* (008/18-21) provide coded equivalents to the first 500 note: contours, shading, gradient tints, and spot heights, respectively. The projection *bh* (008/22-23) indicates that the map is a Transverse Mercator projection. Record group code *a* (008/25) is for a single map.

The first character in field 007 is *a*, defining the material as a map. Given that first character, the rest of the field has the following significance:

- *j:* Specific material designation: *Map.* (As opposed to diagram, profile, remote-sensing image, section, view or other type.)
- |: Original vs. Reproduction Aspect: *Not supplied (fill character).*
- *c:* Color: *Multicolored.*
- *a:* Physical medium: *Paper.* (As opposed to wood, metal, etc.)
- *n:* Type of Reproduction: *Not applicable.*
- *z:* Production/Reproduction Details: *Other.*
- *n:* Positive/negative aspect: *Not applicable (not photocopy or film).*

The record contains matching 034 and 255 fields and includes both an area and a subarea geographic classification code (field 052).

010		‡a___74695549/MAPS¶
040		‡dCStRLIN¶
050	0	‡aG5131.N4 1972‡b.U5¶
052		‡a5131¶
052		‡a5130¶
110	2	‡aUnited Nations.‡bPhysical Planning Office.¶
245	00	‡aGrenada: Electric transmission.‡bJuly 1972.¶
260	1	‡a[New York,‡c1972]¶
300		‡amap‡con sheet 73 x 47 cm.¶
507		‡aScale ca. 1:50,000.¶
500		‡aPhotocopy.¶
500		‡a"Dwg. no. G. 2415."¶
650	0	‡aElectric power distribution‡zWest Indies‡zGrenada‡xMaps.¶
651	0	‡aGrenada, West Indies‡xMaps.¶

Figure 7.6: Map of Grenada (2), Partial Tagged Display

Figure 7.6 illustrates a pre-*AACR2* record using field 507 rather than 034 and 255. The 007 field in this record (not shown) contains only Production/reproduction details:*b—photocopy.* Note that this record also contains two geographic area codes, which provide reasonably precise geographic access using a known set of alphameric codes. Note that in both records the first 052 shows the same number as the LC classification; in fact, the 052‡a is created by dropping the "G" from an LC classification in the "G" category.

```
010         ‡a___80694313/MAPS¶
050    0    ‡aG5130 1976‡b.U5¶
052         ‡a5130¶
110    1    ‡a[United States.‡bCentral Intelligence Agency]¶
245    00   ‡aGrenada.¶
260    0    ‡a[Washington :‡bCentral Intelligence Agency,‡c1976]¶
300         ‡a1 map :‡bcol. ;‡c22 x 17 cm.¶
507         ‡aScale 1:300,000.¶
500         ‡a"502472 1-76 (541646)."¶
500         ‡a"Transverse Mercator projection."¶
651    0    ‡aGrenada, West Indies‡xMaps.¶
```

Figure 7.7: Map of Grenada (3), Partial Tagged Display

```
010         ‡a___77696318/MAPS¶
050    0    ‡aG3984.G8 1967‡b.G7¶
052         ‡a3984‡bG8¶
110    2    ‡aGrenada County Chamber of Commerce.¶
245    00   ‡aMaps, city of Grenada, Grenada Lake, and Grenada County.¶
260    1    ‡a[Grenada, Miss.,‡c1967?]¶
300         ‡amap‡c55 x 43 cm. fold. to 22 x 10 cm.¶
507         ‡bScale not given.¶
500         ‡aFolded title: Grenada--it's all go!¶
500         ‡aIncludes indexes and maps of Grenada/Grenada Lake
       region and Grenada County.¶
500         ‡aText, municipal information, location map, and illus.
       on  verso.¶
651    0    ‡aGrenada, Miss.‡xMaps.¶
```

Figure 7.8: Map of Grenada (Miss.), Partial Tagged Display

Figure 7.7 shows part of the tagged display for a very different record on Grenada. Finally, Figure 7.8 shows part of the tagged version of the map for "the other Grenada." As maps records go, this pre-*AACR2* record is relatively simple. It also has a geographic classification code, including a subarea code that makes the distinction between the two Grenadas abundantly clear.

8

Scores

Printed and manuscript music materials (*scores* as a convenient, if somewhat inaccurate shorthand) have some aspects in common with books and some with sound recordings (treated in chapter 9). Scores require uniform titles much more frequently than most other forms of material and tend to have nondistinctive titles. Arguments that main entries should be scrapped in favor of title main entry, lumping all name entries together, run up against the reality of scores and musical sound recordings. Because titles are so frequently nondistinctive, the name of the composer is the critical identifying element for a high percentage of materials, even more often than for books.

008	006	Code
18-19	01-02	Form of composition
20	03	Format of music
21	04	Undefined (obsolete)
22	05	Target audience
23	06	Form of item
24-29	07-12	Accompanying matter
30-31	13-14	Literary text code (recordings)
32-34	15-17	Undefined (obsolete)

Table 8.1: Specific 008-006 Codes for Music

The Library of Congress created a single MARC format for "music," lumping together printed music and all sound recordings (musical and nonmusical). The two primary shared cataloging services in the United States, OCLC and RLIN, decided independently to treat scores and sound recordings as separate formats. Format integration renders the question moot, since the legend for printed music is distinct from the legend for sound recordings. The historical amalgamation lives on, however, in the format-specific 008 and 006 codes as listed in Table 8.1.

This flavor of 006 is defined by a first character of *c* (Music, printed or microform); *d* (Manuscripts of music); *i* (Sound recordings, nonmusical); or *j* (Sound recordings, musical). Scores are defined by *c* or *d* as the first character of the legend.

Commonly Used Fields in Printed Music

Large samples of scores records suggest that the records have fewer commonly used fields than books, and about the same number as maps. Tables 8.2 and 8.3 show the commonly used fields. Fields in italics appear at least twice as often in records for printed music as in the average of all materials.

Tag	Occ	Description
010	27.8	LC Control Number
020	11.1	ISBN
028	*64.1*	*Publisher Number for Music*
035	3.8	System Control Number
040	85.9	Cataloging Source
041	*21.6*	*Language Code*
043	2.4	Geographic Area Code
045	*56.6*	*Time Period of Content*
047	*4.5*	*Type of Musical Composition Code*
048	*83.2*	*Number of Instruments or Voices Code*

Table 8.2: Scores: Commonly Used Fields, 010-048

Tag	Occ	Description
050	27.3	LC Call Number
100	90.2	Main Entry—Personal Name
110	1.4	Main Entry—Corporate Name
240	*64.8*	*Uniform Title*
250	7.6	Edition Statement
254	*4.9*	*Musical Presentation Statement*
260	98.9	Publication, Distribution, etc. (Imprint)
300	97.0	Physical Description
306	*4.5*	*Playing Time*
440	14.2	Series Statement/Added Entry—Title
490	19.4	Series Statement
500	*146.3*	*General Note*
504	3.1	Bibliography, etc. Note
505	*15.9*	*Formatted Contents Note*
600	*6.1*	*Subject Added Entry—Personal Name*
650	*121.6*	*Subject Added Entry—Topical Term*
700	*64.7*	*Added Entry—Personal Name*
710	*3.9*	*Added Entry—Corporate Name*
740	*19.4*	*Added Entry—Uncontrolled Related/Analytical Title*
800	*1.0*	*Series Added Entry—Personal Name*
830	3.2	Series Added Entry—Uniform Title

Table 8.3: Scores: Commonly Used Fields, 050-830

In addition to the heavy use of uniform titles, with almost two-thirds of all records requiring uniform titles (a ratio that was almost unchanged between 1986 and 1988 samples), four fields are distinctively used for scores and sound recordings: 047, 048, 254, and 306. Field 306 is discussed in chapter 9 since it is far more common for sound recordings than for scores.

> *047 Type of Musical Composition Code*
> __‡aor‡act¶

Field 047 is used when a score includes more than one type of composition; in most cases the type of composition appears in field 008 positions 18-19. The same codes are used here in the repeatable subfield ‡a. This field says that the score includes both one or more oratorios *or* and one or more cantatas *ct*.

> *048 Number of Instruments or Voices Code*
> __‡aba02‡awb03‡awd01‡asa02‡asb01‡asc01‡asz02‡akc01¶

Field 048, with undefined indicators, contains codes for performers or ensembles (in ‡a) and for soloists (in ‡b). The field definition includes a list of two-character codes; the number following each two-character code is the actual number of parts for the particular instrument. This example, for Johann Sebastian Bach's Brandenburg Concerto I in F, BWV 1046, specifies (in the order given) that the concerto has two parts for horns, three for oboes, one for bassoon, two for violin, one for viola, one for violoncello, two for other bowed strings, and one for harpsichord.

Field 048 has great potential for specialized retrieval purposes, and music catalogers have gone to some effort to provide the information whenever possible.

> *254 Musical Presentation Statement*
> __‡aScore and set of parts¶

Field 254 is used to transcribe a statement from the item itself that relates to the edition in hand, which may differ from other editions of the same work. The field is used only for printed and manuscript music and is not used very widely (possibly because it is relatively new to the formats).

Examples

Music catalogers must deal with sheet music for individual songs, miniature scores for classic works, and collections of all sorts. The three examples at the end of this chapter appear chronologically (by date of composition), for no particular reason. The examples are partial, with illustrative fields described in detail.

Bach, Johann Sebastian, 1685-1750.
  [Brandenburgische Konzerte. Nr. 1]
  Brandenburg concerto no. 1, F major, BWV 1046 / Johann Sebastian Bach ;
  edited by Karin Stockl in collaboration with Gudrun Schaub, Christoph
  Schmider, Martin Steinebrunner. -- London ; New York : Eulenburg, c1984.
  1 miniature score (xviii, 41 p.) : facsims. ; 19 cm.
  Edition Eulenburg, no. 280.
  Concertino: 2 horns, 3 oboes, and violino piccolo.
  Eulenburg : 6731.
  1. Concerti grossi--Scores. I. Stockl, Karin. II. Title.

Figure 8.1: Miniature Score, Bibliographic Display

---

028 30   ‡a280‡bEulenburg¶
028 22   ‡a6731‡bEulenburg¶
040   ‡aCL‡cCL¶
041 0   ‡gengger¶
045   ‡av1v2¶
048   ‡bba02‡bwb03‡bsa01‡aoc¶
100 10   ‡aBach, Johann Sebastian,‡d1685-1750.¶
240 10   ‡aBrandenburgische Konzerte.‡nNr. 1¶
245 10   ‡aBrandenburg concerto no. 1, F major, BWV 1046 /‡cJohann Sebastian Bach ; ...*portion omitted*...¶
260 0   ‡aLondon ;‡aNew York :‡bEulenburg,‡cc1984.¶
300   ‡a1 miniature score (xviii, 41 p.) :‡bfacsims. ;‡c19 cm.¶
500   ‡aEdition Eulenburg, no. 280.¶
500   ‡aConcertino: 2 horns, 3 oboes, and violino piccolo.¶
650 0   ‡aConcerti grossi‡xScores.¶
700 10   ‡aStockl, Karin.¶

Figure 8.2: Miniature Score, Tagged Display

Some relevant portions of field 008 are as follows:

> 008/18 cg *Form of composition* Concerti grossi
> 008/20 b *Form of item* Full score, miniature/study
> 008/24 hi *Accompanying matter* Technical information on music;
> historical information

The record includes two publisher's numbers (028), distinguished by their indicators. The first is an "Other number" for which no note or added entry should be made; the second is a plate number for which a note but not added entry should be made (the note appears in the bibliographic display: *Eulenburg : 6731*). Field 041 indicates that the languages of accompanying material (‡g) are English and German.

> 045 *Time period of content*
> __‡av1v2¶

This work is associated with a particular period, specifically 1710-1720 (*v* indicates 1700-1799; the number indicates the decade).

Note that field 048 shows different instrumentation than the earlier example for the same concerto. This field says that this edition is scored for two horns, three oboes, one violin, and a string orchestra.

Moving forward a few years, we come to the score displayed in Figures 8.3 and 8.4. In this case the language field says that the *text* (‡a) is in German and English and that the *original* (‡h) is in English. The German text is a translation; the first indicator 1 says that it "is or includes a translation." Field 045 for this record gives the actual dates, recorded in ‡b: AD 1961-1962. Note that field 028 also generates a note in this record.

Stravinsky, Igor, 1882-1971.
  [Flood. Vocal score. German & English]
  The flood : a musical play : vocal score / [music by] Igor Stravinsky. -- London ; New York : Boosey & Hawkes, c1963.
  1 vocal score (50 p.) ; 31 cm.
  "The text ... chosen and arranged by Robert Craft, is derived principally from the Book of Genesis and the York and Chester cycles of miracle plays (set down between 1430 and 1500)."--Pref.
  For voice and piano, with instrumental cues.
  Duration: 24:00.
  Boosey & Hawkes : B. & H. 18939.
  1. Oratorios--Vocal scores with piano. 2. Ballets--Vocal scores with piano. 3. Noah (Biblical figure)--Drama. I. Craft, Robert. II. Title.

Figure 8.3: Vocal Score, Bibliographic Display

028	22	‡bBoosey & Hawkes‡aB. & H. 18939.¶
040		‡cIdPI‡dIdPI‡dNNC‡dCU-A¶
041	1	‡agereng‡heng¶
045	2	‡bd1961‡bd1962¶
047		‡aor‡abt¶
048		‡bvd01‡bvf02‡bvn06‡aca03‡aka01¶
050	0	‡aM2003.S897‡bF62¶
100	10	‡aStravinsky, Igor,‡d1882-1971.¶
240	10	‡aFlood.‡sVocal score.‡lGerman & English¶
245	14	‡aThe flood :‡ba musical play : vocal score /‡c[music by] Igor Stravinsky.¶
260	0	‡aLondon ;‡aNew York :‡bBoosey & Hawkes,‡cc1963.¶
300		‡a1 vocal score (50 p.) ;‡c31 cm.¶
500		‡a"The text ... chosen and arranged by Robert Craft, is derived principally from the Book of Genesis and the York and Chester cycles of miracle plays (set down between 1430 and 1500)."--Pref.¶
500		‡aFor voice and piano, with instrumental cues.¶
500		‡aDuration: 24:00.¶
650	0	‡aOratorios‡xVocal scores with piano.¶
650	0	‡aBallets‡xVocal scores with piano.¶
600	00	‡aNoah‡c(Biblical figure)‡xDrama.¶
700	11	‡aCraft, Robert.¶

Figure 8.4: Vocal Score, Tagged Display

Field 047 indicates that this is (or contains) both an oratorio and a ballet. Field 048 says that the score is for nine soloists in all (indicated in ‡b subfields)—one tenor *vd01*, two basses *vf02*, and six unspecified voices *vn06*—as well as three-part mixed chorus ‡*caca03* and piano ‡*aka01*.

Finally, Figures 8.5 and 8.6 show a contemporary collection of scores from a slightly different genre, overlapping chronologically with Stravinsky's work.

The compleat Beatles / produced by Delilah Communications/ATV Music Publications ; music arranged and edited by Milton Okun ; art direction and cover design by Ed Caraeff. -- Toronto ; New York : Delilah Communications/ATV Music Publications , c1981.
   1 score (2 v.) : ill. ; 31 cm.

"A Delilah/ATV/Bantam Book."
Discography: v.1, p. 93-104; v.2, p. 63-76.
Contents: v. 1. 1962-1966 -- v. 2. 1966-1970.
ISBN 0-553-01353-X (v.1) : $19.95. -- ISBN 0-553-01354-8 (v.2) : $19.95

1. Beatles. 2. Beatles--Discography. 3. Music, Popular (Songs, etc.)--England. I. Okun, Milton. II. Lennon, John, 1940-1980. III. McCartney, Paul. IV. Beatles.

Figure 8.5: Collection, Bibliographic Display

```
020        ‡a055301353X (v.1) :‡c$19.95¶
020        ‡a0553013548 (v.2) :‡c$19.95¶
045        ‡ax6x7¶
245    04  ‡aThe compleat Beatles /‡cproduced by Delilah Communica-
tions/ATV Music Publications ; music arranged and edited by Milton
Okun ; art direction and cover design by Ed Caraeff.¶
260    0   ‡aToronto ;‡aNew York :‡bDelilah Communications/ATV Music Publi-
cations,‡cc1981.¶
300        ‡a1 score (2 v.) :‡bill. ;‡c31 cm.¶
500        ‡a"A Delilah/ATV/Bantam Book."¶
504        ‡aDiscography: v.1, p. 93-104; v.2, p. 63-76.¶
505    0   ‡av. 1. 1962-1966 -- v. 2. 1966-1970.¶
610    20  ‡aBeatles.¶
610    20  ‡aBeatles‡xDiscography.¶
650    0   ‡aMusic, Popular (Songs, etc.)‡zEngland.¶
700    10  ‡aOkun, Milton.¶
700    10  ‡aLennon, John,‡d1940-1980.¶
700    10  ‡aMcCartney, Paul.¶
710    20  ‡aBeatles.¶
```

Figure 8.6: Collection, Tagged Display

Some portions of the 008 field follow:

008/18 rc *Form of composition* Rock music
008/20 c   *Form of item* Accompaniment reduced for keyboard
008/24 fi *Accompanying matter* Biography; historical information.

Field 045 gives the time period as 1960s-1970s, with x representing 1900-1999. This record also includes three corporate name entries (two subject, 610, and one added entry, 710), not terribly uncommon for music: *The Beatles* is considered to be a corporate name.

9

Sound Recordings

Sound recordings include several media and a wide range of material. A sound recording may be a compact disc, audiocassette, vinyl or shellac audiodisc, reel of tape, or piano roll.[1] It may be a publication or a unique tape recording. It may contain a single classical work, a collection of songs by one popular performer, or a combination of loosely related or apparently unrelated works.

The 008 and 006 fields for sound recordings are identical to those for scores. Sound recordings are identified by *i* (Sound recording, nonmusical) or *j* (Sound recording, musical) as the first character of the legend.

Sound recordings have one thing in common with computer files and many visual materials that differentiates them from books, printed serials, maps, and scores: sound recordings require special equipment for use. Some of the 007 values for sound recordings relate to the needs of potential users to be aware of special reproduction equipment required to use the sound recording.

---

1 Properly, a piano roll is *not* a sound recording at all, but it is treated as such by *AACR2*.

Commonly Used Fields in Sound Recordings

Tables 9.1 and 9.2 show the commonly used fields from two fairly large samples of MARC records for sound recordings. Note that sound recordings use almost as many fields commonly as books, although far fewer than serials. As usual fields used at least twice as often in sound recordings as in all formats appear in italics.

Tag	Occ	Description
007	*70.8*	*Physical Description Fixed Field*
010	24.0	LC Control Number
020	8.1	ISBN
024	*5.9*	*Standard Recording Number*
028	*102.2*	*Publisher Number for Music*
033	*20.0*	*Date/Time and Place of Event Code*
035	*16.9*	*System Control Number*
040	75.6	Cataloging Source
041	*31.2*	*Language Code*
043	9.5	Geographic Area Code
045	*32.6*	*Time Period of Content*
047	*10.7*	*Type of Musical Composition Code*
048	*42.7*	*Number of Instruments or Voices Code*
050	22.1	LC Call Number
100	76.9	Main Entry—Personal Name
110	6.3	Main Entry—Corporate Name
240	*37.3*	*Uniform Title*
260	79.2	Publication, Distribution, etc. (Imprint)
262	*10.3*	*Imprint for Sound Recordings (Pre-AACR2)*
300	86.6	Physical Description
305	*10.4*	*Description for Sound Rec. (Pre-AACR2)*
306	*21.1*	*Playing Time*
440	6.3	Series Statement/Added Entry—Title
490	12.0	Series Statement

Table 9.1: Recordings: Commonly Used Fields, 007-490

Tag	Occ	Description
500	*159.0*	*General Note*
505	*28.3*	*Formatted Contents Note*
511	*61.2*	*Participant or Performer Note*
518	*26.6*	*Date/Time and Place of Event Note*
520	1.7	Summary, Abstract, Annotation, etc.
533	1.2	Reproduction Note
600	4.4	Subject Added Entry—Personal Name
650	120.9	Subject Added Entry—Topical Term
651	1.3	Subject Added Entry—Geographic Name
700	*251.8*	*Added Entry—Personal Name*
710	*51.8*	*Added Entry—Corporate Name*
730	*2.6*	*Added Entry—Uniform Title*
740	*32.6*	*Added Entry—Uncontrolled Related/Analytical Title*
830	1.3	Series Added Entry—Uniform Title

Table 9.2: Recordings: Commonly Used Fields, 500-830

The commonly used and lightly used entry fields should not be surprising. The distribution of sound recordings between personal name and corporate name main entries is not that different from the distribution for books, but very few sound recordings have meeting name entries of any sort. Relatively few sound recordings are about people, but quite a few require a great many added entries for people and groups (conductors, soloists, orchestras, etc.). As with scores, uniform titles play an important part in identifying sound recordings.

Seven fields appear distinctly or predominantly in records for sound recordings. Two of these, fields 262 and 305, represent different practice for recording imprint and physical description prior to *AACR2*. The other five are illustrated below.

---

024 Standard Recording Number
1_‡a75992544472¶
1_‡a64287592268¶

Field 024 could contain either an International Standard Recording Number (ISRN) or a standard music industry code—but there is no ISRN at this time. On the other hand most U.S. recording manufacturers use Universal Product Codes (UPCs) on sound recordings—the ten-digit bar-coded codes that appear on many consumer products and are used, for example, by supermarket laser scanners. That code is a *de facto* U.S. standard with a proper administering body.

Rather than keep field 024 empty until an ISRN was developed, which may never happen, the field name was changed and the first indicator defined to specify what type of standard number is contained in the field. Subfield ‡a carries the *Standard number*; ‡d carries *Additional codes that may follow the number*; ‡z carries *Cancelled or invalid standard numbers*.

Both examples use a first indicator *1*, indicating UPC. The ten-digit number combines a five-digit manufacturer number (assigned by the Universal Product Council), a five-digit selection number (with the first digit being the same as the last manufacturer digit), and a one-digit configuration code. Thus, the first example is for manufacturer 75992 (Warner Bros.), item 25447 (*Graceland*), configuration 2 (compact disc). The second example is for manufacturer 64287, item 75926, configuration 8 (8-track tape).

A constant leading *0* is ignored in recording the UPC. Unfortunately, so is the trailing check digit (which doesn't always print with the label); as a result, it is not possible to check 024 fields for correctness.

Most contemporary recordings use the latter portion of the UPC code as the publisher's number. Thus, as shown later in this chapter, field 028 for the CD release of *Graceland* contains *9 25447-2*.

---

033 *Date/Time and Place of Event Code*
2_‡a1985----‡a1986----¶
0_‡a198402--‡b6299‡cB3¶

The first indicator shows the type of date. Subfield ‡a contains a date coded *yyyymmdd*; ‡b contains a geographic classification area code; ‡c contains a geographic classification subarea code.

In the first example 2 indicates "Range of dates." The two sub-fields show that the recording took place during 1985 and 1986. In the second example *0* indicates a single date. This recording was done in February 1984 in Berlin.

---

306 *Playing Time*
__‡a002018‡a000355‡a000529‡a002055¶

Field 306 has no defined indicators and a single repeatable sub-field ‡a, Playing time. The playing time is stated in hours, minutes, and seconds. The example above is for a recording with four pieces, lasting 20 minutes 18 seconds, 3 minutes 55 seconds, 5 minutes 29 seconds, and 20 minutes 55 seconds respectively.

---

511 *Participant or Performer Note*
0_‡aPaul Simon, with other artists.¶
0_‡aRadio-Symphonie-Orchester Berlin and Chorus ; Riccardo Chailly, conductor.¶

The first indicator shows the type of participant or performer and can generate a display constant; *0* means "General" (no display constant), and *1* generates the constant "Cast:". The only subfield is ‡a. This field is also commonly used for visual materials.

---

518 *Date/Time and Place of Event Note*
__‡aRecorded 1985-1986 in various locations.¶
__‡aRecorded Feb. 1984 in the Jesus Christus Kirche, Berlin.¶
__‡aRecorded and mixed at Sound Stage Studio, Nashville.¶

Field 518 has no defined indicators and a single subfield ‡a. It records notes on the date and place of the recording, and is largely a textual equivalent to field 033.

Field 007 for Sound Recordings

Physical description can be particularly significant for sound recordings, and most contemporary MARC records for sound recordings include field 007. When the first character of 007 is *s* (for sound recording), the remainder of the field carries the information defined in Table 9.3.

007/00 . . . .*s*	**Sound recording**
007/01	Specific material designation
007/02	Original vs. reproduction (not used)
007/03	Speed
007/04	Configuration of playback channels
007/05	Groove width/groove pitch
007/06	Dimensions (sound recordings)
007/07	Tape width
007/08	Tape configuration
007/09	Kind of disc, cylinder or tape
007/10	Kind of material
007/11	Kind of cutting
007/12	Special playback characteristics
007/13	Capture and storage technique

Table 9.3: Field 007 for Sound Recordings

Examples

The five examples given here demonstrate only a portion of the scope of sound recordings. Most examples are partial, with selected fields discussed. The first two examples, Figures 9.1 through 9.4, show two different editions of the same recording as cataloged by two different institutions, one of them the Library of Congress.

Simon, Paul.
  Graceland [sound recording] / Paul Simon. -- [Burbank, Calif.] : Warner Bros., p1986.
    1 sound disc : digital, stereo. ; 4 3/4 in.
    Paul Simon, with other artists.
    Compact disc.
    Program notes by Paul Simon with lyrics to songs (15 p. ; 12 cm.) inserted in container.
    Contents: The boy in the bubble (3:59) -- Graceland (4:48) -- I know what I know (3:13) -- Gumboots (2:42) -- Diamonds on the soles of her shoes (5:34) -- You can call me Al (4:39) -- Under African skies (3:34) -- Homeless (3:45) -- Crazy love, vol. II (4:17) -- That was your mother (2:51) -- All around the world, or, The myth of fingerprints (3:15).
    Warner Bros. : 9 25447-2.
    SRN: 7599254472
    1. Rock music. I. Title.

Figure 9.1: *Graceland* (CD), Bibliographic Display

```
007        sdufzngnnmmne¶
008        871218s1986____caupp____di_____1__eng_d¶
024   1    ‡a7599254472¶
028   02   ‡bWarner Bros.‡a9 25447-2¶
041   0    ‡deng‡eeng‡geng¶
100   10   ‡aSimon, Paul.¶
245   10   ‡aGraceland‡h[sound recording] /‡cPaul Simon.¶
260   0    ‡a[Burbank, Calif.] :‡bWarner Bros.,‡cp1986.¶
300        ‡a1 sound disc :‡bdigital, stereo. ;‡c4 3/4 in.¶
511   0    ‡aPaul Simon, with other artists.¶
...remaining fields (500, 500, 505, 650) omitted...
```

Figure 9.2: *Graceland* (CD), Partial Tagged Display

Simon, Paul, 1941- prf
    Graceland [sound recording] / Paul Simon. -- Burbank, Calif. : Warner
Bros. Records, p1986.
    1 sound disc : analog, 33 1/3 rpm ; 12 in.
    Warner Bros. Records: 1-25447 (on container: 25447-1).
    Popular songs.
    Sung in English and Zulu.
    Performed by Paul Simon and instrumental and vocal ensemble.
    Recorded 1985-1986 in various locations.
    Texts printed on inner envelope.
    Issued also as cassette and compact disc.
    Contents: The boy in the bubble / words by Paul Simon ; music by Paul
Simon and Forere Motloheloa (3:39) -- Graceland / words and music by
Paul Simon (4:48) -- I know what I know / words by Paul Simon ; music by
Paul Simon and General M.D. Shirinda (3:13) -- Gumboots / words by Paul
Simon ; music by Paul Simon, Johnjon Mkhalali, and Lulu Masilela (2:42) --
Diamonds on the soles of her shoes / words and music by Paul Simon ;
beginning by Paul Simon and Joseph Shabalala (5:34--...*portion omitted*....
    1. Popular music--1981- I. Title.

Figure 9.3: *Graceland* (LP), Bibliographic Display

007		sdubsmennmplu¶
008		870709p19861985cauppnn__d_____1_eng_ ¶
028	00	‡a1-25447‡bWarner Bros. Records¶
028	00	‡a25447-1‡bWarner Bros. Records¶
033	2	‡a1985----‡a1986----¶
041	0	‡dengzul‡eengzul¶
100	10	‡aSimon, Paul,‡d1941- ‡4prf¶
245	10	‡aGraceland‡h[sound recording] /‡cPaul Simon.¶
260	0	‡aBurbank, Calif. :‡bWarner Bros. Records,‡cp1986.¶
300		‡a1 sound disc :‡banalog, 33 1/3 rpm ;‡c12 in.¶
500		‡aWarner Bros. Records: 1-25447 (on container: 25447-1).¶
500		‡aPopular songs.¶
500		‡aSung in English and Zulu.¶
511	0	‡aPerformed by Paul Simon and instrumental and vocal ensemble.¶
518		‡aRecorded 1985-1986 in various locations.¶

...remaining fields (500, 500, 505, 650) omitted...

Figure 9.4: *Graceland* (LP), Partial Tagged Display

Consider the 007 in Figure 9.2. Its significance is as follows:

s	Sound recording
d	Sound disc
u	Unknown (not used)
f	1.4 meters per second (disc), the standard speed for CD
z	Other kind of sound
n	Not applicable, item does not contain grooves
g	4 3/4 inches (properly, 12 cm.)
nn	(Not a tape)
m	Mass-produced
m	Metal and plastic
n	Not applicable (no cutting)
e	Digital recording

The 007 in Figure 9.4 differs somewhat, as would be expected for the LP version:

s	Sound recording
d	Sound disc
u	not used
b	33 1/3 rpm
s	Stereophonic
m	Microgroove
e	12 in.
nn	(Not a tape)
m	Mass-produced
p	Plastic
l	Lateral or combined cutting
u	Unknown (special characteristics)

Note that the final *e* in the first example means specifically that the recording requires digital *playback* equipment, not that it was originally stored digitally: every compact disc should be encoded with this *e*. Note also that neither 007 includes the last character currently defined in the 007 for sound recordings.

The interesting portions of field 008 are basically the same in both records (except that the two records differ in the way that dates were handled). The recording was produced in California *cau*, consists of popular music *pp*, and includes libretto or text and historical information *di*. One institution entered a language field showing that the sung or spoken text ‡*d*, librettos ‡*e* and program notes ‡*g* are all in English. The other institution says that the sung or spoken text and librettos are in English and Zulu.

Both institutions gave detailed contents including timing for each piece; only one chose to list credits for each piece. The two differed as to whether this was rock music or popular music.

Neither institution chose to make added entries for the groups involved in the recording. A more complete catalog record could plausibly include at least the following additional fields, or some alternative form of these fields:

```
710  21‡aBoyoyo Boys¶
710  21‡aLadysmith Black Mambazo¶
710  21‡aStimela¶
710  21‡aGood Rockin' Dopsie And The Twisters¶
710  21‡aLos Lobos¶
```

The next example shows a fully cataloged example of a single-composer classical collection. Such MARC records can be long and complex. The record illustrated in Figures 9.5 through 9.7 is twice the size of a typical book record, but is not unusually long for this variety of MARC record.

Stravinsky, Igor, 1882-1971.
  [Selections]
  Symphony de psaumes ; Feux d'artifice ; Le roi des etoiles ; Chant du rossignol [sound recording] / Stravinsky. -- [London] : London, p1985.
  1 sound disc (51 min.) : digital, stereo. ; 4 3/4 in.

  1st & 3rd works for chorus and orchestra (sung in Latin or Russian) ; 2d &
4th works for orchestra.
  Radio-Symphonie-Orchester Berlin and Chorus ; Riccardo Chailly, con-
ductor.
  Recorded Feb. 1984 in the Jesus Christus Kirche, Berlin.
  Compact disc.
  Durations: 20:18 ; 3:55 ; 5:29 ; 20:55.
  Program notes by P. Griffith in English, French, and German and vocal
texts with German, English, and French translations (15 p. : ill.) inserted in
container.
  London : 414 078-2.
  SRN: 2894140782

  1. Choruses with orchestra. 2. Symphonic poems. 3. Orchestral music. 4.
Symphonies. I. Chailly, Riccardo, 1953- II. Stravinsky, Igor, 1882-1971. Sym-
phonie de Psaumes. 1985. III. Stravinsky, Igor, 1882-1971. Feu d'artifice. 1985.
IV. Stravinsky, Igor, 1882-1971. Zvezdolikii. 1985. V. Stravinsky, Igor, 1882-
1971. Chant du rossignol. 1985. VI. Radio-Symphonie-Orchester Berlin. VII.
Radio-Symphonie-Orchester Berlin. Chor. VIII. Title. IX. Title: Feux d'artifice. X. Title: Le roi des etoiles. XI. Title: Chant du rossignol.

Figure 9.5: Stravinsky, Bibliographic Display

```
007        sdufzngnnmmne¶
008        870722s1985___enkmu___di____1_lat_d¶
024   1    ‡a28941407082¶
028   02   ‡bLondon‡a414 078-2¶
033   0    ‡a198402--‡b6299‡cB3¶
040        ‡aNBiSU‡cNBiSU‡dCSt‡dUPB‡dCU‡dCLSU¶
041   0    ‡dlatrus‡elatrusgerengfre‡gengfreger‡hlatrus¶
045   2    ‡bd1900‡bd1939¶
047        ‡asy‡asp‡azz¶
048        ‡aoa‡aca¶
048        ‡aoa¶
048        ‡aoa‡acc¶
100   10   ‡aStravinsky, Igor,‡d1882-1971.¶
240   10   ‡aSelections¶
245   10   ‡aSymphony de psaumes ; Feux d'artifice ; Le roi des etoiles ; Chant
du rossignol‡h[sound recording] /‡cStravinsky.¶
260   0    ‡a[London] :‡bLondon,‡cp1985.¶
300        ‡a1 sound disc (51 min.) :‡bdigital, stereo. ;‡c4 3/4 in.¶
306        ‡a002018‡a000355‡a000529‡a002055¶
500        ‡a1st & 3rd works for chorus and orchestra (sung in Latin or
Russian) ; 2d & 4th works for orchestra.¶
511   0    ‡aRadio-Symphonie-Orchester Berlin and Chorus ; Riccardo Chailly,
conductor.¶
518        ‡aRecorded Feb. 1984 in the Jesus Christus Kirche, Berlin.
500        ‡aCompact disc.¶
500        ‡aDurations: 20:18 ; 3:55 ; 5:29 ; 20:55.¶
500        ‡aProgram notes by P. Griffith in English, French, and German and
vocal texts with German, English, and French translations (15 p. : ill.) in-
serted in container.¶
650   0    ‡aChoruses with orchestra.¶
650   0    ‡aSymphonic poems.¶
650   0    ‡aOrchestral music.¶
650   0    ‡aSymphonies.¶
700   10   ‡aChailly, Riccardo,‡d1953-¶
700   12   ‡aStravinsky, Igor,‡d1882-1971.‡tSymphonie de Psaumes.‡f1985.¶
700   12   ‡aStravinsky, Igor,‡d1882-1971.‡tFeu d'artifice.‡f1985.¶
700   12   ‡aStravinsky, Igor,‡d1882-1971.‡tZvezdolikii.‡f1985.¶
700   12   ‡aStravinsky, Igor,‡d1882-1971.‡tChant du rossignol.‡f1985.¶
710   20   ‡aRadio-Symphonie-Orchester Berlin.¶
710   20   ‡aRadio-Symphonie-Orchester Berlin.‡bChor.¶
```

Figure 9.6: Stravinsky, Tagged Display (Part 1)

```
740   01   ‡aFeux d'artifice.¶
740   31   ‡aLe roi des etoiles.¶
740   01   ‡aChant du rossignol.¶
```

Figure 9.7: Stravinsky, Tagged Display (Part 2)

The fixed fields in this record say, among other things, that the recording contains multiple forms of composition (008/18-19:*mu*) and that the predominant language is Latin (008/35-37:*lat*). The 041 field (Language Code) says that the sung or spoken text is in Latin and Russian; the librettos are in Latin, Russian, German, English, and French; program notes are in English, French, and German; and the original text was in Latin and Russian.

Field 047 gives the specific forms of composition: Symphonies, Symphonic poems, and Other forms. Each 048 field gives the instrumentation and voices for one of the pieces. In order they are: Full orchestra and mixed chorus; full orchestra; full orchestra and men's chorus.

The Gandhi centennial [sound recording]. -- Los Angeles, Calif. : Pacifica Radio Archive, p1983.
 1 sound cassette (44 min.) : analog.
 Radio broadcast.
 Music, Emani Shankar.
 Issued also on reel.
 Summary: On the centennial of the birth of Gandhi, in 1968, features Secretary General of the United Nations U Thant speaking of Gandhi, his life, and his philosophy; Rev. Martin Luther King, Jr., gives a short speech entitled "The spirit of Mahatma"; and Mahatma Gandhi himself is heard addressing the Inter-Asian Relations Conference in New Delhi in 1947.
 Pacifica Radio Archive : BB4578
 1. Gandhi, Mahatma, 1869-1948. 2. Statesmen--India--Biography. 3. Nationalists--India--Biography. I. King, Martin Luther, Jr., 1929-1968. II. Gandhi, Mahatma, 1869-1948. III. Pacifica Radio Archive.

Figure 9.8: Spoken Word, Bibliographic Display

```
007        ssulunjlcnnnu¶
008        870819s1983____caunnnn_____hl0__eng__ ¶
010        ‡a___87753259/R¶
028   02   ‡aBB4578‡bPacifica Radio Archive¶
033   2    ‡a1968----‡a1947----‡b7650¶
245   04   ‡aThe Gandhi centennial‡h[sound recording].¶
260   0    ‡aLos Angeles, Calif. :‡bPacifica Radio Archive,‡cp1983.¶
300        ‡a1 sound cassette (44 min.) :‡banalog.¶
306        ‡a004400¶
500        ‡aRadio broadcast.¶
500        ‡aMusic, Emani Shankar.¶
500        ‡aIssued also on reel.¶
520        ‡aOn the centennial of the birth of Gandhi, in 1968, features
Secretary General of the United Nations U Thant speaking of Gandhi, his
life, and his philosophy; Rev. Martin Luther King, Jr., gives a short speech
entitled "The spirit of Mahatma"; and Mahatma Gandhi himself is heard
addressing the Inter-Asian Relations Conference in New Delhi in 1947.¶
600   10   ‡aGandhi,‡cMahatma,‡d1869-1948.¶
650   0    ‡aStatesmen‡zIndia‡xBiography.¶
650   0    ‡aNationalists‡zIndia‡xBiography.¶
700   10   ‡aKing, Martin Luther,‡qJr.,‡d1929-1968.¶
700   10   ‡aGandhi,‡cMahatma,‡d1869-1948.¶
710   20   ‡aPacifica Radio Archive.¶
```

Figure 9.9: Spoken Word, Tagged Display

Finally, Figures 9.8 and 9.9 show a typical spoken word record-ing—in this case, a limited-release tape from Pacifica Radio. Most of the fields should be self-explanatory at this point.

10

Visual Materials

W hen the first MARC format dealing with pictorial media was prepared in 1970 it was titled *Films: A MARC Format; Specifications for Magnetic Tapes Containing Records for Motion Pictures, Filmstrips, and Other Pictorial Media Intended for Projection.* Almost as soon as the format emerged the name became misleading: when Sony introduced U-matic recording in 1971, libraries began to catalog videocassettes using this format.

As the use of MARC grew, libraries needed to catalog many more forms of visual materials. The films format covered *AACR2* chapter 7, "Motion Pictures and Videorecordings," and part—but not all— of chapter 8, "Graphic Materials." No MARC format covered chapter 10, "Three-Dimensional Artefacts and Realia."

From Films to Visual Materials

P roposal 82-21, "Additions/Changes to the films format so as to accommodate two-dimensional material," was prepared by the Library of Congress in 1982 and first submitted to the USMARC advisory group at meetings in October 1982; the changes were discussed in June and September 1983, and approved during ALA Midwinter 1984. The proposal changed the name of the format to "visual materials," and added a large number of fields, subfields, and indicators to the format. Changes also included editorial revision of *MFBD* for consistency and to reflect the needs of agencies that catalog graphic materials. With the changes, the new format provided full support for chapter 8 of *AACR2* and for the extended rules in LC's publication *Graphic Materials: Rules for Describing Original Items and Historical Collections*.

When this proposal was originally presented, the USMARC advisory group was busily reviewing the archival and manuscripts control (AMC) format. Many of the elements desired for original and historical graphics were also needed for archival materials, and the review group suggested that the newer proposal be modified to take advantage of AMC fields. With Phyllis Bruns' expert guidance and editorial work, the proposal was revised in such a way that it drew the formats closer together and made them more consistent.

Visual materials represents one of the two "catch-all" format areas within USMARC, the other being computer files (considered in chapter 11). The format uses four different codes as the first byte of the legend:

g	Projected media
k	Two-dimensional nonprojectable graphic representations
o	Kits
r	Three-dimensional artifacts and naturally occurring objects

008	006	Code
18-20	01-03	Running time
22	05	Target audience
23-27	06-10	Accompanying matter
28	11	Government publication
33	16	Type of material
34	17	Technique

Table 10.1: Specific 008-006 Codes for Visual Materials

Table 10.1 shows the defined distinctive 008 positions and 006 equivalents for records with any one of these codes (or for 006 fields beginning with one of the codes). These codes are enhanced by field 007 definitions for graphics, motion pictures, and videorecordings, discussed in the examples.

Commonly Used Fields in Visual Materials

Tag	Occ	Description
007	76.6	*Physical Description Fixed Field*
010	8.6	LC Control Number
020	8.4	ISBN
035	22.3	*System Control Number*
040	74.4	Cataloging Source
041	4.2	Language Code
043	16.9	Geographic Area Code
045	1.5	Time Period of Content
050	5.8	LC Call Number
082	6.7	Dewey Decimal Call Number
100	6.0	Main Entry—Personal Name
130	1.3	Main Entry—Uniform Title
257	1.4	*Country of Producing Entity for Archival Films*
260	96.6	Publication, Distribution, etc. (Imprint)
300	103.7	Physical Description
440	11.6	Series Statement/Added Entry—Title
490	21.9	Series Statement
500	146.8	*General Note*
505	3.9	Formatted Contents Note
506	11.3	*Restrictions on Access*
508	27.8	*Creation/Production Credits Note*
511	32.8	*Participant or Performer Note*
518	1.6	*Date/Time and Place of Event Note*
520	65.7	*Summary, Abstract, Annotation, etc.*
521	15.0	*Target Audience Note*

Table 10.2: Visual Materials: Commonly Used Fields, 007-521

Tag	Occ	Description
600	26.8	Subject Added Entry—Personal Name
610	4.2	Subject Added Entry—Corporate Name
650	141.7	Subject Added Entry—Topical Term
651	16.4	Subject Added Entry—Geographic Name
655	12.8	Index Term—Genre/Form
700	*153.3*	*Added Entry—Personal Name*
710	*75.9*	*Added Entry—Corporate Name*
730	1.4	Added Entry—Uniform Title
740	*26.3*	*Added Entry—Uncontrolled Related/Analytical Title*
830	5.8	Series Added Entry—Uniform Title
840	1.6	Series Added Entry—Title (Obsolete)

Table 10.3: Visual Materials: Commonly Used Fields, 600-840

Visual materials records appear to use slightly fewer fields commonly than do books. Tables 10.2 and 10.3 show fields appearing more than once per hundred records in two samples of visual materials records (except for some control fields and field 245), with italicized fields showing those fields appearing more than twice as often in visual materials as in all formats.

As with other nontext formats, visual materials records make heavy use of general notes and specific notes. As with sound recordings, many (but not all) visual materials require special equipment for use, and field 007 is heavily used. Four fields appear distinctively in visual materials records and are described next.

257	*Country of Producing Entity for Archival Films*

‗ ‡aUnited States.¶
‗ ‡aSpain ; Italy ; Austria.¶

This simple field, consisting only of a subfield ‡a, contains the textual equivalent of field 044 (Country of producer code).

506	*Restrictions on Access*
‡a	*Terms governing access*
‡b	*Jurisdiction*
‡c	*Physical access provisions*
‡d	*Authorized users*
‡3	*Materials specified*
__‡arestricted: Material extremely fragile.¶	

Restrictions could reasonably include licensing restrictions as well as restrictions required for archival or security reasons. This field is also used, somewhat more widely, in archival and manuscripts control.

508	*Creation/Production Credits Note*
__‡aMusic, Michael Fishbein; camera, George Mo.¶	

This note generates the display constant "Credits: " and consists of a single subfield ‡a. It provides for credits other than cast members; those credits appear in field 511. Credits deserving added entries may also appear in fields 700 or 710.

521	*Target Audience*
Ind.1	*Display constant controller*
‡a	*Target audience note*
‡3	*Materials specified*
__‡aElementary grades.¶	
8_‡aMPAA rating: R.¶	

The display constant controller may be blank or may contain *8* to *suppress* the display constant "Audience: ".

Examples

LaserVision discs, posters, filmstrips, paintings, fossils, and multimedia educational kits: these are some of the materials that fall into the visual materials category. The four examples shown and described here, fully or in part, represent a small subset of that range but illustrate a few of the features of MARC for cataloging visual materials—and a few of the problems encountered in handling such materials.

Citizen Kane [videorecording] / an RKO Radio Picture ; a Mercury production ; Orson Welles, direction, production. -- Santa Monica, Calif. : Criterion, c1984.

    3 videodiscs (119 min.) : sd., b&w, 1600 rpm ; 12 in. -- (Criterion collection)

    Cast: Orson Welles, Joseph Cotton, Agnes Moorehead, Everett Sloane.

    Credits: Photography, Gregg Toland ; music, Bernard Herrmann ; screenplay, Orson Welles, Herman J. Mankiewicz.

    Originally produced as motion picture in 1941.

    Laserdisc, CAV.

    1941 Academy Award for best screenplay.

    Summary: Videorecording of Citizen Kane, the story of the rise and fall of a great man as the result of his accumulation of wealth and subsequent isolation from the world, plus a visual essay of over 100 photographs, many never before published. Also a theatrical trailer, a rarely seen 3-minute film made by Welles from original footage not contained in the movie.

    Criterion: CC101.

    1. Feature films. I. Welles, Orson, 1915-1985. II. RKO Radio Pictures, inc. III. Mercury Productions. IV. Criterion (Firm)

Figure 10.1: *Citizen Kane*, Bibliographic Display

```
007        vd|bgaiz|¶
008        851031p19841941xxu119_g_____0vleng_d¶
245   00   ‡aCitizen Kane‡h[videorecording] /‡can RKO Radio Picture ; a Mer-
cury production ; Orson Welles, direction, production.¶
260        ‡aSanta Monica, Calif. :‡bCriterion,‡cc1984.¶
300        ‡a3 videodiscs (119 min.) :‡bsd., b&w, 1600 rpm ;‡c12 in.¶
490   0    ‡aCriterion collection¶
511   1    ‡aOrson Welles, Joseph Cotton, Agnes Moorehead, Everett Sloane.¶
508        ‡aPhotography, Gregg Toland ; music, Bernard Herrmann ;
screenplay, Orson Welles, Herman J. Mankiewicz.¶
500        ‡aOriginally produced as motion picture in 1941.¶
500        ‡aLaserdisc, CAV.¶
```

Figure 10.2: *Citizen Kane*, Tagged Display (Part 1)

500		‡a1941 Academy Award for best screenplay.¶
520		‡aVideorecording of Citizen Kane, the story of the rise and fall of a great man...*text omitted*... not contained in the movie.¶
500		‡aCriterion: CC101.¶
650	0	‡aFeature films.¶
700	11	‡aWelles, Orson,‡d1915-1985.¶
710	21	‡aRKO Radio Pictures, inc.¶
710	21	‡aMercury Productions.¶
710	21	‡aCriterion (Firm)¶

Figure 10.3: *Citizen Kane*, Tagged Display (Part 2)

This record illustrates use of field 511 and field 508. Some of the 008 values show (respectively) the following:

851031	Date cataloged: October 31, 1985
p	Dates of distribution and production
1984	Date of distribution
1941	Date of production
xxu	Produced somewhere in the United States
119	Running time: 119 minutes
g	General (intellectual level)
...	
v	Videorecording
l	Liveaction

Field 007 begins with *v*, defining a videocassette. The remaining values are as shown below.

d	Specific Material: *Videodisc*
	Original vs. reproduction: not coded
b	Color: *Black-and-white*
g	Videorecording format: *Laser optical (reflective)*
a	Sound on medium/separate: *Sound on medium*
i	Medium for sound: *Videodisc*
z	Width or dimensions: *Other*
	Kind of sound for moving images: not coded

Why is width coded as *Other*? All available letters *a* through *z* were used for motion pictures, filmstrips, videocassettes, and transparencies.

The 300 field is unusual for a videodisc in that a legitimate playing speed in rpm can be stated, in accordance with *AACR2* rule 7.5C6. That relates to the mysterious last word in the second 500 field, *CAV*. Unlike most entertainment optical videodiscs, which change speed constantly and have no true "rpm" measurement, the Criterion collection uses constant angular velocity (CAV), always spinning at the same speed.

This record is reasonably typical for full cataloging of a motion picture on video, with a handful of added entries and fairly lengthy description. Compare the (topically related) record that appears in Figures 10.3 and 10.4.

Citizen Dull. [Motion picture] / York University. [Toronto] : The University, 1976.
    1 reel, 23 min. : sd., b&w ; 16 mm.
    Credits: Producers, Robert Kennedy, Cam Kieffer, Ernesto Medina.
    Summary: A parody of Citizen Kane.
    1. Short films. 2. Comedy films. I. Citizen Kane. [Motion picture] II. York University, Toronto, Ont.

Figure 10.4: *Citizen Dull*, Bibliographic Display

007		mr|baaad|¶
245	00	‡aCitizen Dull.‡h[Motion picture] /‡cYork University.¶
260		‡a[Toronto] :‡bThe University,‡c1976.¶
300		‡a1 reel, 23 min. :‡bsd., b&w ;‡c16 mm.¶
508		‡aProducers, Robert Kennedy, Cam Kieffer, Ernesto Medina.¶
520		‡aA parody of Citizen Kane.¶
650	0	‡aShort films.¶
650	0	‡aComedy films.¶
730	1	‡aCitizen Kane.‡h[Motion picture]¶
710	21	‡aYork University, Toronto, Ont.¶

Figure 10.5: *Citizen Dull*, Partial Tagged Display

Relatively less information is available on this short film, which is also an initial release rather than a re-release. Compare the 007 values, this time with position 0 *m*, "Motion picture":

r	*Film reel*
|	*Not coded*
b	*Black-and-white*
a	*Standard sound aperture (reduced frame)*
a	*Sound on medium*
a	*Optical sound track on film*
d	*16mm.*
|	*Kind of sound not coded*

Position 04 has a slightly different name when position 0 is *m*: "Motion picture presentation format." (Note for both examples: position 9 [kind of sound] was added to the visual materials 007 fairly recently, primarily to serve the archival community.)

These two examples are typical of commercial films and videos: they have clearly stated titles and enough information on the piece for good descriptive cataloging. The next example, in Figures 10.6 and 10.7, represents the more problematic side of visual materials cataloging.

[Religious sculpture at a mortuary park in California]. -- [195-?].
  1 photoprint : b&w ; 6 x 7 cm. 1 photonegative : col. ; 4.6 x 4.6 cm.
  Contact print (1980) from original photonegative.
  Subject: Religious sculpture, of Jesus and children [?], at a mortuary park in California, possibly Glendale Forest Lawn.

  1. Parks. 2. Sculpture. 3. Jesus Christ--Art. 4. Photoprints. 5.Photonegatives.

Figure 10.6: Photograph, Bibliographic Display

```
007        khobo_¶
007        kgocj_¶
008        860429q19501967xx_____0i____d¶
245    01  ‡a[Religious sculpture at a mortuary park in California].¶
260        ‡c[195-?].¶
300        ‡a1 photoprint :‡bb&w ;‡c6 x 7 cm.¶
300        ‡a1 photonegative :‡bcol. ;‡c4.6 x 4.6 cm.¶
500        ‡aContact print (1980) from original photonegative.¶
520    0   ‡aReligious sculpture, of Jesus and children [?], at a mortuary park in
California, possibly Glendale Forest Lawn.¶
650    0   ‡aParks.¶
650    0   ‡aSculpture.¶
650    0   ‡aJesus Christ‡xArt.¶
655    7   ‡aPhotoprints.‡2ftamc¶
655    7   ‡aPhotonegatives.‡2ftamc¶
```

Figure 10.7: Photograph, Partial Tagged Display

"What do we have here?" More specifically, how does a cataloger describe an object with no known author, certainly no stated title, extremely uncertain provenance, and really nothing more than the object itself? That's a common problem for graphics, particularly photographs, and for realia.

The title was created by the cataloger, as was the date: other than the dimensions, material itself, and apparent subject matter, there's really no hard information about this item. The 008 date area says that the date is questionable, somewhere between 1950 and 1967. The first 007, for Category of Material *k*, "Graphic, nonprojected," has the following information:

h	Specific Material Designation: *Photoprint*
o	Original vs. Reproduction: *Original*
b	Color: *Black-and-white*
o	Primary Support/Base of Emulsion: *Paper*
_	Secondary support material: *None*

The second 007 differs in three values: it is a photonegative *g*, color *c*, with safety film as the base of emulsion.

This record also uses two genre/form headings, field 655. In both cases the source of the genre/form heading is *ftamc*, LC's code for RLG's *Form terms for archival and manuscripts control*.

As a final example we have a two-dimensional graphic, this one with somewhat better bibliographic information than the previous example.

Karsh, Yousuf, 1908-
　Pablo Picasso [poster] / Yousuf Karsh. -- [New York, NY] : Metropolitan
Museum of Art, Dept. of Prints and Photographs, 1954.
　1 poster : b & w ; 89 x 61 cm.

　Original: gelatine-silver print, 1954.
　Gift of Mr. & Mrs. Charles Kromer collection, 1983.

　1. Picasso, Pablo, 1881-1973.--Portraits, etc. I. Title.

Figure 10.8: Poster, Bibliographic Display

```
007        kzucoc¶
008        850509s1954___nyunnn_____1kneng_d¶
100    1   ‡aKarsh, Yousuf,‡d1908-¶
245   10   ‡aPablo Picasso‡h[poster] /‡cYousuf Karsh.¶
260        ‡a[New York, NY] :‡bMetropolitan Museum of Art, Dept. of Prints
and Photographs,‡c1954.¶
300        ‡a1 poster :‡bb & w ;‡c89 x 61 cm.¶
500        ‡aOriginal: gelatine-silver print, 1954.¶
500        ‡aGift of Mr. & Mrs. Charles Kromer collection, 1983.¶
600   10   ‡aPicasso, Pablo,‡d1881-1973.‡xPortraits, etc.¶
```

Figure 10.9: Poster, Partial Tagged Display

This record uses no special bibliographic fields, and represents a properly dated (published) item with a known creator. Field 007, once again for a nonprojected graphic, has the following values:

z	*Other nonprojected graphic*
u	*Unknown (original vs. reproduction)*
c	*Color (multicolored)*
o	*Paper*
c	*Secondary support:* *Cardboard/illustration board*

In other words this is a paper poster mounted on cardboard or illustration board.

11

Computer Files

During 1980 and 1981, a working group of U.S. and Canadian librarians prepared a MARC format for machine-readable data files (MRDF). MARBI and the rest of the USMARC advisory group discussed the proposed format during those two years, finally approving the new format in October 1981. Lenore Maruyama of LC's Network Development Office compiled the format document, while Sue Dodd of the University of North Carolina, Chapel Hill prepared a cataloging manual.[1] Because 1981, 1982, and 1983 were exceptionally busy years for USMARC development, the format was not scheduled for integration into *MFBD* until Update 9 in 1984. MRDF did receive testing prior to approval, as Utlas developed a test system that helped to refine the proposed format. After approval of the format, OCLC began early analysis, resulting in a number of proposed changes to the format prior to publication in *MFBD*.

As defined in *AACR2*,

A machine-readable data file is defined as a body of information coded by methods that require the use of a machine (typically a computer)

---

1   Sue A. Dodd, *Cataloging Machine-Readable Data Files: An Interpretive Manual* (Chicago: American Library Association, 1982), xix, 247 pp.

123

for processing. Examples are files stored on magnetic tape, punched cards (with or without a magnetic tape strip), aperture cards, punched paper tapes, disk packs, mark sensed cards, and optical character recognition font documents. The term *machine-readable data file* embraces both the data stored in machine-readable form and the programs used to process that data.[2]

From Machine-Readable Data Files to Computer Files

The format was developed with primary attention to data files, such as census tapes and raw data from public opinion polls, as used on large computers. When cataloging data files the nature of the data is important, while the physical format is changeable and relatively minor. As a result, both *AACR2* and the MRDF format concentrated on content with little attention to physical form.

The advent of mass-produced microcomputer software required more attention to physical form: physical and technical details are important for microcomputer software, and are constant for a given edition of such software. A patron who wants to check out a LOGO interpreter needs to know what form the interpreter is in and what computers it will run on; if the patron has an IBM PCjr with disk drive, an Atari 1200XL cartridge will be of little use. Microcomputer software requires different rules and elements, and involves a much larger group of users. The name *machine-readable data files*, never really descriptive of the full range of computer-based items requiring cataloging, is being replaced by the more general term *computer files*.

Coded values for computer files are still not well-defined. To date efforts to define one or more 007 fields for computer files have proven futile. The format-specific 008 values, shown in Table 11.1 (when the legend's first character is *m*), include two seriality codes, only two codes specific to computer files, and more blank spaces than in most other material types. Even the two specific positions offer relatively

---

2   *Anglo-American Cataloguing Rules.* 2d ed. (Chicago: American Library Association, 1978), 202-203.

little information: as of this writing "Type of File" has four meaningful values and "Type of Machine" has only one (the values are *a*, "Computer-readable," and *z*, "Other [i.e., readable by a device other than a computer]").

008	006	Code
18	01	Frequency
19	02	Regularity
22	05	Target audience
26	09	Type of computer file
27	10	Type of machine
28	11	Government publication
Other positions	Undefined	

Table 11.1: Specific 008-006 Codes for Computer Files

Commonly Used Fields in Computer Files

While the USMARC bibliographic format may not offer much support for computer files in field 008 (and has no computer-file 007 as of 1988), catalogers of such files make up for the loss with extensive use of special fields and use of fields in general.

The field occurrence tables in chapters 5-10 and 12 come from two six-week samples of current work on RLIN, in every case giving fairly large samples. At this point, however, relatively little computer-file cataloging is being done; a six-week sample would be almost meaningless. Instead the *complete* RLIN computer-file file as of late July 1988 was extracted and studied for Tables 11.2 and 11.3—4,578 records in all.

The first and perhaps most interesting aspect of the records is their average length (which does not appear in the tables): 2,367 characters, a bit more than *twice* as long as the average books record, and even 20 percent longer than archival & manuscripts control records, usually thought of as the most complex MARC records. Almost certainly, this high average length is the result of the large number of Inter-university Consortium for Political and Social Research (ICPSR) records in the database. These records for various data files include extensive details and are much longer than typical records for microcomputer software. As usual, italicized fields appear at least twice as frequently in computer-file records as in the average of all formats.

Tag	Occ	Description
020	6.7	ISBN
035	*18.5*	*System Control Number*
040	91.2	Cataloging Source
100	33.1	Main Entry—Personal Name
110	1.0	Main Entry—Corporate Name
250	18.6	Edition Statement
260	95.0	Publication, Distribution, etc. (Imprint)
300	95.4	Physical Description
440	21.3	Series Statement/Added Entry—Title
490	*43.3*	*Series Statement*
500	*186.3*	*General Note*
503	*1.2*	*Bibliographic History Note*
505	8.7	Formatted Contents Note
506	*16.1*	*Restrictions on Access*
516	*1.8*	*Type of Computer File or Data Note*
520	*69.2*	*Summary, Abstract, Annotation, etc.*
521	*1.7*	*Target Audience Note*
522	*32.3*	*Geographic Coverage Note*
523	*35.2*	*Time Period of Content Note*
536	*3.9*	*Funding Information Note*
537	*22.2*	*Source of Data Note*
538	*63.8*	*System Details Note*
556	*7.2*	*Information About Documentation Note*
565	*64.4*	*Case File Characteristics Note*

Table 11.2: Computer Files: Commonly Used Fields, 020-565

Tag	Occ	Description
567	8.2	Methodology Note
581	24.9	Publications About Described Materials Note
600	2.4	Subject Added Entry—Personal Name
610	3.5	Subject Added Entry—Corporate Name
630	1.0	Subject Added Entry—Uniform Title
650	200.2	Subject Added Entry—Topical Term
651	28.6	Subject Added Entry—Geographic Name
653	*33.3*	*Index Term—Uncontrolled*
700	60.7	Added Entry—Personal Name
710	*134.8*	*Added Entry—Corporate Name*
730	*2.6*	*Added Entry—Uniform Title*
740	*27.7*	*Added Entry—Uncontrolled Related/Analytical Title*
753	*31.5*	*System Details Access to Computer Files*
830	3.6	Series Added Entry—Uniform Title

Table 11.3: Computer Files: Commonly Used Fields, 567-830

Several of these fields pertain specifically to traditional machine-readable data files such as census tapes and survey reports. Relatively few special fields support microcomputer software. Fields 523 and 537 are now obsolete as part of format integration.

536	*Funding Information Note*
‡a	*Text of note*
‡b	*Contract number*
‡c	*Grant number*
‡d	*Project, task, work unit number*

__‡aSponsored by the Advanced Research Projects Agency through the Office of Naval Research.
‡bN00014-68-A-0245-0007‡cARPA Order No. 2616¶

Information concerning the sponsors or agencies appears in ‡a, but a number can be recorded without linking it to an agency. The field is used when the material results from a funded project.

565	*Case File Characteristics Note*
‡a	*Number of cases/variables*
‡b	*Names of variables*
‡c	*Unit of analysis*
‡d	*Universe of data*
‡e	*Filing scheme or code*
‡3	*Materials specified*
__‡a1,546 respondents; approximately 360 variables.¶	

This field, also used in archival and manuscripts control, also has a first indicator to control an optional display constant:

Value	Display constant
_	File size:
0	Case file characteristics:
8	*[no display constant]*

All of these fields serve primarily data files; as of now, most of the RLIN computer-file file appears to be such records. The field described below can be used more broadly in computer-file records.

753	*System Details Access to Computer Files*
‡a	*Make and model of machine*
‡b	*Programming language*
‡c	*Operating system*
__‡aIBM PC‡bPascal‡cDOS 1.1	
__‡aApple II‡bDOS 3.3	

Field 538, which includes only ‡a, is also used quite widely for a textual description of technical details for a program.

Examples

Computer files represent different cataloging problems for different sorts of files. Microcomputer software can involve difficult questions of edition and verification. A fundamental question as to the appropriate primary material format can even arise. Given two 500+

page paperbacks, *PC Magazine DOS Power Tools* and *Turbo Pascal 4.0*—each including a diskette—are both books with software, both software with documentation, or are they different cases?

American public opinion and U.S. foreign policy [computer file] : general public, 1979 / principal investigator, Chicago Council on Foreign Relations. -- Ann Arbor, Mich. : Inter-university Consortium for Political and Social Research [distributor], [1980?]
  data file (logical records) + codebook. -- (ICPSR study ; 7748)

Geographic coverage: United States.
Data collected: November 17-26, 1978.
File size: 1,546 respondents; approximately 360 variables.
Summary: This study includes data for 1,546 United States citizens, 18 years of age and older. The variables measure attitudes toward foreign affairs issues such as the relationship between domestic and foreign policy priorities, the appropriate responses to the growing military power of the U.S.S.R., the sacrifices the American public is prepared to make to implement policies, and the roles of various individuals and institutions in the creation of foreign policy. Variables also include age, income level, race, sex, media attention, religion, educational level, occupation, and political orientation of the respondent. The survey was conducted by the Gallup Organization, Inc., from a stratified systematic national sample.
ICPSR data class: Class IV.
Publications: Reilly, John. American Public Opinion and United States Foreign Policy, 1979. Chicago: The Chicago Council on Foreign Relations, 1979.
  Data and documentation for the machine-readable data files are available from the Inter-university Consortium for Political and Social Research (ICPSR), P.O. Box 1248, Ann Arbor, Michigan 48106/(313)763-5010.

  1. Public opinion--United States. 2. United States--Politics and government--1981- --Public opinion. 3. United States--Economic conditions--1981- --Public opinion. 4. United States--Foreign relations--Public opinion. 5. XIV. Mass Political Behavior and Attitudes. C. Public Opinion on Political Matters. 1. United States. I. Chicago Council on Foreign Relations. II. Gallup Organization. III. Inter-university Consortium for Political and Social Research.

Figure 11.1: Data File, Bibliographic Display

The record illustrated in Figures 11.1 and 11.2 may be fairly typical of the data files cataloged by ICPSR. (A number of local subject headings, field 690, have been omitted from both figures.) Note that the record includes several of the material-specific fields. This record is roughly average length for a computer-file USMARC record, which suggests that it may be shorter than average for ICPSR records.

```
008       010101s1980___miun_____ua_____und_d¶
245   00  ‡aAmerican public opinion and U.S. foreign policy‡h[computer file]
:‡bgeneral public, 1979 /‡cprincipal investigator, Chicago Council on For-
eign Relations.¶
260       ‡aAnn Arbor, Mich. :‡bInter-university Consortium for Political and
Social Research [distributor],‡c[1980?]¶
300       ‡adata file (   logical records) +‡ecodebook.¶
490   0   ‡aICPSR study ;‡v7748¶
522       ‡aUnited States.¶
523       ‡bData collected: November 17-26, 1978.¶
565       ‡a1,546 respondents; approximately 360 variables.¶
     520 omitted
500       ‡aICPSR data class: Class IV.¶
581       ‡aReilly, John. American Public Opinion and United States Foreign
Policy, 1979. Chicago: The Chicago Council on Foreign Relations, 1979.¶
590       ‡aData and documentation for the machine-readable data files are
available from the Inter-university Consortium for Political and Social Re-
search (ICPSR), P. O. Box 1248, Ann Arbor, Michigan 48106/(313)763-5010.¶
     650 and three 651 fields omitted
653       ‡aXIV. Mass Political Behavior and Attitudes.‡aC. Public Opinion on
Political Matters.‡a1. United States.¶
     Three 710 fields omitted
```

Figure 11.2: Data File, Partial Tagged Display

The second example, illustrated in Figures 11.3 and 11.4, is a fairly typical piece of microcomputer software. It also uses fields 538 and 753, and is somewhat simpler than the average ICPSR record.

Reflex [machine-readable data file]. -- [Version] 1.11. -- Scotts Valley, CA : Borland/Analytica, c1986.

ca. 1 program file on 3 computer disks : col. ; 5 1/4 in. + user's guide (1 v. (various pagings) : ill. ; 23 cm.) ; + update ([4] p. ; 23 cm.)

Title on disk labels: Reflex the analyst.

Stamped on edges of pages: Student text.

"Borland International"--Cover of user's guide.

System requirements: IBM PC or compatible; 384K; DOS version 2.0 or later; IBM Color/Graphics Adapter with a display capable of high resolution graphics or Hercules (Monochrome) Graphics Card with regular display.

Contents: [disk 1]. System disk -- [disk 2]. Report & utilities -- [disk 3]. Help disk.

ISBN 087524145X (user's guide)

1. Data base management--Computer programs. I. Borland/Analytica, Inc. II. Borland International. III. IBM PC--DOS IV. Title: Reflex the analyst.

Figure 11.3: Software, Bibliographic Display

```
020        ‡a087524145X (user's guide)¶
245   00   ‡aReflex‡h[machine-readable data file].¶
250        ‡a[Version] 1.11.¶
260        ‡aScotts Valley, CA :‡bBorland/Analytica,‡cc1986.¶
300        ‡aca. 1 program file on 3 computer disks :‡bcol. ;‡c5 1/4 in. +‡euser's
guide (1 v. (various pagings) : ill. ; 23 cm.) ; + update ([4] p. ; 23 cm.)¶
500        ‡aTitle on disk labels: Reflex the analyst.¶
500        ‡aStamped on edges of pages: Student text.¶
500        ‡a"Borland International"--Cover of user's guide.¶
538        ‡aSystem requirements: IBM PC or compatible; 384K; DOS version
2.0 or later; IBM Color/Graphics Adapter with a display capable of high
resolution graphics or Hercules (Monochrome) Graphics Card with regu-
lar display.¶
505   0    ‡a[disk 1]. System disk -- [disk 2]. Report & utilities -- [disk 3]. Help
disk.¶
650   0    ‡aData base management‡xComputer programs.¶
710   20   ‡aBorland/Analytica, Inc.¶
710   20   ‡aBorland International.¶
740   01   ‡aReflex the analyst.¶
753        ‡aIBM PC‡cDOS¶
```

Figure 11.4: Software, Tagged Display

Ongoing Development

One goal of format integration was to eliminate some of the specific notes fields, including some fields used for computer files. Those with special interests in computer files asserted, with some justification, that use of MARC for computer files—and, indeed, bibliographic control of any sort over a broad range of computer files—was, in 1988, still too new to be sure what notes would be most needed. Fields 523 and 537 were made obsolete (as was field 582, almost never used in the RLIN sample), but other material-specific fields such as 516 (Type of File or Data), 538 (System Details), and 753 (Technical Details Access/Computer File) were retained.

12

Archival and Manuscripts Control

Manuscripts had a MARC format beginning in 1973. The format included some fields that took into account the way that some unpublished and archival materials are handled—that is, as collections, not always or generally as individual items. Special fields in the format stored the unit count and linear footage for a collection, and four special note fields supported repository notes, literary rights notes, solicitation information, and biographical tracings.

In the decade following publication of the MARC manuscripts format, it was infrequently used. Fewer than 41,000 manuscripts records were cataloged on OCLC by the end of 1983; RLIN and WLN never implemented the format. The MARC manuscripts format was designed to meet the known needs of manuscripts catalogers, but was perceived by archivists as inadequate for their needs; in fact, the LC manuscripts division itself never used the format.

From Manuscripts Description to Archival Control

Archivists are interested primarily in controlling material. Material is handled in a variety of ways, producing various levels of intellectual and physical control. That control, rather than complete description, is the primary reason to build records. The manuscripts format, couched in the language and needs of library catalogers, appeared to require too much and to provide too little to be suitable for archivists.

Archival and manuscripts materials are, almost by definition, unique (except for microform copies of some collections). As a result, MARC is less useful as a tool for shared cataloging within the community of archivists. Also, most archivists work outside normal library contexts and had not adopted a standard code of descriptive practice prior to the 1980s.

As we know, USMARC has many virtues besides providing a basis for shared cataloging. The format serves to organize information, store complex bibliographic data, allow on-line retrieval on well-established national systems, communicate information in a consistent manner, and manipulate it for a variety of uses. Wider access to archival materials, or at least knowledge of the existence of those materials, could serve scholars and archives well. For archivists to be able to gain these advantages, USMARC needed to provide for the descriptive and control requirements of archives. Steven L. Henson of the Library of Congress described the situation in *Archives, Personal Papers, and Manuscripts: A Cataloging Manual for Archival Repositories, Historical Societies, and Manuscript Libraries:*

> The emphasis is on cataloging of groups of personal papers, and corporate, governmental, and family archives, which can include record groups, series, sub-groups, sub-series, etc. This approach is used and encouraged for two reasons: First, the size of most modern manuscript and archival collections has led archivists and manuscript curators to prefer limited cataloging control over all of their holdings rather than detailed control over only some of their holdings, thus, collective description is the only practical response to the overwhelming cataloging burdens that would be presented by item level description. Second, it is the approach most likely to observe the principle of archival unity which recognizes that, in organically-generated collections at least, it is the collective whole as the sum of the interrelationships of its components that has significance and that the individual item or sub-series within a collection usually derives its importance from its context. In most manuscript cataloging, the analog to the book

is not the individual manuscript, but the collection of which the item may be a part.[1]

Several parties began working on related projects in 1981: a revised MARC format, a descriptive cataloging manual, and an implementation for archival processing. David Bearman headed the National Information Systems Task Force (NISTF) of the Society of American Archivists, working toward a format that would serve the needs of librarians and archivists; Steven L. Henson of the Library of Congress prepared a cataloging manual; and Alan Tucker and Barbara Brown coordinated a Research Libraries Group Special Formats Task Force, working toward implementation. The Library of Congress was represented on both task forces; the Rare Books and Manuscripts section of ALA's Association of College and Research Libraries (ALA ACRL RBMS) was also involved in working toward a new format.

After extensive review by the USMARC advisory group MARBI approved the revisions to the manuscripts format in January 1983, transforming it into the archival and manuscripts control (AMC) format. The Society of American Archivists (SAA) also approved the format, in October 1982, and later published its own interpretive version of the format. LC and SAA share responsibility for maintenance of the format.

Special Aspects of Archival Control

With format integration, archivists have access to the entire range of content designators available within USMARC, and other librarians can use the fields specially designed for archival control.

---

1   Steven L. Henson, *Archives, Personal Papers, and Manuscripts: A Cataloging Manual for Archival Repositories, Historical Societies, and Manuscript Libraries* (Washington, D.C.: Library of Congress, 1983), 1-2.

The significant word is *control*: within most archives, the emphasis is on control of collections of material rather than on detailed description of individual items. A collection in an archive might well include letters, sound recordings, photographs, and other media; when cataloged *as a collection* the level of descriptive detail may be lower for each element, but the cataloging record will provide a record of the status of the collection.

Acquisition and Action

A number of fields support that control function; those fields appear in the section on commonly used fields. Two fields in particular address the issue of control: field 541, "Immediate source of acquisition note," and field 583, "Actions." Within the earliest and most widely used implementation of AMC (RLIN, with some 150,000 records as of mid-August 1988), these two fields have been separated out as separate screens of tagged elements, but within USMARC the fields appear as shown below.

541	*Immediate Source of Acquisition Note*
‡a	*Source of acquisition*
‡b	*Address*
‡c	*Method of acquisition*
‡d	*Date of acquisition*
‡e	*Accession number*
‡f	*Owner*
‡h	*Purchase price*
‡3	*Materials specified*

__‡3Stock transfer register, 1844-1870.‡aPenn Central Corporation‡cdeposit‡fPenn Central Corporation¶

The note above specifies that the material in question came from Penn Central, and that Penn Central retains ownership—an important factor in maintaining archival control, since archives (unlike libraries) frequently do not own the material housed. Subfield ‡3 is crucial to the AMC format since it permits an informal linkage of various control fields relating to one portion of a collection. Note the examples below for field 583, using the same ‡3 value. The same record could have several other 541 fields, each of which might have one or more 583 fields related to it by a matching ‡3: that is, actions taken on that set of materials.

583	Actions
‡a	Action
‡b	Action identification
‡c	Time of action
‡d	Action interval
‡e	Contingency for action
‡f	Authorization
‡h	Jurisdiction
‡i	Method of action
‡j	Site of action
‡k	Action agent
‡l	Status
‡n	Extent
‡o	Type of unit
‡x	Nonpublic note
‡z	Public note
‡3	Materials specified
‡5	Institution to which field applies

__‡3Stock transfer register, 1844-1870.‡aseries description prepared ‡c08/08/88¶

__‡3Stock transfer register, 1844-1870.‡aseries description entered ‡c08/15/88¶

Note that these examples use only a few of the subfields in this fairly complex field; that would be typical of actual practice. Each subfield can play an important part in establishing control. The field as a whole makes it possible to produce past action lists—e.g., material accessioned during the last year— and future action lists—e.g., materials that may be opened for scholarly access after a certain date.

Preservation

Several of the subfields in field 583 as shown—‡n, ‡o, ‡x, ‡y, ‡z and ‡5—were added to the field when it was defined as the primary field for preservation information in bibliographic records.

The statement "This field is also used to record information about preservation actions relating to an item, such as review of condition, queuing for preservation, and completion of preservation" now appears in *UFBD* following the original statement of scope for the field. A few theoretical examples of this field as used for preservation, taken from *UFBD*, follow.

```
583            ‡aQueued for preservation;‡c19861010;‡ePriority;
‡fTitle IIC project‡5DLC¶
583            ‡aFumigate;‡n37‡oarchives boxes;‡n14‡obound
vol.;‡b79-54;‡c19706;‡kJJI¶
583            ‡3V. 1-50‡aCondition reviewed;‡c19860207;
‡kPreservation Dept.;‡lPaper brittle¶
```

Commonly Used Fields in AMC Cataloging

Complex notes and simple coded fields mark AMC records. AMC records are identified by the character *b* as the first character of the legend. The format-specific portion of the 008 field, and the equivalent 006 field, is almost entirely undefined. The only defined character is 008/23 or 006/06, "Form of item."

AMC records run longer than most other bibliographic records, although apparently shorter than computer-file records. The average record in a July 1988 sample of 6,000 AMC records was 1,930 characters long, compared to about 1,130 for books records. The records use more different fields than any format except serials, and most of those fields are either distinctly part of AMC or used at least twice as heavily there as for the average of all formats.

One word of caution about the occurrence tables in Tables 12.1 and 12.2: these represent cataloging *within RLIN*. The RLIN database includes heavy representation from state archives as well as library-related archives and others. The numbers for fields 541 and 583 may be affected by the RLIN implementation, which relies very heavily on these fields for the usefulness of the format

Tag	Occ	Description
007	2.5	Physical Description Fixed Field
010	2.6	LC Control Number
035	*55.6*	*System Control Number*
040	96.7	Cataloging Source
043	3.0	Geographic Area Code
052	*11.6*	*Geographic Classification Code*
072	*8.7*	*Subject Category Code*
100	62.0	Main Entry—Personal Name
110	*32.9*	*Main Entry—Corporate Name*
300	103.1	Physical Description
340	*1.4*	*Physical Medium*
351	*14.8*	*Organization and Arrangement of Materials*
500	57.5	General Note
506	*20.0*	*Restrictions on Access*
510	3.4	Citation/References Note
520	*92.5*	*Summary, Abstract, Annotation, etc.*
524	*18.0*	*Preferred Citation of Described Materials Note*
530	*2.5*	*Additional Physical Form Available Note*
533	*4.3*	*Reproduction Note*
535	*2.9*	*Location of Originals/Duplicates*
540	*1.7*	*Terms Governing Use and Reproduction Note*
541	*106.9*	*Immediate Source of Acquisition Note*
544	*2.1*	*Location of Associated Archival Materials Note*
545	*56.9*	*Biographical or Historical Note*
546	*2.6*	*Language Note*
555	*22.7*	*Cumulative Index/Finding Aids Note*
561	*17.7*	*Provenance Note*
580	*7.1*	*Linking Entry Complexity Note*
583	*166.7*	*Actions*
584	*2.2*	*Accumulation and Frequency of Use Note*

Table 12.1: AMC: Commonly Used Fields, 007-584

Tag	Occ	Description
600	163.4	*Subject Added Entry—Personal Name*
610	80.5	*Subject Added Entry—Corporate Name*
611	1.5	*Subject Added Entry—Meeting Name*
630	3.3	*Subject Added Entry—Uniform Title*
650	184.1	Subject Added Entry—Topical Term
651	95.2	*Subject Added Entry—Geographic Name*
655	74.7	*Index Term—Genre/Form*
656	14.2	*Index Term—Occupation*
657	3.7	*Index Term—Function*
700	72.9	Added Entry—Personal Name
710	36.0	Added Entry—Corporate Name
730	2.3	*Added Entry—Uniform Title*
740	4.1	*Added Entry—Uncontrolled Related/Analytical Title*
773	21.2	*Host Item Entry*
851	78.6	*Location*

Table 12.2: AMC: Commonly Used Fields, 600-851

The index term fields 655-657 entered USMARC with AMC. All three fields include subfield ‡x, *General subdivision*; subfield ‡y, *Chronological subdivision*; subfield ‡z, *Geographic subdivision*; subfield ‡2, *Source of term*; and subfield ‡3, *Materials specified*.

Field 655 also includes ‡a, *Genre/form*. Field 656 includes subfield ‡a, *Occupation* and ‡k, *Form*. Field 657 includes subfield ‡a, *Function*.

Examples

When *MARC for Library Use* was published in late 1984, the RLIN AMC implementation was just beginning. We suspected that real AMC records would be long and complex; that has proved to be the case, with records frequently having more than a hundred added entry fields. The examples here are not among the longest or most complex within AMC.

Weideman, Carl May, 1898-1972.
   Papers, 1921-1972.
   4 linear ft., 2 v. [outsize] and 1 folder (UAm).

   Detroit, Michigan trial attorney, Democratic Congressman, 1933-1935, and
Wayne County Circuit Court Judge.
   Summary: Correspondence and other materials concerning his term in
Congress, national and local politics, and various judicial decisions; miscel-
laneous diaries, newspaper clippings, and scrapbooks concerning his asso-
ciation with the American Turners Association (German-American athletic
society), Detroit, Michigan politics, and the election and recall of Detroit
Mayor Charles Bowles; and photographs.
   Indexes: Finding aid in the library.
   Donor: 5265
   Location: Bentley Historical Library, University of Michigan, Ann Arbor,
Michigan 48109-2113

   1. Diaries. 2. Photoprints. 3. American Turners. 4. Athletics. 5. Bowles,
Charles, 1884-1957. 6. Democratic Party (Mich.) 7. Detroit (Mich.) 8. German
Americans--Michigan. 9. Judges. 10. New Deal, 1933-1939. 11. Strikes and
lockouts. 12. United States. Congress. 13. United States. Congress.--Elections-
-1932. 14. United States. Congress.--Elections--1934. 15. United States--
Politics and government--1929-1938. 16. Wayne County (Mich.). Circuit
Court. I. Abbott, Horatio J. (Horatio Johnson), 1876- II. Brown, Prentiss
Marsh, 1889-1973. III. Bushnell, George E. (George Edward), 1887-1965. IV.
Comstock, William Alfred, 1877-1949. V. Coughlin, Charles Edward, 1891-
VI. Debo, Alfred. VII. Farley, James Aloysius, 1888- VIII. Fitzgerald, Frank D.,
1885-1939. IX. Foley, Thomas. X. Hoover, J. Edgar (John Edgar), 1895-1972.
XI. Hubbard, Orville L. XII. Hull, Cordell, 1871-1955. XIII. Ickes, Harold L.
(Harold LeClair), 1874-1952. XIV. Jeffries, Edward J., 1864-1939. XV. Jeffries,
Edward J., 1900-1950. XVI. Joy, Henry Bourne, 1864-1936. XVII. Lacy, Arthur
J. (Arthur Jay), 1876-1975. XVIII. Lesinski, John, 1885-1950. XIX. Martel,
Frank Xavier, 1888- XX. O'Brien, Patrick H., 1868-1959. XXI. Perkins, Frances,
1882-1965. XXII. Piggins, Edward S., d. 1972. XXIII. Romney, George W., 1907-
XXIV. Tugwell, Rexford G. (Rexford Guy), 1891- XXV. Van Wagoner, Murray
Delos, 1898-

Figure 12.1: Weideman Papers, Bibliographic Display

```
008        860206i19211972miu____|_____eng_|¶
100   1    ‡aWeideman, Carl May,‡d1898-1972.¶
245   00   ‡kPapers,‡f1921-1972.¶
300        ‡a4 linear ft., 2 v. [outsize] and 1 folder (UAm).¶
545        ‡aDetroit, Michigan trial attorney, Democratic Congressman, 1933-
1935, and Wayne County Circuit Court Judge.¶
520        ‡aCorrespondence and other materials concerning his term in Con-
gress, ...remainder of field omitted...¶
555        ‡aFinding aid in the library.¶
500        ‡aDonor: 5265¶
655   7    ‡aDiaries.‡2ftamc¶
655   7    ‡aPhotoprints.‡2ftamc¶
610   20   ‡aAmerican Turners.¶
650   0    ‡aAthletics.¶
600   10   ‡aBowles, Charles,‡d1884-1957.¶
610   20   ‡aDemocratic Party (Mich.)¶
651   0    ‡aDetroit (Mich.)¶
650   0    ‡aGerman Americans‡zMichigan.¶
656   7    ‡aJudges.‡2lcsh¶
650 0 ‡aNew Deal, 1933-1939.¶
           ... six 6xx fields omitted...
700   11   ‡aAbbott, Horatio J.‡q(Horatio Johnson),‡d1876-¶
           ...25 structurally identical 700 fields omitted...
851        ‡aBentley Historical Library,‡bUniversity of Michigan,‡cAnn Arbor,
Michigan 48109-2113¶
```

Figure 12.2: Weideman Papers, Partial Tagged Display

This record also has fields 541 and 583, not displayed here. Note that the record includes two 655 fields and one 656 field, in each case citing the authority for the source used.

Jamestown, Westfield & Northwestern Railroad.
  Records, 1917-1968.
  .2 cubic ft.

  Summary: Order book, timetables, tickets, clippings, and a typescript account of 1917 wreck on the Hartfield curve.
  The Chautauqua Collection is privately owned by the Institution and is therefore not open to the public except by permission and upon written request to the Librarian for the use of the material.
  If any publication is to result, the manuscript must be approved by Chautauqua Institution prior to publication.
  Location: Chautauqua Institution, Smith Memorial Library, Chautauqua, New York 14722.

  1. Railroads--New York (State) 2. Railroads--Accidents.

Figure 12.3: Jamestown Railroad, Bibliographic Display

```
008        010101i19171968nyu_____eng_d¶
110   2    ‡aJamestown, Westfield & Northwestern Railroad.¶
245   00   ‡kRecords,‡f1917-1968.¶
300        ‡a.2 cubic ft.¶
520        ‡aOrder book, timetables, tickets, clippings, and a typescript
account of 1917 wreck on the Hartfield curve.¶
506        ‡aThe Chautauqua Collection is privately owned by the
Institution and is therefore not open to the public except by permission
and upon written request to the Librarian for the use of the material.¶
540        ‡aIf any publication is to result, the manuscript must be approved
by Chautauqua Institution prior to publication.¶
541        ‡3Jamestown, Westfield & Northwestern Railroad records¶
583        ‡3Jamestown, Westfield & Northwestern Railroad records‡aSur-
veyed‡c03/01/81¶
650   0    ‡aRailroads‡zNew York (State)¶
650   0    ‡aRailroads‡xAccidents.¶
851        ‡aChautauqua Institution,‡cSmith Memorial Library, Chautauqua,
New York 14722.¶
```

Figure 12.4: Jamestown Railroad, Tagged Display

This example includes field 506, "Restrictions on Access," and field 540, "Terms Governing Use and Reproduction," as well as fields 541 and 583. This is a relatively simple record, as is the final example below, which includes field 351 (Organization and Arrangement), field 655 (Form/Genre), and field 657 (Index Term—Function).

Erie Canal Company.
  Stock transfer register, 1844-1870.
  0.22 cubic ft. (1 volume).

Organization: Arranged chronologically by date of transfer.
Summary: Record of stock transfer of the Erie Canal Company from November 1844 to November 1870. Entries include folio number for 'Capital Stock Ledger' (PASV88-A315), quantity of shares involved in transaction, identification number of stock certificate issued, identification number of stock certificate cancelled, name of individual relinquishing stock and individual receiving the transfer, and date of transfer.
  Location: Pennsylvania Historical and Museum Commission, Division of Archives and Manuscripts, P.O. Box 1026, Harrisburg, PA 17108-1026.

  1. Pennsylvania Railroad Company. 2. Penn Central Corporation. 3. Pennsylvania Railroad. 4. Penn Central Transportation Company. 5. Railroads--Pennsylvania. 6. Canals--Pennsylvania. 7. Canals--Stockholders. 8. Registers--19th century--Pennsylvania. 9. Canals--Stocks. 10. Canals--Finance. 11. Canals--Securities. 12. Registering. I. Title. II. Title: Stock transfer register of the Erie Canal Company.

Figure 12.5: Erie Canal Company, Bibliographic Display

```
008         880815i18441870pau____|_____eng_d¶
110    1    ‡aErie Canal Company.¶
245   10    ‡aStock transfer register, 1844-1870.¶
300         ‡a0.22‡fcubic ft. (¶
300         ‡a1‡fvolume ).¶
351         ‡bArranged chronologically by date of transfer.¶
520         ‡aRecord of stock transfer of the Erie Canal Company from
    November 1844 to November 1870. Entries include folio number for 'Capi-
    tal Stock Ledger' (PASV88-A315), quantity of shares involved in transac-
    tion, identification number of stock certificate issued, identification num-
    ber of stock certificate cancelled, name of individual relinquishing stock
    and individual receiving the transfer, and date of transfer.¶
541         ‡3Stock transfer register, 1844-1870.‡aPenn Central Corpora-
    tion‡cdeposit‡fPenn Central Corporation¶
583         ‡3Stock transfer register, 1844-1870.‡aseries description prepared
    ‡c08/08/88¶
583         ‡3Stock transfer register, 1844-1870.‡aseries description
    entered‡c08/15/88¶
697   14    ‡aPennsylvania Railroad Company.¶
697   24    ‡aPenn Central Corporation.¶
610   10    ‡aPennsylvania Railroad.¶
610   20    ‡aPenn Central Transportation Company.¶
650    0    ‡aRailroads‡zPennsylvania.¶
650    0    ‡aCanals‡zPennsylvania.¶
650    0    ‡aCanals‡xStockholders.¶
655    7    ‡aRegisters‡y19th century‡zPennsylvania.‡2ftamc¶
650    0    ‡aCanals‡xStocks.¶
650    0    ‡aCanals‡xFinance.¶
650    0    ‡aCanals‡xSecurities.¶
657    7    ‡aRegistering.‡2ssspl¶
740   00    ‡aStock transfer register of the Erie Canal Company.¶
851         ‡aPennsylvania Historical and Museum Commission,‡bDivision of
    Archives and Manuscripts,‡cP.O. Box 1026, Harrisburg, PA  17108-1026.¶
```

Figure 12.6: Erie Canal Company, Tagged Display

13

Authorities

M_{ARC} *for Library Use* deals primarily with the USMARC format for bibliographic data and its implications for libraries. Two other USMARC formats, one long-established and one still in draft stage, may also play important roles in library work but are not used directly for bibliographic description. Each of those two formats, authorities and holdings, deserves and requires book-length treatment on its own. This chapter and the next, on holdings, provide brief introductions and broad commentaries on the two formats and their relationship to the bibliographic format and to bibliographic records.

The Nature of Authority Records

Authorities provide information about headings: names, subjects, uniform titles:

- An authority record may show the *form* of an established heading—that is, the form of a name to be used in building bibliographic records.

- A record for an established heading may also show *other forms* of the name as "see from" tracings and other established headings as "see also from" tracings—or, in some cases, broader terms, narrower terms, and related terms.

- A record may give *explanatory notes*, may note *how* the established form was chosen, or might even note reference works that did *not* serve to establish a form of name.
- An authority record may contain *not* an established heading, but may instead provide explanatory references for non-established headings.
- A *subject authority* record may establish the current form of a subject heading, give earlier forms, related, broader and narrower terms, and scope notes.

Authority files have been maintained manually for decades so that libraries could assure consistent entry of names and avoid repetitive decision-making on form of name. The Library of Congress has one of the largest bodies of authority information on names and subjects; most other libraries follow LC policy where possible to avoid duplicate effort and to allow best use of LC cataloging information.

MARC Authorities: A Brief History

The first version of a MARC format for authority information was prepared by Lenore S. Maruyama of the Library of Congress and published in 1976.[1] That format was used by the Library of Congress to distribute name authority records on a limited basis from 1976 through 1983.

The preliminary format was experimental in some ways, particularly in terms of record maintenance. All other MARC formats have always used full-record maintenance. When anything changes in a record the complete record is redistributed, and the receiving agency can either replace the record blindly or compare fields to see what has changed and what actions should be taken. The preliminary

---

1   Library of Congress, MARC Development Office, *Authorities: A MARC Format*, Preliminary ed. (Washington, D.C.: Library of Congress, 1976)

authorities format used a different method, based on what appeared to be most reasonable at the time. Each variable data field in an authorities record contained a control subfield ‡w with twenty-four characters of information on that field; six of the twenty-four characters gave the date of last transaction. When changes occurred a *partial* record was distributed, containing enough information to identify the record and those fields that actually changed.

Those who suggested this method saw clear advantages to field-level change identification in maintaining authority files, particularly those files that directly control bibliographic information. When an update came in a program could easily establish whether biblio-graphic changes would be needed (because the established form had changed) and, if so, whether those changes could be made by ma-chine. Partial-record updates also reduce record size; if authority records were to be distributed electronically rather than on tape, this would reduce transmission costs.

As use of MARC formats and the authorities format grew, par-tial-record updates became a problem. In order to process partial-record updates, an agency must have already loaded the relevant full records. Any updates must also be loaded in the exact chronological order in which they are received. If that doesn't happen the partial records either won't work at all or, worse, will work incorrectly. New agencies trying to build authority files found it difficult to process the set of tapes; some felt strongly that full-record updates would be easier to maintain.

The Linked Systems Project Begins

Early in the 1980s the Council on Library Resources (CLR) funded the Linked Systems Project (LSP), a joint project of LC, RLG, and WLN, to establish computer-to-computer linkages among biblio-graphic systems. (OCLC joined LSP later in the project.)

The two early phases of LSP were the linkage system itself, to establish a standard set of protocols for computer-to-computer communication, and the first implementation, to establish direct exchange of authorities information.

As part of the authorities phase of LSP (formerly known as the Linked Authority Systems Project or LASP), the authorities format was studied and a number of recommendations were made; among them was a change from field-level status and update information to record-level transaction date/time information, and a change to full-record updates.

Authorities: A MARC Format

Josephine S. Pulsifer and Margaret Patterson of LC worked on a comprehensive revision of the authorities format, with the assistance of Ann Ekstrom. After review by the USMARC advisory group and other interested parties, the first full edition of the format was approved in 1981. The introduction to the first edition defines its scope:

> The MARC authorities format provides specifications for the content and the content designation of authority records containing name, subject, and/or series authority information... The authorities format is designed to accommodate in a single record all of the authority information pertinent to the use of a given heading as a name and/or a subject and/or a series.[2]

USMARC Format for Authority Data

LC's Network Development and MARC Standards Office replaced *Authorities: A MARC Format* in June 1987 with the first of the new USMARC documents: *USMARC Format for Authority Data Including Guidelines for Content Designation.* The thick looseleaf document contains a wealth of detail comparable to *UFBD* and similarly arranged. Most information in the rest of this chapter comes from that document as updated in February 1988.

---

2   Library of Congress, MARC Development Office, *Authorities: A MARC Format* (Washington, D.C.: Library of Congress, 1981), 2.

Summary of the Format

Usmarc for authorities has the same structure as all other US-MARC formats. Table 13.1 summarizes the control fields of the authorities format.

001	Control number
005	Date and time of latest transaction
008	Fixed-length data elements
00-05	Date entered on file
06	Direct/indirect geographic subdivision
07	Romanization scheme
09	Kind of record
10	Descriptive cataloging rules
11	Subject heading system/thesaurus
12	Type of series
13	Numbered/unnumbered series
14	Heading use—main or added entry
15	Heading use—subject added entry
16	Heading use—series added entry
17	Type of subject subdivision
28	Type of government agency
29	Reference evaluation
31	Record update in process
32	Undifferentiated personal name
33	Level of establishment
38	Modified record
39	Cataloging source

Table 13.1: Authorities, 001-008

Kinds of Authority Records

All authority records contain z in Leader/06. Field 008/09, *Kind of record,* further defines seven specific kinds of authority records:

- *Established heading record a*: The most common kind of authority record; may also contain tracing fields for variant and related headings and notes explaining scope, usage, and source of information.

- *Reference record (untraced) b*: An unestablished heading that does not appear as a tracing in an established heading. The record will include either a Complex See reference *260* or a General Explanatory note *666* to guide the user to an established heading.

- *Reference record (traced) c*: An unestablished heading that *does* appear as a tracing in an established heading. The record will include a Complex See reference *664* to guide the user to an established heading.

- *Subdivision record d*: An unestablished term that may be used as a subject subdivision for an established subject heading.

- *Node label record e*: An unestablished term that may be used as a facet indicator in the systematic section of a thesaurus.

- *Established heading and subdivision record f*: An established heading that may also be used as a subject subdivision.

010	LC control number
014	Link to bibliographic record for serial or multipart item
020	International Standard Book Number (ISBN)
022	International Standard Serial Number (ISSN)
035	System control number
040	Cataloging source
042	Authentication code
043	Geographic area code
045	Time period of heading
050	Library of Congress call number
052	Geographic classification code
053	LC classification number
060	NLM call number
070	NAL call number
072	Subject category code
073	Subdivision usage
082	Dewey Decimal call number
083	Dewey Decimal classification number

Table 13.2: Authorities Format, Fields 010-083

- *Reference and subdivision record g*: An unestablished heading that may be used as a reference term and as a subject subdivision.

Table 13.2 shows the coded fields for authorities. Fields 020 and 022 can be used for sets and series; field 050 is used only when a single call number applies to a series. Fields 053 and 083 are not the same as the bibliographic 050 and 082. These fields contain classification numbers or ranges associated with an authority heading; for example, LC class "TH5281" is associated with "Scaffolding."

Headings

100	Heading—personal name
110	Heading—corporate name
111	Heading—meeting name
130	Heading—uniform title
150	Heading—topical term
151	Heading—geographic name

Tracings and References

260	Complex See reference—subject
360	Complex See Also reference—subject
400	See From tracing—personal name
410	See From tracing—corporate name
411	See From tracing—meeting name
430	See From tracing—uniform title
450	See From tracing—topical term
451	See From tracing—geographic name
500	See Also From tracing—personal name
510	See Also From tracing—corporate name
511	See Also From tracing—meeting name
530	See Also From tracing—uniform title
550	See Also From tracing—topical term
551	See Also From tracing—geographic name

Table 13.3: Authorities Format, Fields 100-551

Table 13.3 shows the headings, references, and tracings fields for authorities. There are deliberate parallels in content designation between the authorities and bibliographic families, making it feasible to use authority records to control bibliographic headings. These parallels are stated in the *Underlying Principles*.

For example, field 110 in authorities establishes a corporate name heading which, depending on coded values, can control bibliographic fields 110, 410, 610, 710, and 810; within Authorities, fields 410 and 510 would provide See From and See Also From tracings for other corporate names, allowing systems to generate appropriate See and See Also references.

Series Treatment Information
640   Series date of publication and/or volume designation
641   Series numbering peculiarities
642   Series numbering example
643   Series place and publisher / issuing body
644   Series analysis practice
645   Series tracing practice
646   Series classification practice

References
663   Complex See Also reference—name
664   Complex See reference—name
665   History reference
666   General explanatory reference—name

Notes
667   Name usage or scope note
670   Source data found
675   Source data not found
678   Epitome
680   Subject scope note
681   Subject example tracing note
682   Deleted heading information

Table 13.4: Authorities Format, Fields 640-682

The remaining fields in authorities, shown in Table 13.4, serve different functions and do not follow the patterns just discussed. Fields 640 through 646 contain bibliographic description and local treatment information for series. Fields 663 through 682 contain a variety of information: definition, usage, and scope; free-text references and tracings to explain complex relationships; and sources used to establish a heading or reasons for deleting a heading.

Examples

Figures 13.1 through 13.7 show portions of several different authority records, showing various note fields, headings, and tracings.

---

110 20 ‡aLibrary and Information Technology Association (U.S.)¶
410 20 ‡aAmerican Library Association.‡bLibrary and Information Technology Association¶
410 20 ‡aLITA¶
410 20 ‡aL.I.T.A.¶
510 20 ‡wa‡aAmerican Library Association.‡bInformation Science and Automation Division¶
670   __ ‡aSerials automation for acquisition and control, 1981:‡bintrod. (Library and Information Technology Association (LITA) of the American Library Association; known earlier as the Information Science and Automation Division)¶

Figure 13.1: Name Authority Record, Example 1

---

150 _0 ‡aDenominative¶
260   __ ‡isubdivision‡aDenominative‡iunder names of languages and groups of languages¶

Figure 13.2: Subject Authority Record, Example 1: Untraced Reference

---

150 _0 ‡aElectronic data processing‡xData preparation¶
450 _0 ‡aData preparation in electronic data processing¶
450 _0 ‡aPreparation of data in electronic data processing¶
550 _0 ‡wg‡aComputer input-output equipment¶
550 _0 ‡aInput design, Computer¶

Figure 13.3: Subject Authority Record, Example 2

```
150  _0  ‡aMusic in the Bible¶
430  _0  ‡aBible‡xMusic¶
430  _0  ‡aBible‡xMusical instruments¶
430  _0  ‡aBible.‡pO.T.‡pPsalms‡xMusic¶
450  _0  ‡aMusical instruments in the Bible¶
550  _0  ‡wg‡aJews‡xMusic¶
550  _0  ‡wg‡aMusic‡yTo 500¶
680  __  ‡iHere are entered works on music and musical instruments in the
Bible.¶
```

Figure 13.4: Subject Authority Record, Example 3

```
150  _0  ‡aHoly Year¶
450  _0  ‡aAnno santo¶
450  _0  ‡aJubilee Year¶
450  _0  ‡aYear, Holy¶
450  _0  ‡aYear, Jubilee¶
550  _0  ‡wg‡aAsylum, Right of¶
550  _0  ‡wg‡aIndulgences¶
680  __  ‡iHere are entered works on the holy or jubilee years proclaimed by
the popes. For special holy years (regular or extraordinary) add date,
e.g.‡aHoly Year, 1925.¶
```

Figure 13.5: Subject Authority Record, Example 4

```
100  10  ‡aBrutus, Marcus Junius,‡d85?-42 B.C.¶
400  10  ‡aBrutus, Q. Caepio¶
400  10  ‡wnnaa‡aBrutus, M. Junius,‡d79 (ca.)-42 B.C.¶
500  10  ‡aBrutus, Pseudo-¶
```

Figure 13.6: Name Authority Record, Example 2

```
100   10   ‡aReger, Max,‡d1873-1916.‡tRequiem (Mass)¶
400   10   ‡aReger, Max,‡d1873-1916.‡tLateinisches Requiem¶
400   10   ‡wnnnb‡aReger, Max,‡d1873-1916.‡tTotenfeier¶
400   10   ‡wnnnb‡aReger, Max,‡d1873-1916.‡tDies irae¶
670   __   ‡aHis Lateinisches Requiem [SR] c1980:‡bt.p. (Lateinisches Requiem
: op. 145a ; Dies irae : unvollendeter Requiemsatz (1914))¶
670   __   ‡aNew Grove‡b(Requiem: 1st movt, Totenfeier, 1914; 2nd movt, Dies
irae, 1914)¶
670   __   ‡aStein‡b("Totenfeier" erster Satz eines unvollendeten lateinischen
Requiems: "vom Verleger mit op. 145a bezeichnet" composed in 1914)¶
```

Figure 13.7: Name Authority Record, Example 3

Linked Systems and NACO

Both RLG and LC implemented the software necessary to transfer authorities records using Linked Systems (Open Systems Interconnection) protocols in the mid-1980s, and LC began to distribute new and modified name authority records to RLG electronically. By 1986 the link was well-established, and RLIN users could be sure that the Name Authority File (NAF) on RLIN was rarely more than a day out of synchronization with the Name Authority File at the Library of Congress. OCLC implemented the authorities link in 1987, reaching a similar state of synchronization with the Library of Congress.

The next stage of the interconnection was to pass records the other way. Other libraries have provided name authority information to the Library of Congress in the past, but not electronically or in MARC format. This effort began under the name NACO, standing for the Name Authority Cooperative Project. LSP became a two-way link in 1987 when Yale University Library, a NACO participant, began to contribute name authorities to LC by entering them on RLIN. Records are contributed via LSP from RLIN to LC, where they are checked and distributed—again via LSP, to OCLC and RLIN, or on tape to NAF subscribers.

Other NACO libraries, RLIN and OCLC users alike, have begun to migrate to LSP, which provides faster creation of new authority records with less duplicative effort. NACO itself has been transformed into the National Coordinated Cataloging Operation, a new effort to improve the national availability of original cataloging.

Subject Authorities

Although subject authorities fit within the same USMARC format as name and series authorities, they have been slower to spread throughout the library community in machine-readable form. That is partly because of the nature of LC's subject authority file.

Until recently, the only machine-readable subject authority file at LC was the file used to create the *Library of Congress Subject Headings* ("The Red Book"). This file was not maintained as a normal MARC file would be. When it was transformed to MARC form and distributed there was a fundamental problem: record numbers were assigned as the transformation took place.

This was fine for the first year. For the second distribution, however, it meant that an unchanged record might have a new record number simply because an intervening subject had been added. That meant that a subscribing institution had to *completely* rebuild its online subject authority file each time a new *LCSH* tape was received.

In 1986 LC created its own Subject Authority File (SAF), which overcomes this problem. Subject authority records now have the same consistent numbers and weekly tape distribution as name authorities, making it reasonable for shared cataloging services and some local systems to maintain the same access to subject authorities and to name authorities. However, SAF is not a complete subject authority file. It lacks completeness because floating subdivisions are not attached—that is, the file does not include a record for each possible complete subject heading that can be formed by using such subdivisions.

Library Uses for USMARC Authorities

LC authorities and the USMARC authorities format are used to build and maintain authority files for reference and for control. Authority files can be used to provide references for book and card catalogs, to suggest related headings, to maintain quality control in a bibliographic system, and even to make automatic changes as established headings change.

Authority files can improve efficiency for an online catalog by filtering searches through the authority system and, in some cases, by indexing bibliographic headings indirectly (through an authority file) rather than directly.

Authority files serve catalogers directly, and serve library patrons less directly but no less powerfully. One major function of cataloging and maintenance of catalogs (card, book, or online) is guidance to related works: a patron looking for one book by an author should be able to find other books by the same author easily; a patron should be able to find those books even if the patron brings a different form of name to the search.

14

Holdings

USMARC for bibliographic data provides only two fields for storage or communication of holdings information: fields 850 and 851 (currently limited to archival and manuscripts control). The bibliographic formats lack ways of storing extensive holdings data so as to allow manipulation of that data. Most implementations of USMARC have added local fields to accommodate holdings at various levels of complexity; chapter 19 discusses three such extensions. Serial holdings have always been a problem in library automation, particularly in terms of automatic compression from piece-level holdings—as used in a checkin system—to summary holdings—as needed for most displays.

Serial holdings change over time; new issues are received as pieces, collected and bound, and sometimes discarded or replaced by microfilm. Libraries control unbound serials differently than bound volumes: it is effectively impossible to circulate volume 13 number 5 of a periodical to one borrower and volume 13 number 7 to another once volume 13 has been bound. A library must keep track of what issues are on hand, and of the current status of those issues. Even monograph holdings change over time, when the library considers physical condition and preservation information to be part of holdings information.

History of *USMARC for Holdings and Locations*

In October 1982 eight southeastern research libraries received a Title IIC grant to begin developing a regional resource sharing system for serials.[1] This group project, dubbed the "Southeastern ARL Libraries Cooperative Serials Project," worked with the Library of Congress to develop a proposal for a national format for holdings and locations. The result was Proposal 82-20, "MARC Format for Holdings and Locations", first presented at a meeting of the USMARC advisory group in October 1982.[2] Intensive discussion followed at the October 1982 meeting, at a special three-day conference in November 1982, and at the Midwinter 1983, ALA 1983, and September 1983 USMARC advisory group meetings.

The "final draft" of the *USMARC Format for Holdings and Locations* was published by the Library of Congress in 1984. Since that time— and, to some extent, before actual publication—various agencies have been experimenting with implementations of the format. Update 1 to the document appeared at the end of 1987. As of this writing, however, the format is *still* a "final draft" rather than an adopted USMARC format. That extreme delay stems from two sources:

- the sheer complexity of the format and difficulties in establishing sound implementations that will demonstrate the feasibility of all aspects of the format;

- an unusually long process required to arrive at an American National Standard for Nonserial Holdings Statements and assure that the nonserial standard works properly in conjunction with Z39.44, the standard for serial holdings statements.

---

1 Emory University, University of Florida, Florida State University, University of Georgia, University of Kentucky, University of Miami, University of Tennessee, and Virginia Polytechnic Institute and State University (VPI).

2 Much of this chapter, including all examples of fields, derives from Proposal 82-20.

Summary of the Format

U*SMARC for Holdings and Locations*, in its draft state, is about 150 pages long, with detailed descriptions of subfield and field usage. This brief treatment gives some of the content designation and a few partial examples. Most monographic holdings segments are very simple; serial holdings segments can become exceedingly complex.

001	Control number
004	Control number: parent bibliographic record
005	Date and time of latest transaction
007	Physical description fixed field (as in USMARC Bib)
008	Fixed length data elements
010	LC Card Number
020	ISBN
022	ISSN
023	International film number (SFN)
024	Standard recording number (SRN)
027	Standard technical report number (STRN)
030	CODEN
035	Control number

Table 14.1: Holdings Format, Fields 001-035

The holdings format is designed so that records can be maintained as independent USMARC records or be attached to bibliographic records. When carried as independent records, holdings records have the standard USMARC structure and include field 001, 005, and 008 (as would other USMARC records). Table 14.1 shows the coded and control fields for the holdings format.

Fields 010 through 030 serve to link a holdings record to a bibliographic record. USMARC bibliographic records can be self-contained entities, but holdings records are meaningless unless linked to some bibliographic entity. It doesn't help to know that an institution has volumes 1-117 without knowing what they are volumes *of*. Field 004 provides an explicit link to a single USMARC record; other fields can link to records that may not be in USMARC form by providing unambiguous identifiers such as ISBN or CODEN.

583	Actions
841	Fixed length data elements (alternate storage)
843	Reproduction Note
845	Terms governing use
852	Location / Call Number
853	Definition of enumeration & chronology/publication pattern
854	Definition of enumeration & chronology/publication pattern : supplement or accompanying material
855	Definition of enumeration & chronology/publication pattern : index
863	Enumeration and chronology - basic bibliographic unit
864	Enumeration and chronology - supplement or accompanying material
865	Enumeration and chronology - indexes
866	Enumeration and chronology - bibliographic unit: alternative display
867	Enumeration and chronology - supplement or accompanying material: alternative display
868	Enumeration and chronology - indexes: alternative display

Table 14.2: Holdings Format, Fields 583-868

Table 14.2 shows the remainder of the holdings fields. Field 841 is used when a holdings record is attached to a bibliographic record: it carries the holdings type of record, descriptive cataloging form/ level of description, and 008 values in three subfields.

The rest of the format is made up of three independent fields and three groups of fields, each containing three fields. Fields 843, 845, and 852 are independent; fields 853-855, 863-865, and 866-868 are groups in one respect, while the triplets 853, 863, and 866, 854, 864, and 867, and 855, 865, and 868 are groups in another respect.

---

843 ⎯ ‡aMicrofilm.‡bWashington,‡cLibrary of Congress, Photoduplication Service‡d[1954-]‡e5 reels. 35 mm.‡3v. 1-10.¶
843 ⎯‡aMicrofilm.‡bNew Orleans,‡cRecordak Corp.,‡d[Dec. 8, 1969-]‡e1 reel. 35 mm.‡fJapanese camp papers,‡3v. 1-2.¶

Two 843s for a single newspaper with split holdings:
843 ⎯ ‡aMicrofilm.‡bNew York,‡cRecordak Corp.‡d[1962-]‡e328 reels. 35 mm.‡3Feb. 4, 1883-Aug. 3, 1960¶
843 ⎯‡aMicrofilm.‡bWinston-Salem, N. C.,‡cMann Film Laboratories,‡d[1962-]‡e52 reels. 35 mm.‡3Sept. 1, 1960-Nov. 30, 1962¶

Figure 14.1: Field 843, Examples

Field 843 describes the reproduction when the bibliographic record is for the original, but some (or all) of the holdings are for reproductions. As shown in Figure 14.1, a single record may include multiple 843 fields. Field 845 is used to specify information on lending or reproduction of copies that cannot be specified in coded fields 008/20 and 008/21. Field 852 provides location information for an item, and is the fundamental location and call number field. This field is typical of holdings fields in its wealth of subfields and extended description (nine pages). For some nonserial holdings field 852 would be the single new field. Figure 14.2 shows examples of field 852.

---

852 01‡aViBlbV‡bMain Lib‡bMRR‡kRef‡hHF5531.A1‡iN4273¶
852 01‡aDLC‡bSer Div‡hA123‡i.B456‡zSigned by author.¶

Figure 14.2: Field 852, Examples

The first three related fields (853, 854, and 855) define enumeration and chronology or publication patterns. As with the other groups the first field is for base publications; the second is for supplements or accompanying material; the third is for indices. These fields provide definitions and captions for holdings, but do not provide the holdings proper.

---

853 01‡6l‡av.‡wa¶
863 51‡6l.1‡a1‡p//¶

853 20‡6l‡av.‡bno.‡u12‡vr‡x01‡wm‡tc.¶
863 40‡6l.1‡a1-13‡t1¶
854 20‡6l‡a(year)‡0Buyer's guide‡wa‡tc.¶
864 40‡6l.1‡a1956-1962‡t1¶
[Library has v. 1-13, 1951-1963 with the Buyer's guide for 1956-1962]
Note: *this pattern would NOT be used for a publication like* Consumer Reports, *where the* Buying Guide *is numbered as a regular issue.*

855 __‡6l‡av.‡i(year/year)‡oAuthor index¶
865 41‡6l.1‡a21/25‡i1971/1976‡zin v. 25 of Emory law journal.¶
[Serial published as Journal of public law, *v. 1-23; as* Emory law journal, *v. 23- . Holdings record for* Journal of public law *shows index location in note.]*

Figure 14.3: Fields 853-865, Examples

Fields 853-855 and 863-865 are extensively subfielded to accommodate many levels of information; Table 14.3 shows the subfielding for field 853.

Where fields 853-855 contain the definitions and labels, using whole numbers in subfield ‡6, fields 863-865 contain the actual values, using decimal numbers in subfield ‡6. The format includes fourteen pages of explanation for field 853, which can vary from one occurrence per physical piece down to a single statement for a long run.

The combinations of 853-855 and 863-865 are needed for the anticipated computer support of holdings compression and expansion. For those not using integrated serials checkin, for those who find the scheme too complex for implementation, and for those publications that can't be represented in such a scheme, the format includes a final trio of fields. Fields 866, 867, and 868 allow free text holdings strings, identified as ANSI Z39 notation or nonstandard notation. One or more such fields can replace a portion of the 85x/86x combinations for display purposes, can replace all of them, or can be used without 85x/86x fields.

853	Definition of Enumeration & Chronology/Publication Pattern
‡6	Sequence control number (SCN)
‡a	Term designating first level of enumeration
‡b	Term designating second level of enumeration
‡c	Term designating third level of enumeration
‡d	Term designating fourth level of enumeration
‡e	Term designating fifth level of enumeration
‡f	Term designating sixth level of enumeration
‡g	Term designating alternative numbering scheme, first level of enumeration
‡h	Term designating alternative numbering scheme, second level of enumeration
‡i	Term designating first level of chronology
‡j	Term designating second level of chronology
‡k	Term designating third level of chronology
‡l	Term designating fourth level of chronology
‡m	Term designating fifth level of chronology
‡n	Term designating sixth level of chronology
‡t	Term designating copy
‡u	Bibliographic units per next higher level
‡v	Restart/continuous numbering code
‡w	Issues per year / frequency
‡x	Calendar change
‡y	Regularity pattern
‡3	Definition date span

Table 14.3: Subfields for Field 853

Experimentation and Evaluation

Before LC published the final draft, work had begun to demonstrate the feasibility and usefulness of the format. Since most networks and local systems already defined holdings fields, the USMARC format would mean some shift from current practice for most institutions. That required shift, and the obvious complexity of the format, effectively placed a burden on those advocating the format to demonstrate that it was worthwhile.[3]

A number of libraries, library consortia, and vendors have experimented with or, in some cases, implemented the draft standard during the past few years. In no known case is the implementation either pure or complete—that is, to date no system can fully support compression and expansion of holdings, provide full prediction for checkin, and work with the draft format exactly as published, with no extensions or modifications.

SOLINET's Lambda

The Southeastern ARL Libraries Cooperative Network contracted with SOLINET to develop program designs using the draft format, and to test the workability of the format. SOLINET, in turn, contracted with Burroughs Corporation to design a holdings component for the Lambda system (based on WLN software) that would use the draft format and support addition, editing, deletion, and display of holdings records, with automatic compression from a detailed holdings statement to a summary display. That subsystem first became operational in the fall of 1984.

The designers did not follow the format exactly, adding fields to accommodate OCLC holdings and location information directly (rather than translating it to USMARC fields), and modifying field 852 for more efficient reporting of nonconsecutive multiple copies of monographs.

An early report on use of the Lambda holdings subsystem indicated that staffs did not find the format difficult but that correct coding was time-consuming. The Lambda implementation included extensive error and consistency checks. Early users found acceptable production rates.

---

3   Most material in this section comes from reports in the *LITA Newsletter*, issues 23, 25, 30, 31 and 32, not cited in the bibliography.

For reasons *not* directly connected to the holdings format, SO-LINET shut down the Lambda system in 1987.

Other Implementations

Harvard modified NOTIS (Northwestern's library automation system) to support the draft holdings format and began coding retrospective serials checkin records in 1984. It also found coding time-consuming but not difficult. Harvard estimated $4 per record to go from manual checkin to coded holdings. It also deviated from the format, however: its conclusion was that the NISO (Z39) standard for display was not workable, so it recorded data in an incompatible form.

The University of Georgia implemented the format within its MARVEL integrated system, as have the University of Kansas, VTLS, Inc., and the University of Florida.

Faxon designed a microcomputer-based serials control system (MicroLinx) to store holdings in a form compatible with the format. The system did not use tags and subfields for input or editing, using a mnemonic system instead. Others involved in developing the format looked to Faxon as a possible source of information for publication patterns; as of this writing, however, no such plans have emerged. Faxon uses the draft format extensively to extract and communicate serials holdings to library online catalogs.

OCLC based its microcomputer serials control system (SC350) on the holdings format and also used mnemonics for input and editing. Note that this implementation is for the microcomputer-based system only; as of 1988 neither OCLC nor RLIN has implemented the (still draft) holdings format as part of its national shared cataloging system.

The Standards Problem

The initial developers of the USMARC holdings format were simultaneously working in the National Information Standards Organization (NISO) toward national standards for the storage and display of holdings information at the summary and detail level. Throughout the development of the format, a basic design principle has been that it would fully support the NISO standards.

Serials standards have been adopted: first Z39.42, for summary holdings, then Z39.44, initially for detailed holdings and finally merging both levels of holdings (and replacing Z39.42). Z39.44 was adopted in 1985. By that time a committee had already begun work on a standard for nonserial holdings. That standard, Z39.57, is nearing approval as this is written. We can expect changes in the holdings format based on Z39.57 and, most likely, a fully approved format before 1990.

Conclusion

USMARC for Holdings and Locations represents years of work by the Southeastern ARL group, Library of Congress (particularly Gary McCone), MARBI, and the USMARC advisory group. Most who have been involved with the design agree that, if any USMARC holdings format can serve serials checkin and other serials automation needs, this design can. Even the most pessimistic generally regard fields 852 and 866/868 as reasonable foundations for a national holdings reporting format. Fields 853-855 and 863-865 are far more difficult to establish, but are needed if computers are to generate piece predictions, establish missing-issue claims, and automatically recognize volume ends, compressing holdings at that point. Only experience will show whether the full USMARC holdings format can be implemented in a realistic, cost-effective manner. The design is a careful, thoughtful one; its future will depend on its workability.

15

Linking in USMARC

Before USMARC, there was the catalog card. The Library of Congress developed MARC, at least initially, in order to distribute in machine-readable form the same information used to produce catalog cards at LC—and, for most of its first two decades, the primary end-result of MARC use within libraries was printed catalog cards.

Fundamentally, the cataloging record represented on a catalog card is a *unit record*: a description of a single work. That is particularly true in the case of books. The dominant bibliographic practice in the United States is to treat each item as an integral whole, somewhat isolated from all other items. Unit records do contain links, of course. Subject headings gather together works thought to be on the same topic. Classification numbers also bring similar work together on the shelf, in shelflist catalogs and in some online catalogs. Main entries and added entries collocate works by specific authors, and authority control helps to provide consistent collocation. But the links are indirect, created by sorting different related unit records into contiguous order.

Similarly, USMARC defines fields and records at a single level of significance. Each field within a record may be accessed independently from the directory, and (with few exceptions) each field functions as an independent data element or group of related data elements. Further, most USMARC records are independent, capable

171

of being processed without reference to any other USMARC record. USMARC has not supported hierarchies of information: records within records or fields within fields. Some MARC formats (e.g., UKMARC) do support subrecords or other hierarchical structures within records, but such support has never been part of USMARC.

While the formats have not had formal support for hierarchies, bibliographic data does involve hierarchical relationships—sometimes between elements within a single record, sometimes among various records. In the early 1980s, USMARC designers looked at the problems of links and hierarchies within a record and among records. While USMARC has always had some support for links and certain types of hierarchies, those links have been improved and broadened in recent years. USMARC still does not support formal subrecords, but now defines a sufficient variety of links within and among records to satisfy most bibliographic needs.

Linkage mechanisms fall into two broad categories: intra-record links, linking different elements within a single record, and inter-record links, linking different records. Some forms of inter-record linking support analytic cataloging of one sort or another; others support chronological relationships (successive entry cataloging), collocation, and authority control. Table 15.1 notes intra-record linking techniques, most of which appear in other chapters. Table 15.2 notes inter-record linking techniques discussed in this chapter.

Intra-Record Links

Alternate graphic representation (Vernacular data) (Ch. 16)
   Field 066 . . . . . .Character sets present
   Field 880 . . . . . .Alternate graphic representation
   Subfield ‡6 . . . . .Linking subfield

Materials specified (Ch. 12 & below)
   Subfield ‡3 . . . . .Materials specified

Sequence control (Ch. 14)
   Subfield ‡6 Sequence control number (Holdings)

Table 15.1: Linking Techniques Noted Elsewhere

Analysis
Analytics of monographic and multipart series, using series note
   Fields 4xx . . . . . .Series notes
   Fields 8xx . . . . . .Series added entries
Display of parts in the notes area
   Field 505 . . . . . .Formatted contents note
Analytical added entries
   Fields 7xx . . . . . .Other added entries
"In" analytics
   Field 773 . . . . . .Host item entry

Other Inter-record Links
   Fields 760-787 . . .Linking entry fields
   Fields 010-035 . . .Control & standard number links

Table 15.2: Linking Techniques Discussed Below

Intra-record Links

Fields within a record are inherently linked to one another, in the sense that they all relate to the same overall record. Until 1976 LC MARC had no provision for explicit links between one field and another, or between groups of fields within a record.

Fields 870-873 and Subfield ‡j

In 1976 four fields were added to the serials format which included explicit field-to-field linkage: the 87x "variant name" fields. These fields were used in pre-*AACR2* CONSER records, where the ALA form of a corporate name would be recorded in field 871 while the *AACR* form was entered in field 110 (or 410, 610, 710, or 810). Subfield ‡j, *Tag and sequence number of the field for which this field is a variant*, contained a tag, a slash, and a number: for example, *‡j710/1*. This subfield (which could only appear in an 871) links this field to the first 710 in the record.

    The 87X fields were added to all formats in 1979 and 1980, but were never implemented at the Library of Congress. When LC began using *AACR2*, it stopped using 87X fields in serials. The fields were made obsolete as part of format integration, but may still be used in some systems. The first attempt at precise intra-record linkage was not very successful, for at least two reasons (in addition to cataloging-related reasons):

- Maintenance of a record can disrupt the validity of the links through simple inattention. Inserting a 710 field before an existing 710 (in the example above) without inspecting the 87X fields will leave the field with an incorrect link (the 871 will be treated as a variant form of the new "first 710"),

- The link is unidirectional. The 710 itself contains nothing to show that a variant form exists. Records with 87X fields cannot be processed using normal field-by-field techniques—and most MARC processing programs do work with fields independently as a rule.

The concept of an explicit field-to-field link is sound, and cases exist where such a link is valuable. A newer explicit intra-record link was approved by MARBI in 1982; its first major use in USMARC is to support storage of vernacular (nonroman) text. That use is discussed in the next chapter, which includes examples of its use for cataloging Chinese and Hebrew materials.

Materials Specified: Subfield ‡3

The USMARC bibliographic format still does not have an explicit, formal linking technique to link groups of fields within a record. As discussed later in this chapter, such a technique was proposed but eventually abandoned. An *implicit* linking technique for some fields uses subfield ‡3, *Materials specified*. When used as part of a field, subfield ‡3 restricts applicability of the field to some portion of the record—that is, to the materials specified.

Subfield ‡3, defined in many descriptive and access fields, explicitly identifies a field as pertaining to *part* of the material covered by a record. When the same ‡3 value appears in several different fields, those fields can be treated as a group. For instance field 583, *Actions*, can form a history of processing for material; common ‡3 values link together the stages for a given set of material. Chapter 12 includes some examples of ‡3.

---

541 __‡3Letters, 1890-1913‡aUnidentified collector.¶
541 __‡3Newspaper clippings, 1910-1945‡aJohn Sedgewick Ferwort Foun-
dation¶
583 __‡3Letters, 1890-1913‡aAccessioned‡c11/06/83¶
583 __‡3Letters, 1890-1913‡aDeacidified‡c11/13/83¶
583 __‡3Newspaper clippings, 1910-1945‡aAccessioned‡c11/14/83¶
541 __‡3Letters, 1914-1919‡aJohn Sedgewick Ferwort Foundation¶
583 __‡3Letters, 1890-1913‡aTransferred to offsite storage‡c11/16/83¶
583 __‡3Letters, 1914-1919‡aAccessioned‡c11/16/83¶
583 __‡3Newspaper clippings, 1910-1945‡aDeacidified‡c11/16/83¶
583 __‡3Letters, 1890-1913‡aRemove restrictions‡c1/1/86¶
583 __‡3Newspaper clippings, 1910-1945‡aDeed of gift needed‡c1/1/84¶
583 __‡3Letters, 1914-1919‡aDeed of gift needed‡c1/1/84¶

Figure 15.1: MARC 541 and 583 Fields

Figure 15.1 shows several fields from a hypothetical archival and manuscripts control record, entered in chronological order as material was received and processed; these fields make up the "process control" section of a record within RLIN.

Letters, 1890-1913. Source: Unidentified collector.
      Accessioned, 11/06/83.
      Deacidified, 11/13/83.
      Transferred to offsite storage, 11/16/83.
      Remove restrictions, 1/1/86.
**Newspaper clippings, 1910-1945. Source: John Sedgewick Ferwort Founda-
tion.**
      Accessioned, 11/14/83.
      Deacidified, 11/16/83.
      Deed of gift needed, 1/1/84.
Letters, 1914-1919. Source: John Sedgewick Ferwort Foundation.
      Accessioned, 11/16/83.
      Deed of gift needed, 1/1/84.

Figure 15.2: Grouped Display of 15.1 Contents

Figure 15.2 shows a possible display format, regrouping the fields based on the contents of subfield ‡3. The technique works well for this particular situation, but it is not a formal linking technique and is not explicitly supported by the format documentation.

Subfield ‡3 links are informal and not restrictive. If a box of personal papers is processed as such through three stages, then split into letters and diaries for further processing, the ‡3 values will not provide any link from the larger group to the smaller material groups.

Subfield ‡3 is also defined for many added entry fields. There, as in other cases, it does not appear to be useful as a computer-supported link; rather, the subfield serves as an annotation. Subfield ‡3 is a textual subfield without a controlled vocabulary or controlled usage; it was not intended for computer-supported links, but has some value in such a role.

Inter-record Links

Usmarc has a variety of means for indicating relationships among bibliographic records, ranging from contents notes to record number links. These links are discussed in two general areas, as shown in Table 15.1: links that support analysis and all other inter-record links.

Analytics

"Analysis is the process of preparing a bibliographic record that describes a part or parts of a larger item."[1] Analysis thus involves a smaller item, which can be called a "component part," within a larger item, which can be called the "host item." *AACR2* notes five methods of achieving analysis:

---

1   *Anglo-American Cataloguing Rules*, 2d ed. (Chicago: American Library Association, 1978), 270.

- analytics of monographic series and multipart series, where the larger item is described in a series note;
- display of parts in the note area, normally as a contents note;
- analytical added entries, giving the part's main entry heading and uniform title;
- "in" analytics, with full descriptive cataloging for the part and a brief citation (main entry, uniform title, title proper, edition, and publication details) of the larger item in an "In" note;
- multilevel description, giving relatively complete description of parts within a record for the whole.

USMARC Support of Analysis: Pre-1984

USMARC has always supported the first three methods of analysis. Analytics of monographic series are supported by series notes and tracings, carried in fields 400-490 and 800-840. These fields have worked well for those cases in which the component part is also an independent bibliographic item, as is typically the case with monographic series.

Simple display of parts usually appears in field 505 (Formatted Contents Note). Analytical added entries appear in 7XX fields. Such entries provide access to component parts while maintaining a coherent master record.

Series fields, contents notes, and added entries serve many requirements for analysis; all three are in the core bibliographic formats, and all three have been heavily used in USMARC. There are limitations to the techniques; they are not suitable for some component parts, and do not provide sufficiently detailed description for others. Added entries are unsuitable for articles within serials, as the number of potential entries is unlimited and 7xx fields have no specific place to indicate location within the serial. While added entries can be quite informative, libraries with special needs may wish to record more information on certain elements of a larger work; USMARC has not allowed for such detail. The USMARC formats did not allow for full analytic records.

Analytic Records: Early Proposals

The lack of USMARC support for full analytic records has bothered librarians in LC and elsewhere for years—since 1972 or earlier, by some estimates. In the early 1970s a field was proposed that would link a full component-part record to a host-item record. At the time, the field was felt to be unsatisfactory. There was some feeling that a single record should accommodate full description for the host item and the component part. The 76X-78X linking entry fields, after which the new field was patterned, had never been wholly satisfactory for indexing, partly because the main entry subfields failed to distinguish types of main entry. As a result, it was difficult to determine whether personal name indexing or corporate name indexing procedures should be used, and sometimes difficult to connect linking entries properly.

During the late 1970s a number of different proposals were raised for consideration. A range of possibilities was presented at the 1980 ALA Annual Conference in New York, with some basic requirements appearing to gain acceptance. The requirements, as stated in Proposal 80-5.1, are as follows:

- The technique must be capable of handling a variety of relationships including vertical, horizontal, or chronological.
- The technique must be consistent with the record structure standard as defined by ANSI Z39.2-1979.
- All data fields must be directly accessible through the record directory.
- All data fields should be fully content-designated.
- There should be no restriction on the data fields for the related item that can be selected for inclusion in a record.
- The technique must be able to express relationships between bibliographic units within a single record and between separate

records. The description of related bibliographic units may or may not reside in the same bibliographic record.[2]

Proposal 80-5.1 extended the directory as allowed in ANSI Z39.2-1979: each directory entry may contain a fourth segment, an "implementation-defined portion." As proposed, the "implementation-defined portion" would add a thirteenth character identifying "fields belonging to one subrecord." The proposal also defined field 002, including a three-character "relationship code," the subrecord character, and the legend of the subrecord. Given the set of requirements above, 80-5.1 appeared to be the best technique available. In May 1981 the technique was tentatively approved by the USMARC advisory group. Many other techniques had been considered, including ones that allowed whole fields to be imbedded within subfields, and ones that used fields to delimit portions of the directory.

The Library of Congress surveyed a number of federal agencies (and some other parties) to determine interest in the technique. Response, though interpreted by one participant as "favorable," was lukewarm: most agencies did not use the MARC format and thought the method was "fine, if you use MARC." One agency that did use MARC, via OCLC, thought the proposal was fine, but outlined what OCLC would have to do to make the format work. The needed changes to OCLC, though well-stated, would have been expensive to make and would have made OCLC or any similar system slower and more expensive to operate.

Representatives from OCLC and RLG had reluctantly acceded to the technique, but warned early on that it would be an expensive technique to implement. As the two shared cataloging services spent more time looking at it, the sheer expense and difficulty of the technique became more and more apparent. For the bibliographic services to support subrecords, online displays and data handling techniques would need to be changed drastically; the cost of software

2 *Proposal 80-5.1, MARC Subrecord Technique* (Washington, D.C.: Library of Congress, 1980) (Proposal for consideration by USMARC advisory group.)

changes, documentation changes, and retraining appeared to be excessive.

At the 1981 ALA Annual Conference in San Francisco, RLG and OCLC liaisons asserted that implementation of the subrecord technique would take several years and probably cost upwards of $2 million dollars ($1 million for the bibliographic services alone). Given this expense and difficulty, LC and others agreed that a less disruptive proposal might be reasonable, and that single-record multilevel storage might not be necessary. After further discussion and analysis Sally McCallum of the Library of Congress prepared Proposal 81-13, which affirmed the existing serials linking entry fields and extended the technique to provide for "In" analytics.

Analytic Records: Field 773

Proposal 81-13, *Record-Linking Techniques*, was prepared in October 1981, revised and approved in February 1982, and published in *Information Technology and Libraries* in September 1982.[3] The proposal is an excellent explication of analysis and other linking entry situations, and adds four new elements:

- two new values for Bibliographic Level: *a* for monographic (singly occurring) component parts and *b* for serial component parts (such as a running column within a periodical);
- a new element in the Leader, position 19, "Linked-record code," to be used in those cases where the linked-to record is identified only by a control number;
- a new subfield ‡7 for all linking entries, containing up to four one-character codes providing further information on the linked-to record;
- field 773, "Host item entry," defined in all bibliographic formats.

---

3   Sally H. McCallum, "MARC Record-Linking Technique," *Information Technology and Libraries* 1, no. 3 (September 1982): 281-291.

The heart of MARC support for "In" analytics is field 773, defined in Update 8 to *MFBD*. Field 773 is repeatable and is defined identically across all bibliographic formats, as shown in Table 15.3. The field carries a suggested display constant, "In ." Field 773 and the other elements of proposal 81-13 provide full support for the fourth method of analytic cataloging; additionally, subfield ‡7 strengthens other linking entry fields by defining them more clearly for indexing and other manipulation.

Any MARC format can be used for an analytic record. If a music cataloger wishes to give a full description for a recording of Igor Stravinsky's *Zvezdoliki* on Side 2, Band 1 of "Stravinsky Conducts Stravinsky: Choral Music," a full USMARC music record can be created with legend *ja* (Sound recording, musical; component part, monographic). A continuing (serially appearing) column in a periodical can be cataloged with legend *ab* (Language material, component part, serial); an article in the same periodical would be *aa*, as it is monographic.

773	**Host Item Entry**
‡7	Control subfield
‡a	Main entry
‡b	Edition
‡d	Place, publisher, and date of publication
‡g	Relationship information
‡k	Series data for related title
‡r	Report number
‡s	Uniform title
‡t	Title
‡u	Standard Technical Report Number (STRN)
‡w	Control number
‡x	International Standard Serial Number (ISSN)
‡y	CODEN
‡z	International Standard Book Number (ISBN)

Table 15.3: Field 773 Subfields

Bryant, Keith L.
  Cathedrals, castles, and Roman baths; railway station architecture in the urban south.
  ill.
  Grant St. Station (Aeck Assoc., archts.) and Decatur (Ga.) Station (Stevens & Wilkinson, archts.).
  In Journal of urban history, February 1976, v.2, n.2, p. 195-230.
  1. Atlanta (Ga.)Railroads--Stations. 2. Aeck Associates. 3. Stevens & Wilkinson.

Figure 15.3: Serial Article Analytic, Bibliographic Display

```
100   10   ‡aBryant, Keith L.¶
245   00   ‡aCathedrals, castles, and Roman baths;‡brailway station architec-
ture in the urban south.¶
300   __   ‡bill.¶
500   _‡aGrant St. Station (Aeck Assoc., archts.) and Decatur (Ga.) Station
(Stevens & Wilkinson, archts.)¶
651   00   ‡aAtlanta (Ga.)‡xRailroads‡xStations.¶
610   20   ‡aAeck Associates.¶
610   20   ‡aStevens & Wilkinson.¶
773   0_   ‡tJournal of urban history‡gFebruary 1976, v.2, n.2, p.195-230.¶
```

Figure 15.4: Serial Article Analytic, Tagged Display

Figures 15.3 and 15.4 show a hypothetical serial analytic. In this case, the 773 field uses a textual linkage to the serial record—which need not even be available as a MARC record. Field 773 could also contain an explicit record number, ‡w, in place of or in addition to textual links. Figures 15.5 through 15.8 show a real example in which one portion of an archival collection is explicitly linked to its parent— or parents, since in this case the set of papers is part of three different collections in three different locations. (The second related record shown is the Atlanta copy of the King collection. The third record is a collection of George Romney's papers.)

Romney, George W., 1907-
  Miscellaneous papers, 1965-1967.
  ca. 7 items.
  George Romney was governor of Michigan from 1963-1969, a period of
  much civil rights activity.
  Summary: Photocopies of correspondence between George Romney and
  Martin Luther King, Jr. and other individuals of interest to King.
  Originals in: Bentley Historical Library, University of Michigan.
  Duplicates in: King Library and Archives, Martin Luther King, Jr. Center,
  Atlanta.
  Duplicates in: Martin Luther King, Jr. Papers Project, Stanford University.

Figure 15.5: Romney Papers, Partial Bibliographic Display

```
100_  1    ‡aRomney, George W.,‡d1907-¶
245   00   ‡kMiscellaneous papers,‡f1965-1967.¶
300   __   ‡aca. 7 items.¶
545   __   ‡aGeorge Romney was ...remainder omitted¶
520   __   ‡aPhotocopies of ...remainder omitted¶
535   1_   ‡aOriginals in:‡aBentley Historical Library, University of Michigan.¶
535   2_   ‡aDuplicates in:‡aKing Library and Archives, Martin Luther King,
Jr. Center, Atlanta.¶
535   2_   ‡aDuplicates in:‡aMartin Luther King, Jr. Papers Project, Stanford
University.¶
541   __   ‡3surveyed¶
773   __   ‡w(CStRLIN)CSKV87-A0¶
773   __   ‡w(CStRLIN)GAKV87-A0¶
773   __   ‡w(CStRLIN)MIUV85-A2178¶
```

Figure 15.6: Romney Papers, Partial Tagged Display

Figures 15.5 and 15.6 show use of the control number subfield,
‡w. If field 773 (or any other linking field) lacks any textual identification of the host item, a system must access the host record in order
to prepare a meaningful note. In practice field 773 should almost
always contain textual identification of the host item.

Martin Luther King, Jr., Papers Project Collection, 1870-1968.
c. 20,000 items.
Organization: Bibliographic records in RLIN for the King papers are structured by collection name. Each collection record summarizes material by or about King, either originals or photocopies, received from an archive or donor. In addition, items in original form housed at the King Center are entered by collection name.

The Martin Luther King, Jr., Papers Project is a joint effort of the Martin Luther King, Jr., Center for Non-violent Social Change and Stanford University to collect and publish a twelve volume scholarly edition of the speeches, sermons, correspondence, and other writing of Martin Luther King, Jr.

Summary: The Project collection consists of both original primary resource material located at the King Library and Archives as well as photocopies of King related documents that are part of the collections of various archives around the country. The Collections include correspondence, tape recordings and transcriptions of King's speeches and sermons as well as transcripts and publications of SCLC and other local civil rights organizations. FBI documents and previously published material is also included. In most cases copies of documents are located at both the King Center and at the Stanford University office.

The papers are accessible to scholars at the King Library and Archive, Martin Luther King, Jr., Center, Atlanta. Some restrictions apply from contributors. Permission to use the materials must be obtained from the King Papers Project or the King Library and Archives.

1. King, Martin Luther, Jr., 1929-1968. 2. Afro Americans--Civil Rights.

Figure 15.7: M.L. King Papers, Bibliographic Display

```
245   00   ‡aMartin Luther King, Jr., Papers Project Collection,‡f1870-1968.¶
300   __   ‡ac. 20,000 items.¶
351   __   ‡aBibliographic records in RLIN ...remainder omitted...
545   __   ‡aThe Martin Luther King, Jr., Papers Project is a joint effort ...remainder omitted...
520   __   ‡aThe Project collection consists ...remainder omitted...
540   __   ‡aThe papers are accessible to ...remainder omitted...
600   10   ‡aKing, Martin Luther, Jr., 1929-1968.¶
650   _0   ‡aAfro Americans‡xCivil Rights.¶
```

Figure 15.8: M.L. King Papers, Partial Tagged Display

Textual reference has two limitations. First, it is less precise than a full representation of the host item. Second, it can become obsolete if the description of the host item is modified. When field 773 contains a record number and nothing else, those two limitations are replaced by other problems. Full support of record number linkage in a network or distributed environment requires that the host record be communicated each time any analytic referring to it is communicated. Neither OCLC nor RLIN provides such automatic support. For a processing system, record number linkage involves significant overhead in order to format a small note: a second record must be fetched and processed in the midst of processing the first record.

Field 773 does not allow for multilevel description, the fifth form of analysis; USMARC has no provision for formal multilevel description and does not appear likely to add any such provision. Field 773 does not disrupt existing data, and requires little new training for use; an analytic record is like any other USMARC record, with one new field. The technique is easy to implement without record number links and easy to use.

Only time will tell how heavily field 773 is used. The field appears to handle situations mentioned in other proposals with varying degrees of success. By stipulating that inter-record links are always from the smaller to the larger (whereas added entries can run from the larger to the smaller), field 773 simplifies (and narrows) the choices available for analysis. Field 773 uses a linking technique which has become very familiar to serials catalogers. While linking fields have never been elegant or perfect, they have almost always worked in the real world.

Other Inter-record Links

USMARC has four other varieties of inter-record link, at varying levels of formality. The holdings format requires explicit links to bibliographic records; such links can be provided through control numbers or standard numbers. Control numbers normally link to a unique record, where standard numbers link to a unique bibliographic entity which may exist in any number of USMARC records. Control number and standard number links can also be used within the USMARC bibliographic formats: field 010 (LCCN) and standard number fields help to pull together different records for the same bibliographic item, and field 035 has some potential for tracing a single bibliographic description through various appearances on different systems.

All heading fields, main and added entries alike, serve to link bibliographic records containing common headings. Such links are directly supported by online indexing and by the filing order within card catalogs and represent the primary reason for authority control and establishment of uniform titles and controlled subject headings.

Links between bibliographic records and authority records, and between different authority records, are normally textual links; the USMARC authority format does not generally provide for direct linkage from an authority record to a bibliographic record. Several authority records may relate to a given bibliographic record, controlling different headings, and a single authority record may relate to tens of thousands of bibliographic records. Linkages from bibliographic headings to authority records are indirect in terms of the USMARC formats, but are direct in some system implementations of the formats. If a bibliographic heading is under authority control, that heading must match an existing established heading within an authority record.

Some systems store the record number of the authority record in place of the heading within the bibliographic record, reconstructing the record when it is displayed. This method of implementation adds to display overhead but makes changes in headings very easy to implement: if the authority record changes, all controlled headings are automatically changed without any system effort.

16

Nonroman Text in USMARC

Most bibliographic records for most library collections require only the character set used in English and the three special delimiters required for USMARC. The English language does not use diacritical marks. But USMARC has always supported the broadest possible range of bibliographic descriptions, providing an extended character set able to handle a wide range of special characters and diacritics.

The one real limitation of USMARC has been that the text of a record must be in the roman or Latin alphabet. But libraries in the United States do have materials printed in other writing systems, both alphabetic and ideographic. Ideally libraries should be able to store and retrieve bibliographic information for their entire collections.

Prior to 1983 nonroman text could be represented in USMARC records only by romanized "equivalents," either transliterated or translated. While some libraries and scholars have learned to live with such equivalents, the results are rarely wholly satisfactory. Transliterations may not be totally reversible; other forms of romanization may lose intelligibility.

The romanization problem is particularly severe for Chinese, Japanese and Korean materials (abbreviated CJK®, an RLG trademark). None of the several different romanization systems maintains distinctions present in the original scripts: romanized records include too many homonyms to be fully satisfactory. When the Research Libraries Group planned CJK enhancements for RLIN, it decided that all basic bibliographic fields should be available in romanized form as well as the original form (sometimes called *vernacular form*). This required not only a technique for storing vernacular data, but also a technique for linking the vernacular form to the romanized form and vice-versa.

Alternate Graphic Representation

RLG, the Library of Congress, and MARBI worked together to develop a technique to identify nonroman text and link romanized and nonroman forms. The technique that was approved can be used for *any* alternative form: it links a single field to another single field in an unambiguous manner that is not affected by subsequent changes to the record.

Explicit linkage requires the definition of one new subfield, ‡6, *Nonroman linking subfield*, in all variable data fields. It also requires the definition of a new field to contain the alternative form. Field 880, *Alternate Graphic Representation*, is a repeating field that contains all nonroman text in USMARC records.

Storage of alternate graphics actually requires two new fields in USMARC. The other, field 066, *Character Sets Present*, defines the nonroman character sets used in the record. Any character set outside of ALA Extended ASCII must be defined by a three-character *escape sequence*, so called because the first character is always hexadecimal "27," the ASCII "escape" character. The second character of the escape sequence indicates whether the character set uses one byte per character or multiple bytes per character. The third and final character of the escape sequence defines the nonroman character set.

Field 066 contains one or more subfield ‡c's, each subfield containing a two-character escape-sequence completion for a character set used in a record. A single record may have more than one nonroman character set, and each such set will be represented in a subfield ‡c within field 066. The field can be used in a local system to determine whether it will be able to process all the text within a given record. The field also, through its appearance, indicates that the record contains at least one occurrence of field 880.

The Linking Technique

066		‡c$1¶
245	00	‡6880-02‡aTitle [romanized]¶
250	__	‡6880-22‡aEdition [romanized]¶
260	0_	‡6880-03‡aImprint [romanized]¶
300	__	‡aCollation (no alternate representation)¶
650	_0	‡aSubject (no alternate representation)¶
650	_0	‡aSubject (no alternate representation)¶
650	_0	‡aSubject (no alternate representation)¶
650	_0	‡aSubject (no alternate representation)¶
650	_0	‡aSubject (no alternate representation)¶
710	20	‡6880-01‡aAdded entry [romanized]¶
710	10	‡6880-04‡aAdded entry [romanized]¶
880	00	‡6245-02/$1‡aTitle [CJK data]¶
880	__	‡6250-22/$1‡aEdition [CJK data]¶
880	0_	‡6260-03/$1‡aImprint [CJK data]¶
880	__	‡6500-00/$1‡aNote (unlinked) [CJK data]¶
880	__	‡6500-00/$1‡aNote (unlinked) [CJK data]¶
880	20	‡6710-01/$1‡aAdded entry [CJK data]¶
880	10	‡6710-04/$1‡aAdded entry [CJK data]¶§

Figure 16.1: Schematic Representation of CJK Record

Field 880 and subfield ‡6 work together in the following manner, illustrated in schematic form in Figure 16.1 and in other figures in this chapter.

- The romanized field (a 245, for instance) contains a leading ‡6 consisting of the string *tag-number*. The tag is always 880 for this function and the occurrence number (a two-digit whole number) is a neutral matching number. A typical subfield ‡6 might be ‡6880-03.

- The 880 ‡6 contains the tag with which it is paired and the same occurrence number. The number in field 880 ‡6 must match the number in the romanized field; the number has no other significance. The alternate graphic representation of the 245 field above would be in an 880 field beginning ‡6245-03. Note that the numbers need not be in any order, and are not in order in the example.

- A variation is used when a vernacular field has no romanized equivalent: the 880 ‡6 contains the tag, a hyphen, and two zeroes. The special occurrence number 00 can appear as often as needed; it signifies that there is no matching field. The two note fields in Figure 16.1 are examples; each 880 begins with ‡6500-00. These two notes do not have romanized equivalents.

- Subfield ‡6 in field 880 contains three additional characters: a slash and the last two characters of the initial escape sequence used in that field. The characters do not constitute an escape sequence but indicate what the first escape sequence in the field will be. For CJK records the second and third characters are $1 in RLG's implementation (the $ is standard notation for multiple-byte character sets).

- Even though the subfield ‡6 has indicated the first alternate graphic representation to be used, the escape sequence must appear before any alternate graphics. Following a string of alternate graphics, another escape sequence returns to the default character set (always ANSEL in USMARC) or, potentially, to yet another graphic representation.

- Alternate graphic representations may not cross subfield or field boundaries. Proper data entry (or computer support) explicitly escapes back to ANSEL before the next subfield delimiter or field terminator. This practice is important, since subfields are not always processed in the order in which they appear, and the escape sequences might otherwise not be interpreted properly.

The technique is generalized; it is not specific to CJK. While the initial implementation was for CJK information, RLG has since added Cyrillic, Hebrew, and Yiddish support using precisely the same technique. Other alternate graphic representations can and will be added.

CJK Usage

```
TEMP      Books       FUL/BIB   HAUO86-B1351              Search          CRLG-KSS
FIN SP JOINT VENTURE#JAPAN ALS LG JPN - Cluster 6 of 15 - CJK
+
  ID:HAUO86-B1351     RTYP:c    ST:p    FRN:     MS:       EL:      AD:05-05-86
  CC:9114  BLT:am     DCF:a     CSC:d   MOD:     SNR:      ATC:     UD:05-05-86
  CP:ja     L:jpn     INT:      GPC:    BIO:     FIC:0     CON:
  PC:s      PD:1980/            REP:    CPI:0    FSI:0     ILC:a    MEI:0   II:0
  MMD:      OR:    POL:   DM:    RR:     COL:     EML:      GEN:    BSE:
  040       HU#cHU
  043       a-ja---
  245 00   Waga kuni oyobi ˉO-Bei shokoku ni okeru kokusai konsˉoshamu jittai chˉ
           osa kenkyˉu hˉokokusho.
  245 00   我 が 国 及 び 欧 米 諸 国 に お け る 国 際 コ ン ソ ー シ ャ ム 実 態 調 査 研 究
           報 告 書 。
  260 0    [Tˉokyˉo] :#bNihon Kikai Yushutsu Kumiai,#cShˉowa 55 [1980]
  260 0    [東 京 ] :#b日 本 機 械 輸 出 組 合 ,#c昭 和 55 [1980]
  300       [6], 320 p. :#bill. ;#c26 cm.
  500       #6#a"通 商 産 業 省 委 託 "
  500       #6#a別 添 I-II (p. 275-320): Specimen consortium agreement for a
           particular contract ; Consortium agreement for tender and execution of
           turnkey project.
  650  0   Joint ventures#zJapan.
  650  0   Joint ventures#xAddresses, essays, lectures.
  650  0   International business enterprises#xAddresses, essays, lectures.


TEMP      Books       FUL/BIB   HAUO86-B1351              Search          CRLG-KSS
Cluster 6 of 15 - CJK
+
  650  0   Syndicates (Finance)#zJapan.
  650  0   Syndicates (Finance)#xAddresses, essays, lectures.
  710 20   Nihon Kikai Yushutsu Kumiai.
  710 20   日 本 機 械 輸 出 組 合 。
  710 10   Japan.#bTsˉushˉo sangyˉoshˉo.
  710 10   Japan.#b通 商 産 業 省 。
```

Figure 16.2: RLIN Editing Screen for CJK (1)

Figure 16.2 shows a portion of a CJK record as it would appear when editing the record on RLIN. The record includes the same fields as Figure 16.1 (and some additional fields not shown in that figure).

Note that roman text may appear in 880 fields; subfield codes are always roman text. In some cases, such as the second note (the second 880 field with ‡6500-00), the CJK portion of a field may be quite small, two characters in this case.[1]

Note that linked field pairs appear together and unlinked CJK fields (marked by the leading ‡6) appear with normal tag numbers. Translation to tag 880 and assignment of linking numbers takes place when the records are written out for tape or other communications.

```
066        ‡c$1¶
245   00   ‡6880-01‡aWaga kuni oyobi O-Bei shokoku ni okeru kokusai konso-
shamu jittai chosa kenkyu hokokusho.¶
260   0    ‡6880-02‡a[Tokyo] :‡bNihon Kikai Yushutsu Kumiai,‡cShowa 55
[1980]¶
300        ‡a[6], 320 p. :‡bill. ;‡c26 cm.¶
650   0    ‡aJoint ventures‡zJapan.¶
650   0    ‡aJoint ventures‡xAddresses, essays, lectures.¶
650   0    ‡aInternational business enterprises‡xAddresses, essays, lectures.¶
650   0    ‡aSyndicates (Finance)‡zJapan.¶
650   0    ‡aSyndicates (Finance)‡xAddresses, essays, lectures.¶
710   20   ‡6880-03‡aNihon Kikai Yushutsu Kumiai.¶
710   10   ‡6880-04‡aJapan.‡bTsusho sangyosho.¶
880   00   ‡6245-01/$1‡a°$1!...(B.¶
880   0    ‡6260-02/$1‡a[°$1!D&!0a°(B]:‡b°$1!Bs...°(B 55 [1980]¶
880        ‡6500-00/$1‡a"°$1!\(!6F°(B °$1EKz!E-!MI°(B °$1!9f!XB°(B"¶
880        ‡6500-00/$1‡a°$1K3[!Gr°(B I-II (p. 275-320): Specimen consortium
agreement for a particular contract ; Consortium agreement for tender
and execution of turnkey project.¶
880   20   ‡6710-03/$1‡a°$1!Bs!...°(B.¶
880 10 ‡6710-04/$1‡aJapan.‡b°$1!\(!6F°(B °$1EKz!E-!MI°(B.¶
```

Figure 16.3: Tagged CJK Record (1)

---

1   As with all other reduced figures in this chapter, the record was printed on a high-resolution dot matrix printer, then photoreduced to 60 percent of its original size for inclusion in this book.

Figure 16.3 shows most of the record displayed in Figure 16.2 as it would actually be written to tape. The character "°" has been used as a printable version of the "escape" character. Most of the CJK fields have been shortened, with missing characters replaced by "…".

CJK text looks like long, random strings when displayed in this manner. This is because each CJK character is represented by three ASCII characters—thus, the second note in Figure 16.2 has six ASCII characters between the first escape sequence "°$1" (escape to CJK) and the second escape sequence "°(B" (escape to ANSEL). Fortunately neither catalogers nor scholars need to deal with CJK in such a cumbersome manner.

```
TEMP      Books        LON       HAUO86-B1351              Search          CRLG-KSS
FIN SP JOINT VENTURE#JAPAN ALS LG JPN - Cluster 6 of 15
+B
   我 が 国 及 び 欧 米 諸 国 に お け る 国 際 コ ン ソ ー シ ャ ム 実 態 調 査 研 究 報 告 書 . --
   [東 京 ] : 日 本 機 械 輸 出 組 合 , 昭 和 55 [1980]
   [6], 320 p. : ill. ; 26 cm.

   "通 商 産 業 省 委 託 "
   別 添 I-II (p. 275-320): Specimen consortium agreement for a particular
   contract ; Consortium agreement for tender and execution of turnkey project.

   1. Joint ventures--Japan. 2. Joint ventures--Addresses, essays, lectures. 3.
   International business enterprises--Addresses, essays, lectures. 4. Syndicates
   (Finance)--Japan. 5. Syndicates (Finance)--Addresses, essays, lectures. I. 日 本
   機 械 輸 出 組 合 . II. Japan. 通 商 産 業 省 .

   ID: HAUO86-B1351              CC: 9114        DCF: a      [CJK]
   CALL: HD9708.J3W33 1980
```

Figure 16.4: Long CJK Display for CJK (1)

When a CJK record is displayed for use as a bibliographic record, there is no need to display romanized fields when the CJK version exists. Indeed, the romanized fields may represent a distraction for users. Figure 16.4 shows the same record as displayed in RLIN Long form, the most complete cardlike display available on RLIN.

But what of other users and libraries, those that cannot read the alternate graphics or that don't have the special display hardware required for CJK? The USMARC provisions, as implemented by RLG (and, more recently, OCLC and others), provide for this case as well. Figure 16.5 shows the same record (omitting some diacritics) as it would appear in an RLIN Long display *on a non-multiscript terminal.*

Waga kuni oyobi O-Bei shokoku ni okeru kokusai konsoshamu jittai chosa kenkyu hokokusho. -- [Tokyo] : Nihon Kikai Yushutsu Kumiai, Showa 55 [1980]
   [6], 320 p. : ill. ; 26 cm.

   1. Joint ventures--Japan. 2. Joint ventures--Addresses, essays, lectures. 3. International business enterprises--Addresses, essays, lectures. 4. Syndicates (Finance)--Japan. 5. Syndicates (Finance)--Addresses, essays, lectures. I. Nihon Kikai Yushutsu Kumiai. II. Japan. Tsusho sangyosho.

Figure 16.5: Long Roman Display for CJK (1)

The RLIN East Asian Character Code

Full use of CJK for cataloging requires two things: a USMARC storage technique (explained above) and a known mapping of Chinese, Japanese, and Korean characters to ASCII equivalents. Extensive analysis and work with a variety of East Asian groups resulted in REACC, the RLIN East Asian Character Code. This code is defined in such a manner that additional characters can be added in the future; the total number of Chinese characters extant in historical materials is not known. The structure of the code is further defined in such a manner that some normalization of variant character forms can take place for indexing and retrieval purposes.

A dictionary containing codes and graphics for 13,645 Chinese characters, 174 kana, and 2,028 hangul was published in 1986 as the *USMARC Character Set, Chinese, Japanese, Korean* by LC's Cataloging Distribution Service. With this publication REACC became a known standard for CJK bibliographic usage, adopted by OCLC, RLG, LC and others in the U.S. bibliographic community. The character set was also proposed to the National Information Standards Organization as a national standard. In 1988 the character set was adopted by

NISO as Z39.64, *American National Standard for Information Sciences—East Asian Character Code for Bibliographic Use.*

Use and Remaining Problems

Since the original RLIN implementation in 1983, records containing CJK scripts have been entered describing books, maps, sound recordings, scores, and visual materials. Some existing USMARC records created before 1984 (thus containing only romanized text) have been enhanced with CJK scripts. More than 400,000 CJK records appear in the RLIN database as of August 1988.

The Library of Congress uses RLIN to prepare all of its own CJK monographic cataloging. Plans are also under way for RLG and OCLC to send CJK records created by their users to LC for subsequent distribution by the Cataloging Distribution Service.

One remaining problem vexes CJK users, as well as users of more recently implemented alternate graphic representations. As of late 1988 the USMARC authorities format does not support alternate graphic representations. Thus, there is no authority file to establish the form of a nonroman name—and no authoritative way to distinguish between two nonroman names with the same established romanized form. This problem will eventually be solved through changes to the USMARC authorities format.

```
TEMP        Books        FUL/BIB    ONTG85-B773              Search            CRLG-KSS
FIN TW シ ル ク   ロ ー ド  ALS NOTE 絲 - Cluster 1 of 1 - SAVE record - CJK
+
  ID:ONTG85-B773      RTYP:c    ST:s    FRN:     MS:       EL:        AD:02-22-85
  CC:9114  BLT:am      DCF:a    CSC:     MOD:     SNR:      ATC:       UD:02-22-85
  CP:ja       L:jpn     INT:     GPC:     BIO:d  FIC:0     CON:
  PC:s        PD:1980/            REP:     CPI:0  FSI:0     ILC:af    MEI:1   II:0
  MMD:        OR:   POL:    DM:   RR:           COL:      EML:       GEN:   BSE:
  010        82805475/AJ
  020        ‡cY1700
  040        ‡cNjP-G‡dNjP-G‡dCaOTU
  043        ac-----
  050 0      PL830.N63‡bZ469  1980
  100 10     Inoue, Yasushi,‡d1907-
  100 10     井上  靖,‡d1907-
  245 10     Ryūsa no michi :‡bSeiiki nando o yuku /‡cInoue Yasushi, Nagasawa Kaz
             utoshi, NHK Shuzaihan.
  245 10     流砂  の  道 :‡b西域  南道  を  行 く /‡c井 上  靖,  長 澤  和 俊,    NHK
             取材班.
  260 0      Tokyo :‡bNihon Hoso Shuppan Kyokai,‡cShowa 55 [1980]
  260 0      東京 :‡b日 本  放 送  出 版  協 会,‡c昭 和  55 [1980]
  300        271 p., [64] of plates :‡bill. (some col.) ;‡c22 cm.
  440  0     Shiruku Rodo ;‡vdai 4-kan
  440  0     シ ル ク   ロ ー ド  ;‡v第  4巻


TEMP        Books        FUL/BIB    ONTG85-B773              Search            CRLG-KSS
Cluster 1 of 1 - SAVE record - CJK
+
  505 0      Shichu nando o kyomeguru / Inoue Yasushi -- Ryūsa no nando, Wigur
             u no machi Hotan / NHK Shuzaihan -- Seiiki nando no nazo / Nagasawa Ka
             zutoshi.
  505 0      絲綢南道を経巡る  / 井上靖 -- 流砂の南道・ウィグルの街ホータン /
             NHK取材班 -- 西域南道の註  / 長澤和俊.
  600 10     Inoue, Yasushi,‡d1907-        ‡xJourneys‡zAsia, Central.
  600 14     井上  靖,‡d1907-      ‡xJourneys‡zAsia, Central.
  651  0     Asia, Central‡xDescription and travel.
  650  0     Authors, Japanese‡y20th century‡xBiography.
  700 10     Nagasawa, Kazutoshi,‡d1928-
  700 10     長澤  和俊,‡d1928-
  710 20     NHK Shuzaihan.
  710 20     NHK  取材班.
```

Figure 16.6: Tagged CJK Record (2)

Figure 16.6 shows another CJK record in tagged editing form. In this case the Japanese characters were used to search for the material (note the second line, beginning *FIN TW*). This record uses a wider variety of bibliographic fields and would have eight 880 fields in its pure USMARC form. Figure 16.7 shows the long CJK bibliographic display for the same record.

```
TEMP      Books      LON       NJPX83-B1585          Search          CRLG-KSS
FIN TW シルク　ロード　ALS NOTE 絲 - Cluster 1 of 1

Inoue, Yasushi, 1907-
    流沙　の　道 : 西域　南道　を　行く / 井上　靖，　長澤　和俊，　NHK 取材班．　-
  - 東京 : 日本放送出版協会，昭和　55 [1980]
    271 p., [64] of plates : ill. (some col.) ; 22 cm. -- (シルクロード　; 第4巻 )

    Contents: 絲綢南道を径巡る / 井上靖 -- 流沙の南道・ウィグルの街ホータン /
  NHK取材班 -- 西域南道の註 / 長澤和俊．
    Y1700

    1. Inoue, Yasushi, 1907-     --Journeys--Asia, Central. 2. Asia, Central--
  Description and travel. 3. Authors, Japanese--20th century--Biography. I.
  Nagasawa, Kazutoshi, 1928- II. NHK Shuzaihan. III. Title. IV. Series.

    LCCN: 82805475/AJ
    L.C. CALL NO: PL830.N63.Z469   1980
    ID: NJPX83-B1585               CC: 9114       DCF: a     [CJK]
    CALL: J3079/650(4)
```

Figure 16.7: Long Display, CJK (2)

Cyrillic, Hebrew, and Yiddish

Cyrillic text, as used in Russian and several other languages, seems simple by comparison to East Asian text. The Cyrillic alphabet is just that, an alphabet, and has a relatively small character set—although inclusion of Old Church Slavonic and some other special cases requires a few more characters. Also the Cyrillic alphabet is written left-to-right, as is the roman alphabet (and East Asian character sets).

Additionally, standard representations for Cyrillic already exist. There are International Standards Organization (ISO) standards for ASCII representation of Basic Cyrillic and Extended Cyrillic.

Indeed, implementation of Cyrillic in RLIN was somewhat easier than implementation of CJK. Cyrillic characters have one-character ASCII equivalents, and can be represented with less sophisticated displays than are required for CJK. Cyrillic became available on RLIN in 1986. Perhaps surprisingly, it has not been heavily used. The Library of Congress continues to produce transliterated records for such materials, and most libraries are satisfied with transliteration.

Hebrew and Mixed Scripts

Hebrew presents a different problem, and a thorny one to solve for online cataloging. Hebrew is written right-to-left rather than left-to-right. To make matters more complicated, bibliographic descriptions will frequently mix Hebrew and roman text in a single field—and the roman text must appear left-to-right while Hebrew appears right-to-left.

```
BKS/PROD Books        FUL/BIB   MABX88-B1142          Catalog        CRLG-JAE
FIN TW תולדות - Cluster 15 of 66 - HBR
+
   ID:MABX88-B1142      RTYP:c    ST:p   FRN:     MS:       EL:       AD:07-18-88
   CC:9114  BLT:am      DCF:a    CSC:d   MOD:      SNR:      ATC:      UD:07-29-88
   CP:nyu    L:heb      INT:     GPC:    BIO:      FIC:0     CON:
   PC:m      PD:1979/9999         REP:   CPI:0     FSI:0     ILC:      MEI:0   II:0
   MMD:      OR:        POL:     DM:     RR:       COL:      EML:      GEN:    BSE:
   040       MWalB‡cMWalB
   130 00    Talmud Yerushalmi.‡f1979.
   130 00                                                      ‡6a תלמוד ירושלמי.‡f1979.
   245 00    Talmud Yerushalmi.
   245 00                                                               תלמוד ירושלמי.
   260 0     New York, N.Y., U.S.A. :‡bMakhon mutsal me-esh,‡c740 [1979 or 1980-
   260 0     New York, N.Y., U.S.A. :‡bמאש מוצל מכון, ‡c740 [1979 or 1980-
   300       v. ;‡c35 cm.
   500       Aramaic and Hebrew.
   500       Includes commentaries by Elijah ben Solomon, Mordecai Ze'ev ben Isaac
             Aaron Segal Ettinger, Yitzhak Issac Krasilschikov.
   500       Vol. 2 (Berakhot, pt. 2) includes commentaries by Joseph Sirillo, Samu
             el Jaffe ben Isaac Ashkenazi, and Joshua Raphael ben Israel Benveniste.
   500       ‡6‡aTitle on spine:‡hמי כל עם, תבונה, יצחק תולדות פרושי עם ירושלמי תלמוד
             פרשים.
   505 1     ‡6‡a.תרומות ¿6¿ שביעית.¿.¿5¿ פאה.¿.¿3¿ ברכות,ב.¿.¿2¿ א.¿.¿1¿ ברכות ¿0¿
BKS/PROD Books        FUL/BIB   MABX88-B1142          Catalog        CRLG-JAE
Cluster 15 of 66 - HBR
+
   630 00    Talmud Yerushalmi.‡xCommentaries.
   700 00    Elijah ben Solomon,‡d1720-1797.
   700 10    Ettinger, Mordecai Ze'ev ben Isaac Aaron Segal,‡d1804-1863.
   700 10    Krasilschikov, Yitzhak Issac,‡d1888-1965.
   700 10    Sirillo, Solomon ben Joseph,‡dd. ca. 1558.
   700 10    Ashkenazi, Samuel Jaffe ben Isaac,‡d16th cent.
   700 10    Benveniste, Joshua Raphael ben Israel,‡d1590?-1665?
   740 01                    .תבונה ,יצחק תולדות פרושי עם ירושלמי תלמוד‡a‡6‡
   796 00                             .1797¯1720d‡,שלמה בן יהו שלמהa‡6‡
   796 10                      .1863¯1804d‡,ואב, מרדכי אטינגא,נa‡6‡
   796 10               .1965¯1888d‡,אייזיק יצחק ,שצ'יקוב קראסיל'a‡6‡
   796 10                       ?1558d‡,יוסף בן שלמה ,סירילואa‡6‡
   796 10          .16¯ה הממאה‡,יצחק בן יפה שמואל ,אשכנז'ורי,a‡6‡
   796 10        ?1665¯?1590d‡,ישראל בן יהושע ,בנבנשתיa‡6‡
```

Figure 16.8: Tagged Hebrew Record

As of this writing there is no ISO or NISO standard for representation of Hebrew in ASCII form, but a draft proposal is in progress. RLG considered that draft proposal, recommended enhancements to the ISO proposal, and used it as the basis for the RLG Hebrew and Yiddish implementation in January 1988.

Figure 16.8 shows a Hebrew record (retrieved using a Hebrew search key). Note that Hebrew fields appear right-to-left. Note also that the Hebrew equivalents for the 700 added entries are tagged 796 rather than 700 (796 is an RLIN MARC local extension). This is because of the lack of authority control for nonroman data; the cataloger chose to consider these fields as locally defined added entries. Figure 16.9 shows the same record in a Long display.

```
BKS/PROD  Books        LON       MABX88-B1142          Catalog        CRLG-JAE
FIN TW הזהות - Cluster 15 of 66
+
Talmud Yerushalmi. 1979.
                                                          .1979 .תלמוד ירושלמי
                                                              .תלמוד ירושלמי
-- New York, N.Y., U.S.A. : מאש מוצא מכון,   740 [1979 or 1980-
   v. ; 35 cm.

   Aramaic and Hebrew.
   Includes commentaries by Elijah ben Solomon, Mordecai Ze'ev ben Isaac Aaron
Segal Ettinger, Yitzhak Issac Krasilschikov.
   Vol. 2 (Berakhot, pt. 2) includes commentaries by Joseph Sirillo, Samuel Jaffe
ben Isaac Ashkenazi, and Joshua Raphael ben Israel Benveniste.
   Title on spine:.המפרשים כל עם ,תבונה ,יצחק תולדות פרושי עם ירושלמי תלמוד
   Contents: .תרומות ר53 .שביעית ר43 .מאה ר33 ברכות,ב. ר23 ברכות,א. ר13
BKS/PROD  Books        LON       MABX88-B1142          Catalog        CRLG-JAE
Cluster 15 of 66
+B
   1. Talmud Yerushalmi.--Commentaries. I. Elijah ben Solomon, 1720-1797. II.
Ettinger, Mordecai Ze'ev ben Isaac Aaron Segal, 1804-1863. III. Krasilschikov,
Yitzhak Issac, 1888-1965. IV. Sirillo, Solomon ben Joseph, d. ca. 1558. V.
Ashkenazi, Samuel Jaffe ben Isaac, 16th cent. VI. Benveniste, Joshua Raphael
benIsrael, 1590?-1665? VII. .1797-1720 שלמה בן אליהו VIII. איטינגא, מרדכי זאב.
סירילאו, שלמה בן יוסף, X. קראסילשצקוב, יצחק איזיק. IX. .1965-1888 ,1863-1804.
XI. .16-ח המאה ,יצחק בן ימח שמואל אשכנזי, XII. .ישראל בן יהושע בנבנשתי,
XIII. Title: .תבונה ,יצחק תולדות פרושי עם ירושלמי תלמוד 1590?-1665?

   ID: MABX88-B1142          CC: 9114       DCF: a      [HBR]
   CALL: \+\BM\498\1980
```

Figure 16.9: Long Display, Hebrew Record

The Library of Congress uses RLIN to catalog Hebrew records. Other libraries also prepare Hebrew records; some libraries are now cataloging on RLIN using Cyrillic; and some records mix more than one script within the same record. Figures 16.10 and 16.11 show one such record, in this case prepared as part of RLG's internal testing for multiple scripts.

```
BKS/PROD  Books      FUL/BIB  CRLGSIMULATED-B       Catalog        CRLG-JAE
FIN PN RAN, L - Cluster 1 of 2 - CYR, HBR

  ID:CRLGSIMULATED-B  RTYP:c    ST:p    FRN:    MS:      EL:?      AD:11-13-87
  CC:9124   BLT:am     DCF:a    CSC:d   MOD:    SNR:     ATC:      UD:11-13-87
  CP:nyu    L:yid      INT:     GPC:    BIO:    FIC:0    CON:b
  PC:s      PD:1974/            REP:    CPI:0   FSI:0    ILC:ab    MEI:0   II:1
  MMD:      OR:        POL:     DM:     RR:     COL:     EML:      GEN:    BSE:
  041 0     yidenghebrus
  043       e-ur-li
  245 00    Yerusholayim de-Li.ta :‡billus.trir.t un do.kumen.tir.t /‡cgezamel.t u
            n tsuzamengesh.tirt.t Leyzer Ran = Jerusalem of Lithuania : illustrated
            and documented / collected and arranged by Leyzer Ran = Yerushalayim de-
            Li.ta : me'uyar u-meto'ad / li.ke.t ve-'arakh Leizer Ran = Litovskiʸi Ie
            rusalim : v ill'iʸustr'tʸsi'iʸakh i dokumentakh / sobral i sostavil Leʸi
            zer Ran.
  245 00    ירושלים דליטא :‡bאילוסטרירט און ד,אקומענטירט/‡cגעזאמלט אמסט און צו.אמענ_גרט
            Jerusalem of Lithuania : illustrated and documented = און ר_א, רא‏יער עשטעלט
            / מאויר ומתועד דליטא ירושלים = / collected and arranged by Leyzer Ran
            ליקט וערך לייזר ראן / Литовский Иерусалим : в иллюстрациях и документах
            . / собрал и составил Лейзер Ран
  260 0     Nyu-Yor.k :‡b,Vilner Albom ,Komi.te.t [distributor],‡c1974.
  260 0     .1974c‡,ווילנ:ער קאמ_יטעט אם א,ב_ל_ אלבם נ_ס_ארש·מרייטסער‡‏ ,ארק‡‏,י-י_וונ
  300       3 v. :‡bchiefly ill., map ;‡c28-37 cm.
BKS/PROD  Books      FUL/BIB  CRLGSIMULATED-B       Catalog        CRLG-JAE
Cluster 1 of 2 - CYR, HBR

  500       English, Hebrew, Russian, and Yiddish; bibliographical notations also
            in Belorussian, German, Lithuanian and Polish.
  500       ‡6‡aDevice of ערל_ס אר_א×‡‏ וו‏יל_וגער on t.p.
  500       TESTER'S NOTE: This is the actualization of a title used for the RLIN
            simulations (August 1985).
  650  0    Jews‡zLithuania‡zVilnius‡xPictorial works.
  651  4    ‡6‡aוילנ‏ס.
  700 10    Ran, Leyzer,‡d1912-
  700 10    ‡6‡2d, לייזער‡‏ ,ראן_ר
  740 10    Jerusalem of Lithuania.
  740 10    Yerusalayim de-Li.ta.
  740 10    Litovskiʸi Ierusalim.
  740 10    Литовский Иерусалим.
```

Figure 16.10: Tagged Cyrillic/Hebrew/Yiddish Record

```
BKS/PROD Books        LON        CRLGSIMULATED-B       Catalog        CRLG-JAE
FIN PN RAN, L - Cluster 1 of 2
+B
          ,פֿאַרשװענדעט_אין גאַ_אמעריקע / װיעאָקומענטירט דאַ,אילוסטרירט אין : דליטא יﬦיﬦ ירושﬥ
     Jerusalem of Lithuania : illustrated and documented / collected = ראַ_ן ריעﬦיﬤ
     ﬥיﬤﬦ ערך ﬡון ﬡיﬤﬨ / ﬦﬨ ﬦﬡﬤﬦ : דליטא ﬦﬦ ירושﬥ = and arranged by Leyzer Ran
     Литовский Иерусалим : в иллюстрациях и документах / собрал и составил / ראַ_ן
          .1974 , פֿרייﬨﬦﬥﬦ_נﬦﬥﬨ ﬦﬦﬤﬨﬦ ﬡﬦ,ﬡﬦﬥ_ ﬦﬦﬦﬤ ﬦﬦﬦ, ﬡﬤﬨﬦ -- .Лейзер Ран
     3 v. : chiefly ill., map ; 28-37 cm.

     English, Hebrew, Russian, and Yiddish; bibliographical notations also in
     Belorussian,German, Lithuanian and Polish.
     Device of ראַ_ן_לﬦﬨ_ﬦ ﬦﬦﬦﬤ on t.p.
     TESTER'S NOTE: This is the actualization of a title used for the RLIN
     simulations(August 1985).

        1. Jews--Lithuania--Vilnius--Pictorial works. 2. ﬦﬦﬥﬦﬦ. I. ﬦﬥﬦ1912 , ﬦﬦﬦﬤﬦ , ראַ_ן
     II. Title: Jerusalem of Lithuania. III. Title: Yerusalayim de-Li.ta. IV. Title:
     Литовский Иерусалим.

     ID: CRLGSIMULATED-B          CC: 9124       DCF: a      [CYR/HBR]
     CALL: hebrewdemo
```

Figure 16.11: Long Display, Cyrillic/Hebrew/Yiddish

More scripts will certainly be added to RLIN and other processing systems to meet the varied needs of libraries. The relatively simple, wholly generalized technique of ‡6 and field 880, together with standardized ASCII representations and agreed escape sequences, make it possible to represent almost any nonroman script in a bibliographic record and communicate it to other libraries.

17

USMARC: A Brief History

USMARC evolved from MARC II or LC MARC. MARC II emerged from years of effort and study, led by Henriette Avram of the Library of Congress and others. The Council on Library Resources provided early and continuing funding to encourage the development and spread of the formats. Courageous and innovative library leaders such as Frederick Kilgour of OCLC acted to build a massive and successful structure of shared bibliographic data on the solid foundation of the MARC formats. Innovators continue to expand uses of the format, while dedicated workers strive to make the formats more consistent and more useful.

The Beginnings: 1961-1965

The Library of Congress began to consider automation in the late 1950s.[1]. The Council on Library Resources (CLR) paid for a study, published in 1963, that recommended a group within LC to design and implement automated procedures for cataloging, searching, indexing, and document retrieval; another CLR project considered methods for converting LC catalog card data to machine-readable

---

1   Henriette Avram, *MARC, its history and implications* (Washington, D.C.: Library of Congress, 1975), 3.

form. LC, CLR, and the Committee on Automation of the Association of Research Libraries (ARL) cosponsored a conference in January 1965 to consider the two studies and their significance. The conclusions are as follows:

- Availability of machine-readable catalog records produced and distributed by LC would help those libraries that have automated systems.

- The machine-readable record should include all the data presently available on LC's printed card, plus additional information to produce a multipurpose record.

- Agreement by a broad segment of the library community on the elements to be included in the record was most desirable, and the design of the record at LC was probably the best means of achieving standardization.

Henriette Avram, Ruth Freitag, and Kay Guiles analyzed LC cataloging data and, in June 1965, prepared a proposed record format. Many LC staff members and others in the library field commented on the proposal, which was followed by another CLR-sponsored conference in November 1965. Given the warm reception of the library community, LC sought and CLR provided funds for a pilot project. The pilot project needed a name, which was derived from *ma*chine-*r*eadable *c*ataloging: MARC was born.

MARC Pilot Project: 1966-1968

Lc's pilot plan was ambitious. The CLR grant of $130,000 was received in December 1965; by February 1966 contractors were chosen to write software and evaluate the project, and sixteen libraries were selected as project participants from forty who had expressed willingness. Initial participants were the Argonne National Laboratory, Georgia Institute of Technology, Harvard University, Indiana University, Montgomery County Public Schools, Nassau (County) Library System, National Agricultural Library, Redstone

Scientific Information Center, Rice University, University of California Institute of Library Research (Los Angeles), University of Chicago, University of Florida, University of Missouri, University of Toronto, Washington State Library, and Yale University.

Those contractors and participants met with LC staff on February 25, 1966. Expectations were that MARC I would be completed in April, with weekly tape distribution beginning in September 1966.

The project ran late, but only by two months. A test tape was distributed in October, and weekly distribution began in November 1966. The original plan called for eight months of distribution; interest and enthusiasm were high enough to extend it through to June 1968. In fact, LC had been ready to extend the project almost from its inception. The extension announcement was made at the ALA Midwinter Meeting in January 1967, only two months after initial tape distribution.

LC MARC staff began to evaluate the MARC I format in March 1967; a preliminary MARC II format was presented at ALA in June 1967. Another CLR-sponsored conference on December 4, 1967 considered the MARC II format and proposed bibliographic character set, and four more libraries were added to the pilot project, expanding the group of agencies cooperatively involved in evaluating and testing MARC.[2]

The pilot project ended in June 1968; some 50,000 MARC I records were distributed in all. Twenty agencies evaluated the format and programs distributed with it, reporting back to LC.[3] Some of those agencies actually used the tapes for processing; others did not.

---

2   California State Library, Illinois State Library, Cornell University Library, and SUNY Biomedical Communications Network.

3   Henriette Avram, *The MARC Pilot Project* (Washington, D.C.: Library of Congress, 1968), 91-173.

MARC I was intended as an experiment. The timing and scope were ambitious, and the actual speed of implementation was little short of remarkable. In 1966 few libraries had significant automation, and available computers were barely capable of handling the most rudimentary library needs. Henriette Avram states in the *Final Report* that "there is no doubt that eventually standards would have been designed for machine-readable bibliographic records, character sets, and codes for place and language."[4] Mrs. Avram's energy, enthusiasm, and tenacity made such standards possible before most libraries saw any need or use for them.

The pilot program included distribution of computer programs to handle MARC I records. Given the severe limitations of the machines used, the programs had to be coded in languages that were difficult to read and maintain. The programs were coded rapidly and with little overall success. Programs implemented at LC after the pilot project did form the basis for much of the batch processing software of the early and middle 1970s: for example, SKED and BIBLIST, two major programs, are familiar to many involved in library automation at the time.

The original format was different from MARC II, which was heavily influenced by the results of the experiment. The MARC Pilot Project established a common ground for machine-readable bibliographic data, and provided the basis for the success of MARC II. Reports from the participants show wide-ranging degrees of success or failure, but almost unanimous enthusiasm for the fundamental ideas behind MARC. MARC I established the feasibility; MARC II began the real work of building a national system of shared cataloging.

---

4   Ibid., 1.

MARC II: 1968-1974

$\mathbf{M}$ARC I was an innovative format, described in detail in the final report on the MARC Pilot Project. That report also outlines the original MARC II format for monographs and compares the two formats. Both formats are designed to carry information on monographs in a consistent form, but the two have very little else in common. The separate directory, subfield codes, and structured tags of MARC II are all innovations of the newer format. The structure of MARC II has remained essentially fixed since the original draft was issued in January 1968,[5] and has proven flexible and valuable, handling a range and volume of materials far greater than that of any similar development. The structure has survived for two decades with no substantial change, while content designators and content continue to evolve.

The Library of Congress did *not* set out to provide software for MARC II. Instead, LC released detailed specifications for the new format as early as August 1968 in a publication originally titled *Subscriber's Guide to the MARC Distribution Service* (later *Books: A MARC Format*).[6]: Library of Congress, 1972)

LC and ALA's Information Science and Automation Division (ISAD) launched a series of workshops to introduce MARC II. The MARC Institutes began in Seattle in July 1968 and continued for several years, introducing over 2,000 people to MARC II. MARC II became operational in March 1969, when the first MARC Distribution Service got under way.

---

5   Henriette Avram, John F. Knapp, and Lucia J. Rather, *The MARC II format: A Communications Format for Bibliographic Data* (Washington, D.C.: Library of Congress, 1968)

6   Library of Congress, MARC Development Office, *Books: a MARC Format; Specifications for Magnetic Tapes Containing Catalog Records for Books*, 5th ed. (Washington, D.C

MARC Distribution

In 1969, and for many years thereafter, the primary role of MARC II was to distribute Library of Congress cataloging data in machine-readable form to other institutions. The Library of Congress and the American Library Association used a number of methods to publicize the formats and inform current and potential users. The MARC Institutes were one method; the MARC Users' Discussion Group within ISAD was another.

Weekly distribution of MARC records for English-language monographs began in March 1969. At first the tapes included only U.S. imprints, about 1,000 records per week. Coverage expanded rapidly to include other English-language monographs. Since then other languages have been added, so that by the late 1970s nearly all languages using the roman alphabet were included in LC MARC tapes.

Other Formats

With the books format well on its way, the Library of Congress began work on other formats. Formats for serials and maps were published in 1970. The films format was published in 1971 and the original manuscripts format in 1973. The last material format of the 1970s, and the final bibliographic format to be published as a separate publication, was for music; the draft version of this format was published in 1973.

After MARC formats appeared, LC MARC distribution generally followed. Distribution of films cataloging began in 1972; distribution of serials and maps began in 1973. Since 1973 the Library of Congress has concentrated on broader coverage of current formats, adding languages as funding permits. The Library of Congress never distributed manuscripts cataloging in MARC form and distribution of MARC records for scores and sound recordings began in the mid-1980s.

Standardization

"The impetus given to standardization by LC/MARC is doubtless one of its most important results."[7] MARC has focused standardization efforts while providing the means to allow diversity within standards. The early development of MARC II or LC MARC contributed to standardization efforts and to the development of MARC formats in other countries. The structure of MARC was proposed as a national and international standard. ANSI standard Z39.2 was adopted in 1971;[8] the international equivalent, ISO 2709, was adopted in 1973.[9]

Local Uses and Developments

Quite a few library automation projects began in the late 1960s and early 1970s. Many of these succeeded, and some are still in operation. Dozens of universities and other institutions began working with MARC during this period. The period from 1969 to 1974 was one of enormous growth in library automation.

Four projects that began in the late 1960s resulted in the four major shared cataloging services of today. The Ohio College Library Center was founded in 1967, though provision of online services did not begin until 1971. At Stanford, Project BALLOTS (Bibliographic Automation of Large Library Operations Using a Time-Sharing System) also began in 1967; the project eventually resulted in an online multilibrary network in the 1970s, and was transformed into the Research Libraries Information Network (RLIN) at the end of that

---

7   Avram, *MARC, Its History and Implications*, 21.

8   American National Standards Institute, *American National Standard Format for Bibliographic Information Interchange on Magnetic Tape* (New York: ANSI, 1971) (ANSI Z39.2-1971)

9   International Organization for Standardization, *Documentation--Format for Bibliographic Information Interchange on Magnetic Tape.* (1973) (ISO 2709-1973(E))

decade. Developments at the Washington State Library and the University of Toronto, both participants in the MARC Pilot Project, eventually led to the Washington Library Network (WLN, later Western Library Network) and University of Toronto Library Automation System (Utlas, now a commercial service).

Use of MARC in 1972

In 1972 the Library of Congress contracted for a survey of MARC users, carried out by the firm of Becker & Hayes, Inc., and conducted and reported by Josephine S. Pulsifer.[10] There were fifty-four MARC subscribers as of August 8, 1972; fifty-two of these were doing or planning some work with MARC. Those fifty-two included twelve research libraries, fifteen other university libraries, eleven commercial firms, four special libraries, six national libraries, two state libraries, and two "library centers": OCLC and the College Bibliocentre in Don Mills, Ontario. Most users had small development staffs: the largest group of librarians was six, the largest group of "computer people" seven. Nine subscribers had operational online systems, and thirty-two had operational offline (batch) systems; at least eleven had no operational systems at the time of the survey.

Table 17.1 gives the number using each category of service set forth in the 1972 survey. One particularly significant use is redistribution; the fifty-two subscribers provided LC MARC records in machine-readable form to at least 178 other agencies in 1972. In 1972 OCLC was serving fifty-five agencies. The largest single constituency appeared to be Richard Abel & Company, producing catalog products for 375 customers. Even in 1972 more than 1,000 agencies were using LC MARC data, directly or indirectly.

---

10   Library of Congress, MARC Development Office, *MARC User Survey, 1972* (Washington, D.C.: Library of Congress, 1972)

Users	Service
97	Selection (lists for selection purposes)
36	Ordering
514*	Catalog cards
10	Book catalogs
63	Union catalogs
118*	Catalog products (spine labels, pockets, bookcards)
10	Machine-readable charge cards
120	New book lists
159*	Bibliographies
107*	On-demand searches
134	Selective dissemination of information (SDI)
178*	Secondary distribution (tape, lists, online)
265	Microform distribution
1148	**Apparent number of distinct users for all services**

* One commercial vendor did not release numbers of customers for these five services. Thus, each number is too low by some unknown factor.

Table 17.1: MARC Use in 1972

MARBI and the USMARC Advisory Group: 1974-1980

ALA, the American Library Association, has several committees made up of representatives from more than one ALA division. One of these, established prior to 1974, is the Committee on Representation in Machine-Readable Form of Bibliographic Information, known as MARBI. This committee includes representatives from RTSD (Resources and Technical Services Division), RASD (Reference and Adult Services Division), and LITA (Library and Information Technology Association), formerly known as ISAD (Information Science and Automation Division).

The Library of Congress approached MARBI in 1973 suggesting that a MARC advisory committee be formed to work with LC on changes to the MARC formats. MARBI decided to make itself that advisory committee. At MARBI's request LC drew up proposals and recommendations, which were adopted by MARBI at the ALA 1974 Midwinter meeting.[11]

Later in the 1970s, LC began a series of quarterly meetings at which liaisons from the bibliographic services and national libraries considered MARC changes. The network group and MARBI were brought together to form a group informally called the USMARC advisory group. During the 1980s MARBI meetings have always included the rest of the advisory group (as non-voting liaisons); spring and fall meetings at LC have been held only when needed.

Consolidation and Growth

If the early seventies were years of major new undertakings, the late seventies were years of consolidation, cooperation, and growth. No new material formats were developed, but the old ones were refined, with better explanations and more explicit detail. Use of the formats grew rapidly during the seventies, and continues to grow as systems become more available and more sophisticated. The middle 1970s were the start of explosive growth for the bibliographic services. The smallest of the four major bibliographic services had four times as many users in 1983 as OCLC had in 1972; OCLC itself had at least thirty times as many.

The mid-1970s saw the development of the preliminary authorities format, discussed in chapter 13. This format was initially designed so that LC could share its authority control information with the library world; as with other MARC formats, the authorities format quickly took on significance beyond its original purpose.

Specifications for shared records were established during the decade with the publication of the National Level Bibliographic Record (NLBR) documents for various materials. NLBR uses MARC

---

11   Henriette Avram, "The Library of Congress View on its Relationship to the ALA MARC Advisory Committee." *Journal of Library Automation* 7, no. 2 (June 1974): 119-125. Also in: *Library of Congress Information Bulletin* 33, no. 9 (March 1, 1974): A60-A65.

as a base and common vocabulary, specifying essential and recommended data elements for various levels of completeness.

CONSER, a project for CONversion of SERials, began in 1974 with CLR funding. A cooperative project based at OCLC, CONSER has built a database of hundreds of thousands of serials records now distributed by LC.

Expansion, Linkage, and Integration: 1980 to the Present

Changes in MARC seem to come in waves—not surprisingly, since a major group of changes require time to implement and understand. The first big wave of MARC development was in the early 1970s. Aside from authorities, which was a major development, the late 1970s were relatively quiet.

MARC development was active and complex between 1980 and early 1984. Some of the developments already mentioned include the following:

- a linked-record technique to support "In" analytics, discussed in chapter 15;
- the archival and manuscripts control format, discussed in chapter 12;
- the machine-readable data files (now computer files) format, discussed in chapter 11;
- the visual materials format (evolved from the films format), discussed in chapter 10;
- The draft holdings format, discussed in chapter 14;
- Techniques to support nonroman data, discussed in chapter 16.

The period from 1984 through early 1987 was, superficially, another quiet one for MARC development, as agencies implemented the new formats and major changes made during the preceding years. That period was the developmental period for another major change that will be implemented over the next few years: format integration.

Format Integration and *Underlying Principles*

Chapter 18 gives the history and significance of MARC format integration, which also began in the early 1980s but was not completed until 1988. Related to format integration was preparation of a written set of underlying principles for content designation.

Those who founded and developed LC MARC have worked from a set of principles. While there have been articles on the design principles of MARC, no codified set of principles was available for use by the USMARC advisory group or those advocating changes in MARC.

John Attig of Pennsylvania State University prepared a discussion paper setting forth the principles of LC MARC as determined from the actual formats. During 1981 and 1982, this draft was thoroughly examined by the USMARC advisory group and other interested parties. A preliminary version was published in 1982 and an open hearing was held at the ALA Annual Conference in Philadelphia that year.[12]

After further changes and review, the document was approved on October 29, 1982, in a meeting of the USMARC advisory group at the Library of Congress. The resulting document, *The USMARC Formats: Underlying Principles*, appears with annotations as Appendix A in this book.

MARC XX

In 1987 a group of interested parties formed the MARC XX Committee, to commemorate the 20th anniversary of MARC. The group held fundraising parties during ALA conferences in 1987 and 1988,

---

12   John Attig, "The USMARC Formats—Underlying Principles," *Information Technology and Libraries* 1, no. 2 (June 1982): 169-174.

and may continue. Funds will go to prepare an oral history of the founding of MARC.

Maintaining USMARC

LC publishes USMARC formats and has the final authority over the formats. The Library of Congress does not act unilaterally, however. Changes in USMARC are discussed thoroughly in open sessions involving the Library of Congress, MARBI and liaisons from the bibliographic services, other national libraries, and other interested parties.

Many proposals for USMARC revisions originate in the Library of Congress. Others originate in other agencies and associations, or are submitted by interested librarians. The shared cataloging services take an active role in proposing USMARC revisions and in discussing such proposals. Some proposals arise directly out of discussions during MARC review sessions, and some proposals result from special projects. Proposals are channeled through the MARC Development and Network Standards Office in the Library of Congress, which gathers and coordinates proposals, sees that proposals reach the appropriate parties within LC, and sees that proposals ready for open discussion are copied and sent to interested parties.

Role of the Library of Congress

The Library of Congress initiates some proposals and reviews others prior to open discussion. Internal review at LC can help to assure that proposals are consistent with USMARC, can coordinate multiple proposals, and can raise issues that need to be resolved. LC internal review can also eliminate proposals that have already been dealt with, proposals clearly outside the scope of USMARC, and other proposals that are not ready for open discussion.

The Library of Congress puts proposals into a standard format, assigns proposal numbers, and copies and distributes the proposals to a wide mailing list, including those agencies that specifically subscribe to receive proposals. LC also prepares agendas for review sessions and determines the needs for and dates of spring and fall sessions. Finally, LC reviews the results of MARBI discussions.

Following revision and approval of changes, LC acts on the changes as the publisher of the MARC formats. Revisions are printed by the Government Printing Office (GPO) and distributed by LC's Catalog Distribution Service (CDS).

The Library of Congress does not implement most changes to USMARC immediately after approval by MARBI. Some changes require more editorial effort than others, and post-approval review sometimes turns up problems with approved revisions. On occasion the Library of Congress has returned to the review sessions with proposed changes in approved USMARC revisions.

The Library of Congress plays a critical role in the timing of changes to USMARC. LC has established a policy that it will not distribute records containing given changes until at least ninety days after those changes have been published in an update to the formats. When major changes such as format integration appear to require coordinated planning within the American bibliographic community, LC helps to establish that coordination, which also involves liaisons to MARBI.

MARBI Meetings and Other Review Sessions

Two review sessions are held at the American Library Association Midwinter Meeting and Annual Conferences each year. These sessions are MARBI committee meetings and are open to all ALA members. When format change proposals require more intensive work, LC may hold additional review sessions in the spring, the fall, or both. The spring and fall review sessions are held at the Library of Congress, are typically one or two days long, and involve some MARBI members and other active participants.

Major changes in USMARC are always discussed at least once during Midwinter or Annual Conference MARBI meetings, and final review of major changes usually takes place at those meetings.

Divisions differ in the amount of publicity provided for MARBI work. Recently, summary reports on MARBI activity have been appearing in the three divisional newsletters with good regularity. MARBI members represent themselves, their institutions, and their divisions. They are appointed for two-year terms and can be reappointed once, as with other ALA committee appointments. Some divisions now appoint interns to gain a year's experience with MARBI before taking office.

Each of the four major shared cataloging services sends a liaison to MARC review sessions. These liaisons are expected to gather the views of staff and to represent the needs of their services. Liaisons are also invited from the National Agricultural Library, National Library of Medicine, and the National Library of Canada. The Music Library Association, Society of American Archivists, Map & Geography Round Table, and Online Audiovisual Catalogers also have liaisons at some MARC review sessions.

Liaisons do not have votes but do have voices. The importance of the shared cataloging services and national libraries is well known, and objections raised by liaisons are rarely ignored. Each shared cataloging service has an ongoing program to maintain MARC within the system. The liaisons work to see that MARC is effective and meets their needs, which are generally the needs of the library community.

Because the services are involved in review, they usually have some advance knowledge of upcoming changes in the formats, although the gap from approval to publication can be anywhere from three months to three years or more. Once changes are published, teams of analysts, programmers, testers, trainers, and writers must work to make the changes part of the bibliographic service's operation and to reflect the changes in documentation.

USMARC review group meetings air the difficulties with US-MARC, generate useful changes in the formats, and generally work well to keep the formats contemporary and useful. In some ways the machinery of USMARC may seem cumbersome. Compared to typical standards organizations, however, USMARC maintenance is stream-lined and effective. MARBI members and liaisons give up nearly half of ALA conference time to meetings, and those who continue with MARBI do so because they believe in the benefits of USMARC and wish to improve the formats. The combination of LC's editorial work and leadership and the careful analysis and discussion typical of the quarterly review sessions makes USMARC a living, vital standard for recording and manipulating bibliographic data.

USMARC Today

Use of MARC has continued to expand since its inception. OCLC now has more than fifteen million titles in its database; RLIN has more than thirty million records (not equivalent to titles); other databases have also grown rapidly.

The American bibliographic scene includes complex inter-changes of records. OCLC and RLG exchange tapes regularly, includ-ing all records for preservation microfilming, many records for grant-funded retrospective conversion, and other categories of infor-mation. It is not unheard of for a record to begin on one shared cataloging system, go to a local system, go from there to another shared cataloging system, and eventually find its way back to the original location. Fortunately, system control numbers (field 035) and time-date stamps (field 005) can, if used consistently, help to identify such cases and to determine which version of a record is most current.

The final chapters of this book discuss guidelines for and uses of MARC records, with some comments on the limits of the format and its future uses. The clearest measure of the current role of MARC is the shift in expectations for local library automation systems, both those developed by libraries and those purchased from vendors. A decade ago, whether to support MARC fully was still an open question for a vendor or system designer. Today, any designer that does *not* provide for full MARC support must make a convincing case for ignoring the established national standard for communicating bibliographic data.

The Impact of MARC: A Summation

Through its history, USMARC has served as a format for communication from one to many, and as a format for local use. USMARC is unusual among standards: by establishing a common basis it allows and even encourages diversity to meet local needs. When a public library can derive 90 percent to 97 percent of its cataloging (as seems common in 1988) and can manipulate those records, cataloging time and talent is freed to add entry points that meet the needs of the community.

It seems fitting to close this brief history, largely based on Henriette Avram's work, with the closing paragraphs from *MARC, Its History and Implications*. Mrs. Avram speaks specifically of standards; her hopes for the future are being realized largely because of the success of LC MARC and USMARC.

> The benefits that accrue to a library and its clients from the establishment of and the conformity to standards are many. Products from different sources will mesh. Records from different libraries will be interchanged. Machine systems will be more easily developed and shared. Union catalogs will be possible without costly editing for consistency, thus facilitating interlibrary loan. Cost of local changes to catalog records will be minimized. It will be advantageous for vendors to manufacture hardware to handle the requirements of libraries. The process of ordering, cataloging, etc. will be more uniform. Therefore, less searching and bibliographic verification will be necessary and duplication of effort will be avoided. Networking will

be facilitated. Various data bases will be accessible through the use of standard protocol. Service to the user will be improved and that is really what MARC is all about.[13]

---

13   Avram, *MARC, Its History and Implications*, 31-32.

18

Format Integration

During 1988 and 1989 the family of USMARC formats will shrink from nine to three as the seven MARC bibliographic formats become the single integrated USMARC format for bibliographic data. The Library of Congress made the name change in 1988, when the first edition of *USMARC Format for Bibliographic Data Including Guidelines for Content Designation* replaced *MARC Formats for Bibliographic Data* as the primary document for USMARC bibliographic records. That change in name will be matched by a significant change in content as MARBI proposal 88-1, *Format Integration*, makes its way into the document. This chapter discusses the history and effects of format integration.

The Problems

Work with the bibliographic formats within catalog departments, at LC and in MARBI, revealed several problems that arise from the growth and maintenance of seven distinct bibliographic formats:

- *Seriality*. Serial publications have many special aspects that should be described in cataloging. Provisions for seriality in MARC formats other than serials varied and were inconsistent in methodology. The serials format did not provide for inclusion of special characteristics of nonprint materials. Catalogers were forced to choose between seriality and material characteristics.

Serial maps are quite common, serial video publications are increasingly common, and serial sound recordings and data files are not unheard of. All of these could logically use the special fields and codes defined for serials.

- *Flexibility.* Many books now include machine data files in the form of diskettes; some include sound recordings. Some materials have characteristics of more than one medium. Separate formats preclude certain coded information for such cases, and allow complete cataloging only if fields are replicated from format to format.

- *Consistency.* Because separate formats were maintained separately, elements that appear to have the same significance sometimes had different names or tags in different formats.

- *Simplicity.* An integrated format could be published in a more legible and informative manner. Systems supporting an integrated format could move to a single validation table and simplify computer support in other ways.

- *Maintainability.* The Library of Congress and MARBI could study specific changes to the bibliographic format once, without the fear that a given change would later need to be made in other bibliographic formats. Since the phenomenon of a new field in one format being brought back for addition to other formats, either one at a time or all at once, was moderately common during the 1970s and early 1980s, this would represent a real (although not major) savings for LC and MARBI. It would also save money for institutions supporting MARC, since fewer system changes would be required.

History of Format Integration

Format integration as a topic of conversation must be almost as old as MARC itself. There were surely librarians who, first seeing MARC formats for serials and maps in 1970, wondered why those materials could not be handled within a single MARC bibliographic format. Indeed, that question was raised before the MARC format for books was ever published; at the time, LC staff felt that a universal bibliographic format would be too difficult to build and maintain.

Development of larger and more sophisticated MARC-based systems during the 1970s and the addition of formats for manuscripts, films, and music made inconsistencies between formats more obvious and more troublesome. More widespread use of MARC also made its gaps and shortcomings more noticeable. Even with the benefit of hindsight, LC's decision *not* to attempt a universal bibliographic format in the 1960s was probably a correct one for the time, if not for all time.

Work during the Early 1980s

The Library of Congress combined and edited six individual MARC bibliographic formats into the *MARC Formats for Bibliographic Data* (*MFBD*) published in 1980. This document, prepared using a special database designed and implemented by RLG, included columns for each format running down the right-hand side of each page. The columns identified field and subfield validity, also noting which formats were applicable for specific examples and descriptions.

Placing all six formats side by side clarified the inconsistencies and the common core of the formats. LC and MARBI were now confronted with the set of formats whenever change arose. Many more in the library community began to think of MARC as a single format with variations, and wondered why the variations were as extensive as they were.

MFBD also accelerated a tendency that had already begun. Users of one MARC format would begin exploring the other formats, and see fields for which they had applications. New fields would be proposed by one special-interest group, and adopted in a single format. After that adoption other groups would come to LC and MARBI and suggest that the same field be added to other formats, often with minor changes in details of content designation, terminology, or application. Beginning in 1980, MARBI and LC worked steadily to bring the formats closer together. Approval of an existing field for a new format became almost automatic; in some cases, MARBI or LC simply recommended that a new field be adopted across formats when it was first proposed.

The Weisbrod Study

At LC's request, David Weisbrod of Yale University studied the MARC formats and, as a result, wrote *Principles of MARC Format Content Designation* in early 1981.[1] That document raised a large number of questions about the formats and suggested some answers, projecting some proposed principles for the future. As a result of Weisbrod's study, two MARBI projects began in 1981 and continued through 1982. The first was a long list of potential areas for future consideration, including those raised by Weisbrod's report and others raised during discussion. Over the course of a year's analysis, the bulk of the list was eliminated (either because the problems had been solved or were being worked on, or because the issues were determined to be insignificant or outside the scope of MARBI). A final short list of a dozen or so topics included "format integration" as one of the highest priorities, noting that "several encoding problems would be solved if the *MFBD* were integrated across formats and codes/subfields/fields could be assigned as appropriate without concern for their validity within a particular format."[2]

Format Integration as an Ongoing Project

Publication of *The USMARC Formats: Underlying Principles* (discussed in chapter 17) did not change USMARC but did articulate the conceptual bases for the formats. One obvious deduction from the

---

1   David Weisbrod, *Proposal No. 81-4. Principles of MARC Format Content Designation* (Washington, D.C.: Library of Congress, 1981)

2   Elaine W. Woods, *Discussion Paper No. 5* (numerous versions with differing pagination produced during 1981 and 1982)

statement of principles is that all bibliographic formats are based on common assumptions and work in a similar manner: the principles make no distinctions among bibliographic formats and apply equally to all. The principles identify a group of individual formats within the "bibliographic family." The family was continuing to grow, and more people involved with MARC were thinking of the family as a single organism.

Several members of the USMARC advisory group took action to increase discussion of format integration during 1983. John Attig published an article in March 1983 which proposed merging US-MARC bibliographic formats into a single format and considering revision of the legend.[3] Attig later prepared a discussion paper for Marbi suggesting a strategy for format integration, beginning with a statement of intention and objectives and ending with re-evaluation of the legend.[4]

Attig's discussion paper reached the USMARC advisory group agenda in September 1983. The first stage in Attig's strategy was reached when the following statement was approved by MARBI at January 1984 meetings in Washington, D.C.:

Statement of Intention and Objectives:

In its discussions of format integration, MARBI has agreed on the following definition of an integrated format. The USMARC bibliographic formats are considered a single integrated format. Content designation defined therein is valid in any record in which it is appropriate.

In order to begin the process of format integration, MARBI has agreed to identify inconsistencies among the various existing formats and to evaluate the advantages and disadvantages of eliminating these inconsistencies (including the impact of such changes on ex-

---

3   John Attig, "The Concept of a MARC Format," *Information Technology and Libraries* 2, no. 1 (March 1983): 7-17.

4   John Attig, *Integration of USMARC Bibliographic Formats.* (MARBI Discussion Paper no. 7)

isting systems). Where the advantages predominate, the inconsistencies will be removed. Any inconsistencies that remain will be clearly labeled in the format documentation.

Work toward these objectives accelerated during 1984. The Research Libraries Group liaisons to the USMARC advisory group (Kathleen Bales and Walt Crawford) prepared two omnibus proposals, contributed to the Library of Congress for its own internal work on format integration. The first proposal, 84-1, identified a number of specific inconsistencies among existing formats and suggested possible ways of eliminating them. The second, 84-3, proposed a method of carrying information on seriality in other material formats and recommended extending a large number of fields from the serials format to other formats. The Library of Congress had already begun a systematic review of the formats in September 1983. LC worked with RLG's proposals and a variety of other ideas generated internally for the next two years.

Discussion Paper 10

Strategies for Format Integration (Discussion Paper 10), a sixty-nine page document including cover letter from Henriette Avram, was mailed to principal users of the MARC formats, including the presidents of the shared cataloging services (OCLC, RLG, WLN, Utlas), on September 3, 1985. The cover letter suggested that format integration might have considerable financial impact but that LC could not accurately predict what that impact might be. LC requested "institutional cost impact statements" from users and set out assumptions to be used for institutional analysis.

Discussion Paper 10 laid out one possible set of changes to achieve an integrated format, and broke aspects of format integration down into six parts:

- the definition of a new fixed field (006) for seriality and secondary material characteristics;
- the extension of all serials variable fields across all formats;
- the extension of all other variable fields across all formats;

- the deletion, conversion, or designation as obsolete of fields determined to be redundant or duplicative of other fields in the format;
- the modification of certain fields to make them consistent with other parallel fields (e.g., the 1xx and 700-730 fields);
- the issuing of separate guidelines for each type of material with indications at the tag level (only) that the field was Required if Available, Mandatory, Mandatory if Applicable, Optional, or Unlikely to Be Used in a standard national-level record (though not actually prohibiting the use of any field.[5]

When RLG received this document, we carried out a thorough analysis of the implementation cost of the proposals, using much the same methodology we would use for any other major project; other shared cataloging systems did the same. We concluded that a moderate approach to format integration would be cost-effective for RLG over a three-to-five year period. We recommended work on the first three aspects, with work on the fourth and fifth aspects limited to changes that could be made without disrupting existing records. Responses from other agencies were clearly along similar lines.

Discussion Papers during 1987

Given the responses, LC continued to work deliberately on format integration proposals. In April 1987 LC brought together the chair of MARBI and liaisons from the U.S. shared cataloging services for a special two-day discussion of an unnumbered discussion paper, *Select Format Integration Considerations*. This lengthy document spelled out proposed changes in great detail, including a fairly large number of proposals to delete fields or make them obsolete.

The two-day discussion resulted in many refinements to the discussion paper based on experience at OCLC, RLG, and WLN and our sense of what could reasonably be accomplished. The discussion

---

5   *Strategies for Format Integration*, Discussion Paper No. 10 (Washington, D.C.: Library of Congress, 1985), 9.

also relied heavily on actual indications of field usage, taken from OCLC's one percent sample of the database, RLG's six-week record of current activity, and LC's analysis of the complete LC MARC database. The latter figures were used as background for proposals to make values obsolete: lack of real use made a potent argument for getting rid of the values. After two days of intense discussion and changes resulting from that discussion, the proposals were nearly ready to bring before MARBI.

Discussion Paper No. 16: Format Integration Considerations, 132 pages long, came before MARBI during its meeting in San Francisco. The discussion paper took up most of the agenda on June 29 and June 30, including straw votes of the committee and audience on many specific proposals within the overall paper.

It was made clear that the discussion paper generally took a "least change" approach, avoiding any *required* changes to existing records and generally retaining the bulk of existing practice, even at some expense in theoretical elegance. Given the size of the existing MARC database, the sheer number of MARC users, and the variety of systems involved, most people recognized that it was impractical to issue changes that would require the rebuilding of existing databases.

Some MARBI members and liaisons who had been considering format integration for some time feared that this open discussion, well-publicized in advance, would bring out many visitors opposed to any massive changes in the formats. That turned out not to be the case. The visitors in San Francisco were far more numerous than usual and represented many vendors and system suppliers, but almost everybody had already decided that the benefits of format integration outweighed the costs.

Once again, the Library of Congress considered people's reactions and refined its proposals. Another massive document emerged in the fall of 1987; this time, however, it was not a discussion paper but a proposal: Proposal 88-1: *Format Integration*.

Proposal 88-1

Proposal 88-1 consists of three parts totaling 214 pages. The first part (88-1/Preface) contains introductory material, including a general model and a discussion of handling multiple aspects of items in the 008 field. 88-1/General makes up the general proposal to validate fields for all forms of materials, and other proposals that apply to all bibliographic forms. 88-1/XXX consists of proposals that require more explanation, including proposals to delete fields, subfields, and indicators or make them obsolete.

Discussion of Proposal 88-1 began during the ALA Midwinter Meeting in San Antonio on Sunday, January 10, 1988. The long and sometimes grueling process took up specific points first, postponing the general issues until specifics could be clarified. Many issues were discussed and voted on during the remaining three meetings at Midwinter. Twenty-seven specific proposals were discussed and acted on during the January meeting, with twenty-four approved (some with amendments, and two of them sent back for further discussion by LC) and three rejected or partially rejected. Most of these proposals were to make fields and other elements obsolete or delete them.

Recognizing that much more discussion was needed, the chair of MARBI scheduled a fifth three-hour meeting slot for ALA 1988 in New Orleans. She was determined that MARBI would complete Proposal 88-1 during the conference, as were LC and most of those involved. Hours of difficult discussion ironed out most remaining points; after a final day consisting almost entirely of MARBI meetings, the committee finally passed the proposal as a whole. A few items were left somewhat open to further proposals; seven specific subproposals were rejected; but the spread of fields across formats was accepted, as was the general approach to format integration.

At this writing, remaining portions of Proposal 88-1 are undergoing final review at the Library of Congress. Some details of the changes mentioned below may be modified during 1989 and later, but that is always true, since specific proposals will continue to be considered by LC and MARBI. The tables and discussion in the following section should represent a fairly accurate picture of changes brought about by format integration as those changes are eventually reflected in USMARC documentation and practice.

Effects on the Format

Format integration could be done in two ways. One way, suggested as a talking point by David Weisbrod in 1981, would rebuild the formats into a single internally consistent format with no redundant fields, no overlap, and no confusion between different tags. That method would also almost certainly require rebuilding all or most MARC records throughout the universe of USMARC use. Old records would be misinterpreted in new systems and vice-versa.

The other extreme would simply take all existing fields and spread them across all formats, without regard to conflicting definitions. That method would not require any changes to existing records, but would make the integrated format ungainly and more awkward than necessary.

The Library of Congress, aided by feedback from the library community, chose a middle ground. Format integration does not require that *any* existing records be modified, but does reduce the total universe of defined fields considered suitable for new records. Format integration also adds a fairly elegant new mechanism to permit storage of fixed length data elements pertaining to *any* form of material, even if that form of material is not the primary form for the bibliographic record.

Proposal 88-1 opens with four paragraphs offering a definition of format integration. Those four paragraphs serve well as an introduction to the changes actually involved in format integration.

> An ideal integrated bibliographic format would be one that contains data elements that can be used to describe many forms of material. An integrated format would also provide the means for describing the

serial-related aspects of any of these items as well as any archival characteristics present, regardless of the medium or form of material.

For USMARC, the process of format integration would involve the elimination, insofar as possible, of restrictions on data elements that currently make them valid only for specific forms of material. The USMARC bibliographic format would become chiefly a list of data elements and data definitions along with MARC structural specifications.

Integrating the USMARC formats would also inevitably require addressing the inconsistencies, ambiguities, and redundancies that would result when all fields, subfields, and indicators were extended across all forms of material.

Changing USMARC to allow all fields to be used for all forms of material and removing the resulting inconsistencies and redundancies would have direct implications for automated systems using USMARC. These implications would be greater or lesser, depending on how administrators and system designers decided to accommodate these changes in the communications format.[6]

Fixed Length Data Elements

While format integration makes it possible to describe any material or mix of materials in any record, to treat archival characteristics of any material, and to handle seriality for any record, it does not eliminate the type of record and bibliographic level as leader codes (Leader/06 and Leader/07). Those two codes still define the contents of field 008, *Fixed Length Data Elements*. Format integration does provide a means of recording fixed length data elements that don't fit in the 008 defined by the type and level of the record.

---

6   Proposal 88-1: *Format Integration*, (Washington, D.C.: Library of Congress, 1987)

008/00-05 . . . . . . .Date Entered on File
008/06 . . . . .Type of Date/Publication Status
008/07-10 . . . . . . .Date 1
008/11-14 . . . . . . .Date 2
008/15-17 . . . . . . .Place of Publication, Production, Execution
008/35-37 . . . . . . .Language
008/38 . . . . .Modified Record
008/39 . . . . .Cataloging Source

Table 18.1: Common Elements of Field 008

The first eighteen positions and last five positions of field 008 record the same information regardless of record type and level, as shown in Table 18.1. The seventeen positions from 008/18 through 008/34 depend on record type and level. The new field 006, *Fixed Length Data Elements—Additional Material Characteristics*, contains eighteen positions. The first position, 006/00, is either one of the Leader/06 codes for type of record or the value "s" for serial control. The remainder provide exactly the same codes as the appropriate 008, but offset by seventeen positions. Thus, 008/18 becomes 006/01, 008/19 becomes 006/02, and so on through to 008/34, which becomes 006/17. Definitions for field 006 appear in chapters 4 through 12.

Fields Spread across Formats

Format integration does one of three things for each and every field, subfield, and indicator defined in any bibliographic format as of 1988 (and automatically for any new fields):

- extends the definition across all bibliographic formats; or
- defines the value as obsolete (i.e., valid for existing records but not to be used for new material); or
- deletes the value from the formats if it can be shown that the value has not been used and could not properly be used.

Tables 18.2 through 18.5, on the following pages, show fields extended across all formats as part of format integration, except for field 851, still uncertain as of this writing.

In all, 117 fields become valid in formats that previously did not include them. That figure is across the formats as a whole: no individual type of material or treatment finds the list of fields expanded by nearly that many fields. Subfields and indicator values also become uniform across fields. That list is too long to reproduce here, particularly with the explanation that would be needed to make it sensible.

011	Linking LC Control Number
015	National Bibliography Number
017	Copyright Registration Number
018	Copyright Article-Fee Code
020	International Standard Book Number (ISBN)
022	International Standard Serial Number (ISSN)
023	Standard Film Number
024	Standard Recording Number
025	Overseas Acquisition Number
027	Standard Technical Report Number
028	Publisher Number for Music
030	Coden Designation
032	Postal Registration Number
033	Date/Time and Place of Event
034	Coded Cartographic Mathematical Data
036	Original Study Number
037	Source of Acquisition
042	Authentication Code
043	Geographic Area Code
044	Country of Publishing/Producing Entity Code
046	Type of Date Code, Date 1, Date 2 (BC Dates)
047	Type of Musical Composition Code
048	Number of Musical Instruments or Voices Code
050	Library of Congress Call Number
051	LC Copy, Issue, Offprint Statement

Table 18.2: Fields Extended Across Formats (1)

055	Call Numbers/Class Numbers Assigned in Canada
061	National Library of Medicine Copy Statement
071	National Agricultural Library Copy Statement
074	GPO Item Number
080	Universal Decimal Classification Number (UDC)
082	Dewey Decimal Call Number
086	Government Document Classification Number
088	Report Number
210	Abbreviated Key Title
222	Key Title
243	Collective Uniform Title
246	Varying Form of Title
247	Former Title or Title Variations
254	Musical Presentation Statement
255	Cartographic Mathematical Data
256	Computer File Characteristics
257	Country of Producing Entity for Archival Films
261	Imprint Statement for Films (Pre-AACR1 Revised)
262	Imprint Statement for Sound Recordings (Pre-AACR2)
263	Projected Publication Date
306	Playing Time
310	Current Publication Frequency
321	Former Publication Frequency
340	Physical Medium
351	Organization and Arrangement of Materials
362	Dates of Publication and/or Volume Designation
400	Series Statement/Added Entry—Personal Name
410	Series Statement/Added Entry—Corporate Name
411	Series Statement/Added Entry—Meeting Name
440	Series Statement/Added Entry—Title
490	Series Statement
501	With Note
502	Dissertation Note
504	Bibliography, etc. Note
505	Formatted Contents Note

Table 18.3: Fields Extended Across Formats (2)

507	Scale Note for Graphic Material
508	Creation/Production Credits Note
511	Participant or Performer Note
513	Type of Report and Period Covered Note
515	Numbering Peculiarities Note
516	Type of Computer File or Data Note
518	Date/Time and Place of Event Note
521	Target Audience Note
522	Geographic Coverage Note
524	Preferred Citation of Described Materials Note
525	Supplement Note
530	Additional Physical Form Available
533	Reproduction Note
534	Original Version Note
536	Funding Information Note
538	System Details Note
540	Terms Governing Use and Reproduction Note
541	Immediate Source of Acquisition Note
544	Location of Associated Archival Materials Note
545	Biographical or Historical Note
546	Language Note
547	Former Title Complexity Note
550	Issuing Body Note
555	Cumulative Index/Finding Aids Note
566	Information About Documentation Note
561	Provenance Note
562	Copy and Version Identification Note
565	Case File Characteristics Note
567	Methodology Note
581	Publications About Described Materials Note
584	Accumulation and Frequency of Use
585	Exhibitions Note
653	Index Term—Uncontrolled
655	Index Term—Genre/Form
656	Index Term—Occupation

Table 18.4: Fields Extended Across Formats (3)

657	Index Term—Function
740	Added Entry—Uncontrolled Related/Analytical Title
752	Added Entry—Hierarchical Place Name
753	System Details Access to Computer File
754	Added Entry—Taxonomic Identification
760	Main Series Entry
762	Subseries Entry
765	Original Language Entry
767	Translation Entry
770	Supplement/Special Issue Entry
772	Parent Record Entry
775	Other Edition Entry
776	Additional Physical Form Entry
777	Issued With Entry
780	Preceding Entry
785	Succeeding Entry
787	Nonspecific Relationship Entry
800	Series Added Entry—Personal Name
810	Series Added Entry—Corporate Name
811	Series Added Entry—Meeting Name
830	Series Added Entry—Uniform Title
850	Holding Institution

Table 18.5: Fields Extended Across Formats (4)

Fields and Values Made Obsolete

The Library of Congress began with a long list of fields that it felt could safely be made obsolete. That list included many specific note fields. MARBI and LC did agree on a new underlying principle for USMARC, to clarify the need for specific note fields:

A specific 5XX note field is needed when at least one of the following is true:

1) Categorical indexing or retrieval is required on the data defined for the note. The note is used for structured access purposes but is not a true 6XX-8XX access point.

2) Special manipulation of that specific category of data is a routine requirement. Such manipulation includes special print/display formatting or selection/suppression from display.

3) Idiosyncratic structuring of information for reasons other than those given in 1) or 2), e.g., certain archival and manuscripts control notes.

211	Acronym or Shortened Title
212	Variant Access Title
214	Augmented Title
265	Source for Acquisition/Subscription
302	Item Count/Page Count
305	Physical Desc./Sound Recordings (Pre-AACR2)
308	Physical Desc./Films (Archival)
315	Frequency
350	Price
503	Bibliographic History
512	Earlier or Later Vols. Sep. Cataloged
523	Time Period of Content Note
527	Censorship Note (Archival)
537	Source of Data Note
570	Editor Note
582	Related Machine-Readable Files

Table 18.6: Fields Made Obsolete

MARBI and LC also agreed on the meaning of the terms "Obsolete" and "Deleted" when applied to USMARC elements. Paraphrasing the meaning of "obsolete," the content designator continues to appear in format documentation; institutions are not expected to eliminate the content designator from existing records; the content designator should not be used for new records, even for retrospective conversion: documentation will provide instructions to map the data into current content designation.

After discussion only sixteen fields became obsolete. A number of subfields, indicators, and indicator values were also made obsolete.

Fields and Values Deleted

When can a field or value be deleted? When it meets one of two criteria:

- It had been reserved but not defined in the format. For example, tags are sometimes reserved but the indicators and subfields never specified (thus making it impossible to use the field),
- It can be known with near certainty that the content designator has not been used.

The latter test is a tough one to meet, and LC proposed very few deletions as part of format integration. Deletion means just that: the content designator disappears from future versions of USMARC documentation. As a result, it becomes possible to use the content designator for another purpose at a later date.

That last sentence states the second of two critical differences between obsolete and deleted content designators:

- Obsolete designators will appear in existing records and do not represent errors. Deleted designators should never appear.
- Obsolete designators *must not* be reused for new elements, while deleted elements *may* be used for new elements.

002	. . . . .Subrecord Map of Directory
003	. . . . .Subrecord Relationship
004	. . . . .Related Record Directory
246/12	. . . . .Value *9* within USMARC
320	. . . . .Current Frequency Control Info.
330	. . . . .Publication Pattern
331	. . . . .Former Publication Pattern
490/‡n	. . . . .National Library of Canada Call #
500/‡n	. . . . .National Library of Canada Call #

Table 18.7: Content Designation Deleted from USMARC

The small set of elements listed in Table 18.7 meet one or both criteria. Fields 002, 003, 004, 320, 330, and 331 never contained full definitions in MARC documentation and could not legitimately be used. Unfortunately fields 002 and 003 are defined by ANSI Z39.2, the underlying standard for USMARC, and cannot be reused unless that standard is revised. Fields 002-004 would have been used in a subrecord structure that was proposed but rejected for USMARC.

Value 9 in the second indicator of field 246 (*Varying Form of Title*) appeared in the 1975 edition of *Serials: A MARC Format* defined as "Unspecified titles reported to LC by other libraries." A year later, the name of the value was changed to "Undefined." The value was never used, and conflicts with the current principle that reserves 9 in any content designation for locally defined values.

The last two deletions represent provisions made for the National Library of Canada (NLC) and are useful only for that library. NLC never used ǂn in those fields, had no plans to use them, and saw no reason to retain the content designation. LC found no occurrences of the subfield in its serials database, which includes NLC's contributions to CONSER.

The tiny number of deletions will have no effect on any user of USMARC, except to remove a few pages from the documentation, but certainly made sense in the interests of overall USMARC clarity.

Effects on the USMARC Community

What does format integration mean to you? It does *not* mean disruption of existing databases. It does *not* mean relearning basic aspects of assigning MARC content designation. It does *not* mean significant changes in searching or in product generation: many product-generation systems already treated all bibliographic records identically, and many online systems already contain all bibliographic records in a unified database. It does *not* prevent online systems from maintaining distinctions by type of material or treatment, although such systems need to give some consideration to handling of items containing aspects of more than one format.

It *does* provide format support for the kind of materials that need to be cataloged. Books do sometimes include machine data files or sound recordings; maps are frequently issued as serials; videocassettes do appear serially; collections treated archivally include all forms of material.

Cataloging

Catalogers will find promise and challenge in the integrated US-MARC format. The promise is manifested as follows:

- All significant aspects of an item can be described and coded, regardless of the primary aspect of the item,
- Seriality can always be described and coded if appropriate,
- Archival control can be maintained over any form of material without losing description or coding for that form,
- If a field is appropriate for the work in hand, it can be used.

The challenge is that there are more possible fields for any given material format. The USMARC documentation will help in this respect, since it will specify whether fields are not normally used in national-level records for a given format. As is always true with MARC, the set of fields is a set of possibilities, not a set of requirements. You rarely have use for a field *Playing Time* when cataloging a book—but, if the book includes an audiocassette, the field might come in handy.

Format and System Maintenance

The short-term effect of format integration will be some level of maintenance in most systems that use USMARC. That maintenance will have a cost; in most cases, the cost should be fairly modest.

The long-term effect should be less maintenance and simpler systems. For systems that maintain careful validation over MARC, one set of validity tables should be less cumbersome than seven sets. The validation tables needed for fields 006 and 008 are no different in kind than those needed for field 007, where validity for the remaining positions is determined by the first character. There will be less maintenance because fields will be added only once, to all formats.

Format maintenance, the work of the Library of Congress and MARBI, should also be slightly simplified in the long run. A lull in MARC format changes seems likely during 1989 and 1990, just as format changes came more slowly after the sustained high of activity that resulted in the archival and manuscripts control format, computer file format, visual materials changes, and holdings format. During and after that probable lull, those working on the bibliographic format need only consider a field for adoption once. Once adopted, it will be valid for all bibliographic formats.

19

Extending USMARC

U SMARC is unusual in that the definition explicitly allows for extensions. The Library of Congress distributes pure USMARC records, by definition. Other agencies that generate USMARC tapes tend to add extensions to the format as defined in *UFBD*. Even the Library of Congress maintains extensions to USMARC in its own internal format.

Proper extensions to USMARC are *supersets* of USMARC: any pure USMARC record will fit into the extended format, but some of the extended format's information won't fit into pure USMARC. The tape formats used by the two largest shared cataloging services in the United States and the largest such service in Canada are all proper supersets of USMARC.

Extensions to USMARC do not change the format itself. They consist of additional content designation: subfields, indicator values, characters, and fields. Other shared cataloging services and other agencies also extend USMARC. OCLC MARC, RLIN MARC, and Utlas MARC are used in this chapter as three of the most prominent examples of extended USMARC formats, and as formats that, in some cases, use different means to achieve similar ends.

OCLC MARC

OCLC bases its content designation and cataloging standards firmly on USMARC as defined in *UFBD*. Online displays show full USMARC content designation, and OCLC was, until the mid-1980s, the only bibliographic service to implement *every* USMARC format.

OCLC defines three types of extensions to USMARC content designation: additional subfields, additional fields for general local use, and additional fields reserved for use by national libraries.

Subfield Extensions

OCLC defines additional subfields for USMARC fields in two cases. One of these cases affects a single field; the other is defined for a great many fields:

- *Subfield ‡b in Field 035.* Field 035 contains System Control Numbers. Use of the field is not well-controlled. As defined by OCLC, "Field 035 may be used by a participating institution for its own control number."[1] The current USMARC definition includes only ‡a, Local system number, consisting of an NUC code (in parentheses) followed by a local system number. OCLC defines ‡b as *Institution code*, the OCLC symbol rather than the NUC code. When ‡b is used, the NUC code is not entered in ‡a.

- *Subfield ‡w: AACR2 verification.* "Subfield 'w' contains a two-character code that: (1) verifies that the field contains the *AACR2* form of name heading, and (2) indicates the verification's source." This subfield is directly related to OCLC's massive reconstruction of its database in 1981, changing headings to conform to *AACR2* whenever possible. Subfield ‡w is explicitly labeled as an extension to USMARC, and is defined for this purpose in all fields subject to name authority control and a few others: 100, 110, 111, 130, 240, 400, 410, 411, 600, 610, 611, 630, 651,

---

1   OCLC, Inc., *Serials Format* (Columbus, Ohio: OCLC, Inc., 1980)

700, 710, 711, 730, 800, 810, and 811. The subfield is also defined for OCLC's local subject entry fields 691, 692, 693, 694, and 695.

Field Extensions

OCLC defines a number of fields that are not part of USMARC. Most of these fields carry local call numbers, local holdings, and local subject headings. One field is provided for any desired local use, without definition or restriction.

---

049   **Local holdings**
‡a   Holding library code; text associated with call number
‡c   Copy statement
‡l   Local processing data
‡o   Local processing data
‡d   Definition of bibliographic subdivisions
‡v   Primary bibliographic subdivision
‡p   Secondary bibliographic subdivision
‡q   Third bibliographic subdivision
‡r   Fourth bibliographic subdivision
‡s   Fifth bibliographic subdivision
‡t   Sixth bibliographic subdivision
‡u   Seventh bibliographic subdivision
‡y   Inclusive dates of publication or coverage
‡m   Missing elements
‡n   Notes about holdings

049   __ *‡aXXXr‡c2‡d[‡vser.‡pvol.‡qno.]‡vl‡p1‡q1-2‡p2‡q1-4‡d[‡vser.‡pvol.‡qpt.]‡vll‡p1‡p2‡q1-3¶*

Table 19.1: OCLC Field 049, Subfields and Example

Table 19.1 shows OCLC's field for local holdings together with an example of that field. Field 049 contains location, copy, and volume information for an item. Groups of libraries have frequently established explicit guidelines for coding 049 so that holdings can be manipulated easily. In addition to the wealth of subfields, OCLC has provided structure within and among the subfields. The primary subfield ‡a can include text to be printed above or below a call number, with each line of text surrounded by square brackets and the position of lines given by the position of text within the subfield: text before the holdings symbol appears above the call number; text after appears below. Subfield ‡d defines a sequence of other subfields, as does subfield ‡m.

Subfield ‡a of 049 is used by OCLC to control catalog card generation. Most other subfields are provided so that OCLC users can record holdings in a meaningful way, and so that networks and other processing centers can manipulate them. The field can be complex: OCLC devotes ten single-spaced pages to "general guidelines" for its use. Field 049 allows complex and sophisticated storage of holdings. The example shown in Table 19.1 says the following:

Holding library XXXr holds one copy, numbered 2. The publication has two customary numbering schemes: (1) "series" divided into "volumes" divided into "numbers," and (2) "series" divided into "volumes" divided into "parts." Series I consists of volume 1 in two numbers, and volume 2 in four numbers. Series II consists of volume 1 in one physical volume, and volume 2 in three parts.

019	OCLC control number cross-reference
090	Locally assigned LC-type call number
092	Locally assigned Dewey call number
096	Locally assigned NLM-type call number
098	Other classification schemes
099	Local free text call number

Table 19.2: OCLC Extended Fields 019, 090-099

Table 19.2 shows other OCLC extensions in the 0xx area. Field 019 contains OCLC control number(s) for duplicate records that have been deleted; the field is useful for processing agencies in tracing a record that has disappeared.

OCLC's field 090, which contains only LC-type call numbers, is a local extension. OCLC defines the same subfields for 090 as for 050: ‡a, LC class number, and ‡b, Local cutter number (book number).

OCLC adds two new subfields to support classified catalogs: ‡e, Feature heading, and ‡f, Filing suffix. Subfield ‡b in OCLC's 092 is *not* the same as subfield ‡b in the standard Dewey call number field 082, and has special rules for specifying line breaks on a printed card.

Field 098 represents an attempt by OCLC to represent all known standard schemes for classification. As stated in the field's scope note, "Classification schemes defined in this field are generally available in printed form, but are neither major schemes (such as LC or Dewey) nor completely local schemes." The special character of field 098 is in its indicators, which specify the classification scheme used. Both indicators are taken together, carrying a number from "00" (National Center on Educational Media and Materials for the Handicapped) to "24" (Swank Classification for State, County, and Municipal Documents). Other numbers are reserved and added as required. Field 099 contains call numbers that don't fit elsewhere—local systems unique to a given library, text used in place of call numbers, and call numbers that can't be formatted properly from other fields. Like field 098, field 099 has a repeatable ‡a (where each subfield contains a printing line of the call number) and also contains ‡e and ‡f. Unlike field 098, the indicators in 099 are undefined.

590	Local note
690	Local subject added entry - topical heading
691	Local subject added entry - geographic name
692	Local subject added entry - personal name
693	Local subject added entry - corporate name
694	Local subject added entry - conference / meeting
695	Local subject added entry - uniform title heading
910	‡a User-option data
936	‡a Dates or volume designations of pieces used for cataloging
949	Local processing information

Table 19.3: OCLC Extensions, Fields 590-949

Table 19.3 shows the remaining OCLC field extensions available to all libraries. Field 590 is used for notes that pertain only to a single library or single copy of an item. The field can be used for any note that a library wishes to place in the notes section of a catalog card. Examples could be ‡aLibrary retains latest 3 years only¶ or ‡aCopy is missing pages 300-325¶.

Field 690 contains a topical subject heading that is not based on a standard thesaurus. It has the same subfields as field 650 and is used in the same way. Field 691 is comparable to field 651; the same notes apply as for field 690. Fields 692, 693, 694, and 695 are local equivalents for fields 600, 610, 611, and 630 respectively, and have the same subfields. These fields were defined for CONSER, and are used only in Serials; in that format, they are used for subject headings not assigned by national libraries.

Field 910 contains information of local interest; the first twenty-one characters of ‡a can be used as a footnote on catalog cards. Field 936 is used when serial cataloging is based on something other than the first issue published.

Field 949 is open for any desired use. To quote OCLC's documentation, "this field may be defined in any manner by any OCLC participating library or affiliated network, according to its needs for local processing information." The field is repeatable, and may contain any indicators and any subfields. Provision of field 949 is another attempt by OCLC to allow libraries and networks to meet their own needs; OCLC does not do any validation of the field or its internal content designation. Any user is free to use the field for any purpose whatsoever.

While OCLC extensions for local data include only a few fields, the fields allow for a moderately wide range of local data. The local call number fields offer unique capacity for specifying use of lesser-known classification schemes, and field 049 allows well-structured specification of holdings. Field 949 is an essential conduit, allowing libraries to "talk to themselves" and to processing agencies. Field 949 is of no use to OCLC itself, but can be valuable if well-defined within a library or group of libraries.

Field Extensions for National Libraries

012	Terminal Display
680	PRECIS Descriptor String
890	Holdings (Local LC)
900	Personal Name Equivalence or Cross-reference
901	Numbered Copy Information
911	X-copy Information
920	Corporate Name Equivalence, Cross-ref, History Note
921	Conference/Meeting Name Equiv. , etc.
930	Uniform Title Heading Equivalence or Cross-reference
940	Uniform Title Equivalence or Cross-reference
980	Series (Personal Name) Equivalence or Cross-reference
981	Series (Corporate Name) Equivalence or Cross-reference
982	Series (Conference or Meeting) Equivalence or Cross-reference
983	Series (Title) Equivalence or Cross-reference
990	Link to Equivalence, Cross-references, and History Notes

Table 19.4: OCLC Extensions for National Libraries

OCLC has defined several fields that are not present in USMARC and are not available for use by most libraries. Most of these fields, shown in Table 19.4, are used in the CONSER project for records entered by the National Library of Canada or the Library of Congress. Some fields are equivalents for fields in Canadian MARC (CAN/MARC), and some provide for LC internal needs.

RLIN MARC

RLG also produces tapes in a superset of USMARC, with additional subfields and additional fields. RLIN MARC has an unusually wide range of additional fields, including a number of fields with alphabetic tags. The tables shown here represent a condensation of the actual definitions.

Subfield Extensions

RLIN MARC defines four subfields not included in USMARC: ‡9, ‡*, ‡=, and ‡%. The first is obsolete for bibliographic data; the second and third are used only for internal control of archival and manuscripts control fields.

Subfield ‡% contains coded values to identify special tracings, such as tracings for fine printers, special bindings, and the like. Currently ‡% is used only in local added entry fields. In RLIN these fields represent those added entries that are strictly local in form or of strictly local interest. The RLG-defined local added entry fields are shown below, together with their USMARC equivalents. Note that some of these deliberately duplicate OCLC extensions.

```
690 = 650; 691 = 651
696 = 600; 697 = 610; 698 = 611; 699 = 630
796-799 = 700-730 (as for 6xx)
896-899 = 800-830 (as for 6xx)
```

Field Extensions

In addition to the local added entry fields noted above, RLIN MARC adds a large number of other fields to USMARC. None of the others are displayed as MARC tags in RLIN online. All other extensions are tagged with mnemonics, and translated to fields and subfields for RLIN MARC tape transmission. RLIN MARC extensions can be broken down into three groups: call numbers and holdings; miscellaneous local information and errors; and acquisitions information.

---

930 Summary Holdings Statement
‡a   Institution code - location data
‡b   Sublocation identifier - location data
‡c   Copy identifier - location data
‡d   Call number - location data
‡e   Date of report - general holdings data
‡f   Completeness code - general holdings data
‡g   Acquisition status code - general holdings data
‡h   Retention code - general holdings data
‡i   Local notes - general holdings data
‡j   Enumeration - specific holdings data
‡k   Chronology - specific holdings.

930   _‡aMiU‡bNAT‡cCopy 1‡dSH 11. A45‡j1-23‡k1881-1903‡e8007‡f0‡g5‡h_¶

Table 19.5: RLIN Field 930

Holdings and Call Numbers

RLIN provides extensive holdings support, but has no single field with the sophistication of OCLC's field 049. RLIN does include an implementation of the ANSI Serials Holdings at the Summary Level standard, field *SHS* (RLIN MARC 930), shown with an example in Table 19.5. Field 930 is specifically designed to contain holdings statements recorded according to ANSI summary standards. Coded values, subfields ‡f, ‡g, and ‡h, use the codes defined by the standard. The example in Table 19.5 defines the following:

A serial held in location NAT at institution MiU (NUC code), copy 1, with call number SH11. A45. The library holds volumes 1-23 published from 1881-1903. The report was created in July 1980. Completeness is not known; the serial is not currently received and is permanently retained.

---

090   Record-Level Information
      Includes call number ‡a & ‡b, volumes ‡v, dates ‡y, retention ‡z, additional local notes ‡n, output instructions and history ‡i & ‡h, and card-specific subfields ‡f, ‡p and ‡t

950   Location-Level Information
      Includes location ‡l, all 090 subfields for location-level call number, holdings and card instructions, and stamps above and below call number ‡d & ‡e.

955   Copy-Level Information
      Includes location ‡l, copy-level call number ‡a & ‡b, copy designation ‡c, acq. & circ. control numbers ‡q & ‡r, shelflist note ‡s, non-printing note ‡u and copy status ‡i.

Table 19.6: RLIN Call Number and Holdings Fields

Three RLIN MARC fields, shown in Table 19.6, provide for three levels of call number, holdings, and card-related information.

Other RLIN MARC Extensions

901	Local data element A
902	Local data element B
903	Local data element C
904	Local data element D
905	Local data element E
906	Local data element F
907	Local data element G

Fields 901-907 all carry the same definition and the same rules. "LDx is used for information needed by a library that is not provided by existing fields. Each library may use LDx for its own purposes."[2] Each field is repeatable, and a library may define indicators and subfields to suit its own needs.

---

2   All citations in this section are from various RLIN Field Guides or from RLIN internal documentation.

910	RLG standards note
936	Piece used for cataloging
948	Series part designation
94a	Analysis treatment note
94b	Treatment codes
998	Local control information
b99	Private local information

RSN, field 910, is used to record variant practice from RLG standards. The primary use for RSN is to note changes that a library has made in the bibliographic content of LC data, either MARC or non-MARC. The note serves as a guide and warning to other users. RLG has defined field 936 to conform to OCLC's definition of 936, which does appear on distributed CONSER records.

RLIN provides PVT, field b99, to allow libraries to store confidential local information, such as donors of rare books. Libraries may define indicators and subfield codes for PVT as needed. The field differs from other local data elements in terms of display: PVT is displayed only to the library that owns a record.

RLIN Acquisitions Data

USMARC has never included tags containing alphabetic characters, but such tags have always been legitimate possibilities. When RLG implemented an acquisitions system and decided to integrate acquisitions data with bibliographic data, initial analysis showed that the 9XX range of locally defined tags would become overcrowded if all acquisitions data was defined as 9XX fields. RLG chose to place all acquisitions data in fields having tags beginning *u*, and at the same time began using alphabetic characters in some other extended fields (such as b99, 94a, and 89e).

RLIN defines "units" to contain acquisitions data: a single unit reflects one order or other acquisition. A single bibliographic entity can have as many as ninety-nine units, each identified by a one or two digit number. Data relating to a specific unit is grouped by indicators; all acquisitions fields carry the UID, or unit identification number, in the indicator positions.

u01	Unit identification and type
u02	Standard number
u08	Additional coded information
u10	Requester field
u11	Departmental report request
u20	Supplier name and address
u21	Library codes for vendor and order
u22	Supplier codes and catalog information
u25	Supplier report
u30	Claim intervals
u31	Claim counts
u33	Claim for invoice
u34	Extended procurement claim & review
u40	Extended procurement codes
u50	Acquisitions note
u51	Selection note
u52	Supplier instruction notes
u53	Claim notes
u54	Serials note
u55	Cataloging note
u5f	Accounting note
u70	Item control elements
u71	Library fund identification code
u75	Item details
u7f	Price information
ufi	Fiscal information

Table 19.7: RLIN Acquisitions Fields

Table 19.7 shows RLIN acquisitions fields. This is a highly compressed version of the actual fields since some fields have several subfields, each representing a named element of acquisitions information.

Utlas MARC (LCF)

While Utlas accommodates both CAN/MARC (the Canadian MARC format) and USMARC and produces tapes in a number of MARC formats, the system also defines additional elements as part of the Library Communications Format or LCF, another name for Utlas MARC.[3]

Fixed-Field Extensions

The most surprising differences between USMARC and LCF come in field 008. The LCF 008 field is 110 bytes long rather than forty. In most cases, the first forty bytes of an LCF 008 are identical to those in an equivalent USMARC LCF, but in two cases LCF deviates slightly from USMARC within the first forty characters. The changes and additions carry either CAN/MARC information not present (or defined differently) in USMARC, the four-character intellectual level code in LCF (as compared to the single-character code in USMARC), or the many added fixed fields requested by Utlas customers such as Circulation code, Catalogue status code, Bookplate code, and Incunabula code. (The 110-character 008 includes twenty characters at the end reserved for future use.)

Field Extensions

Utlas defines a large number of fields that are not part of USMARC, for a variety of purposes including most of those served by OCLC MARC and RLIN MARC extensions. An additional set of LCF extensions supports bilingual records in a manner somewhat akin to USMARC support for alternate graphic representations.

---

3 All information in this section was provided directly by Sydney Jones, Manager of Bibliographic Services at Utlas.

Holdings and Call Numbers

090	**Local call number**
‡a	Call number
‡l	Reserved
‡b	Location
‡f	Collection
‡s	Shelving code
‡n	Ownership code
‡x	Alternate call number
‡u	National agency call number
‡c	Copy designation
‡e	Accession number
‡d	Summary volume holdings
‡g	Non-date volume designations
‡h	Date volume designations
‡m	Microform holdings
‡k	Set code
‡t	Circulation code
‡r	Remarks
‡y	Number of sets
‡j	Extra main entry cards
‡p	Number of copies
‡q	Ownership code
‡z	Region code

Table 19.8: Utlas Field 090

The primary LCF field for local information is field 090, including the subfields shown in Table 19.8. This field combines some elements of OCLC fields 049 and 09x and RLIN fields 090, 950, and 955. Additional fields for holdings and classification information and for acquisitions appear in Table 19.9; some of these fields are richly subfielded, with as many as nineteen subfields (fields 098 and 398).

089	User own classification scheme
091	Special byproducts
092	Extra cards
097	Pre-catalogue holdings description
098	On-order information
398	Archival on-order information
695	Acquisitions list subject term/KWIC enrichment

Table 19.9: Other Utlas Fields for Local Data

PRECIS

Utlas provides extended support for the PRECIS descriptor string, as used by the British Library. Table 19.10 shows the five PRECIS fields; field 690 includes twenty-two subfields such as ‡b, "Salient focus" and ‡k, "Non-lead indirect difference."

680	PRECIS descriptor string (UKMARC)
681	PRECIS SIN (UKMARC)
682	PRECIS RIN (UKMARC)
690	PRECIS descriptor string
691	PRECIS descriptor SIN number

Table 19.10: Utlas PRECIS Fields

Bilingual Records

Much of the cataloging done in Canada is bilingual, with fields appearing in French and in English. Utlas uses eight indicator positions online. Two of these carry USMARC or CAN/MARC indicators; five are for system use; the last indicates the language of a heading in the case of bilingual records. Figure 19.1 shows a portion of a record as it might appear online in Utlas; Figure 19.2 shows the same information as it would appear in LCF.

```
110    20____0_  ‡aCanada Post Corporation¶
110    20____0F  ‡aSociete canadienne des postes‡6110/001¶
245    10_____   ‡aAnnual report.¶
245    10____F   ‡aRapport annuel.‡6245/001¶
260    1_____    ‡a[Ottowa] :‡bCanada Post.¶
260    1_____F   ‡a[Ottowa] :‡bPostes Canada.‡6260/001
300    _____   ‡av.¶
500    _____   ‡aText in English and French with French text on inverted
pages.¶
500    _____F  ‡aTexte en francais et en anglais disposees tete-
beche.‡6500/001¶
```

Figure 19.1: Bilingual Record, Online Form

```
110    20   ‡aCanada Post Corporation¶
245    10   ‡aAnnual report.¶
260    1_   ‡a[Ottowa] :‡bCanada Post.¶
300    __   ‡av.¶
500    __   ‡aText in English and French with French text on inverted pages.¶
910    20   ‡aSociete canadienne des postes¶
945    10   ‡aRapport annuel.¶
947    1_   ‡a[Ottowa] :‡bPostes Canada.¶
950    __   ‡aTexte en francais et en anglais disposees tete-beche.¶
990    01   ‡a91001a‡b11001a¶
990    01   ‡a94501a‡b24501a¶
990    01   ‡a94701ab‡b26001ab¶
990    01   ‡a95001a‡b50001a¶
```

Figure 19.2: Bilingual Record, LCF Form

As these figures should make clear, the 990 fields explicitly link English and French equivalent fields within the record. Tables 19.11 and 19.12 show the large set of fields used to communicate bilingual information.

900	Personal name
910	Corporate name
911	Meeting or conference
912	Varying form of title
913	Former title or title variations
914	Main series entry
915	Subseries entry
916	Original language entry
917	Translation entry
918	Supplement/special issue entry
919	Parent record entry
920	Other editions available entry
921	Additional physical forms available entry
922	"Issued with" entry
923	Preceding entry
924	Succeeding entry
925	Nonspecific relationship entry
930	References - uniform title
931	Other language notes - Dates and volume designation
932	Other language notes - Limited use / restrictions
933	Other language notes - Citation note
934	Other language notes - Numbering peculiarities
935	Other language notes - Supplement
936	Other language notes - Additional physical forms
937	Other language notes - Issuing bodies
938	Other language notes - Cumulative index
939	Other language notes - Linking entry complexity
940	Uniform title
941	Romanized title
943	Collective title
945	Title
946	Other language edition statement
947	Other language imprint
948	Other language collation
949	Other language 3xx field without direct equivalent
950	Other language notes - general
951	Other language notes - "with" note
952	Other language notes - dissertation note
953	Other language notes - bibliographic history
954	Other language notes - bibliography/discography

Table 19.11: Utlas Bilingual Fields (1)

---

955   Other language notes - contents (formatted)
956   Other language 5xx field without direct equivalent
957   Other language notes - scale
958   Other language notes - abstract, annotation, summary
959   Other language notes - photoreproduction

960   Other language subject - personal name
961   Other language subject - corporate name
962   Other language subject - conference name
963   Other language subject - uniform title
965   Other language subject - topical

966   Other language subject - geographical name
967   Other language subject - reversed geographic
968   Other language subject - genre heading
970   Other language added entry - personal name
971   Other language added entry - corporate name

972   Other language added entry - conference name
973   Other language added entry - uniform title
974   Other language added entry - title
980   Series statement - author/title - personal name
981   Series statement - author/title - corporate name

982   Series statement - meetings and conferences
983   Series statement - title, uniform title or cross reference
984   Series statement - uniform title heading
989   Series statement - not traced or traced differently
990   Reference link

Table 19.12: Utlas Bilingual Fields (2)

Other Field Extensions

Utlas has two other categories of field extension. One group of six fields is used when the information in a field is of a known type, but the specific MARC tag cannot be determined—as might be the case if MARC records are being created mechanically from local systems using simpler content designation. Table 19.13 shows these fields; Table 19.14 shows the remaining Utlas extensions.

199	Main entry - type unknown
499	Series statement - type unknown
599	Note - undefined
699	Subject added entry - undefined
799	Added entry - undefined
899	Series added entry - undefined

Table 19.13: Utlas "Unknown" Fields

012	BNQ bibliographic control number
013	NLM catalogue citation number
014	British National Bibliography control number
016	National Library of Canada bib. control number
018	InterMARC control number
019	OCLC control number
021	Related ISSN
029	French National Bibliography number
031	CIHM control number
056	NLC copy, issue, offprint statement
059	Bowker record control number
073	NLC subject category code
081	CLSI author/title key
190	Greek title
539	Producer/director note
590	Local note
591	Microfilm copy and taped-from note
592	Note pertaining to a copy
595	Authority record link - general explanatory - authors
596	Authority record link - general explanatory - titles
597	Authority record link - general explanatory - subjects
649	NASA subject term
790	List of bound withs
890	Copy statement
891	Unit statement

Table 19.14: Miscellaneous Utlas Extensions

Why Extend USMARC?

Utlas, RLIN, and OCLC extend USMARC as nationally defined, and so do most other agencies. Extensions are needed because US-MARC is designed as a communications format for bibliographic data. Local extensions support local processing needs. In this sense, even OCLC is a "local" system. Extensions serve functions not handled by USMARC, such as:

- *Holdings:* OCLC, RLIN, Utlas, and many others have supported storage of holdings data for many years, long before USMARC took up the issue. Holdings information is vital for resource sharing and for local systems; bibliographic services must provide holdings support to serve their members and users.

- *Acquisitions:* Information on acquisitions can serve cooperative collection development programs. Some of the bibliographic services also provide specific acquisitions services. Most acquisitions data is of strictly local interest, and technically inappropriate for a national communications format. Since much US-MARC communications is from a library to itself (using a bibliographic service as an intermediary), such data still needs a place.

- *Circulation:* A local system might well add new fields to contain circulation information, although such information would rarely be communicated to other agencies.

Extensions to USMARC allow support for functions beyond the scope of USMARC, and make it possible to experiment with functions not yet standardized in USMARC. USMARC's explicit provision for extensions, reserving ranges of tags, makes it possible for designers to add local functions without fear of conflict when USMARC changes. This explicit provision protects the generality of the formats and reduces the need for extensions that violate the normal structure of USMARC.

20

MARC-Compatible Systems and Formats

Very few library automation systems use pure USMARC internally. Most systems and most internal formats are, at best, MARC-compatible. *MARC compatibility* has become a stock term in library automation, but the term does not have a precise meaning and may be used in a way that is misleading. More recently, the related but even more confusing term *MARClike* has been used in some cases.

MARC compatibility may relate to systems or formats:

- A MARC-compatible system should be able to process USMARC records directly, reading any standard USMARC records and, as needed, writing or restoring them without loss of content, content designation, or structure.

- A MARC-compatible format is typically "somehow related to MARC." Ideally, however, a MARC-compatible format is one to which USMARC records can be converted reversibly: without loss of content or content designation on import or export. Alternatively, a MARC-compatible format may be one that can be processed using the same programs that process pure US-MARC.

No single meaning for MARC compatibility will suffice, but a clear distinction can be made between full compatibility and partial compatibility. This chapter and (generally) this book reserve the term *MARC-compatible* for systems and formats that can accept and regenerate USMARC records without loss of information. Other formats and systems are partially compatible at best. In practice most systems and formats called *MARC-compatible* or *MARClike* are only partially compatible. Chapter 21 discusses partially compatible formats.

The Significance of Compatibility

Why is MARC compatibility important? A circulation system does not require a full bibliographic record and can store a limited record more efficiently. Acquisitions records need not be comprehensive; you don't need tracings for orders. Why should a library care whether a system is fully MARC-compatible?

MARC compatibility means *flexibility*, and allows a library to move toward an integrated system. A brief record may suffice for a circulation system, but will reduce access in an online catalog. If you can use an existing bibliographic record to produce an order, you'll do less keying than you would to enter even the most minimal acquisitions record—and the item will be cataloged, needing only call numbers and locations to complete processing.

MARC-compatible systems are designed for the future: with full compatibility, a library can provide data for regional union lists, can use new programs to provide new services, and can take advantage of advances in library automation. MARC provides a common ground for sharing data; without compatibility, a library is foreclosing such sharing.

Precise Compatibility: USMARC

What constitutes precise compatibility? One definition stated a few years ago is almost certainly too strict:

The highest level of USMARC compatibility is identity. Identity normally results from common implementation of a single comprehensive standard by more than one agency. Identity implies that all processes working on one case will work the same on other cases. It requires that the character set, record structure, content designation, data element identification, coded values, and rules for content be the same in all cases.

An implementation of USMARC would be identical to USMARC if it included all (and only) data elements contained in the *MARC Formats for Bibliographic Data*, stored in ALA Extended ASCII, using the structural definitions given in *MFBD*, and using ISBD punctuation and *AACR2* cataloging rules as used in *MFBD*.[1]

In fact, non-*AACR2* cataloging can still be USMARC in its purest form, as can records with non-ISBD punctuation, as long as all content designation is precisely as stated in *UFBD*. The purest form of USMARC, however, is usually represented only by LC MARC—that is, records distributed by the Library of Congress.

The problem with identity is that the only fields allowed are those fully defined in *UFBD*. While those fields allow comprehensive descriptive cataloging and access points, they do not allow for local call numbers, locations, or other local data. Library practitioners tend to include fields as part of USMARC that are not actually defined in the national formats, such as OCLC fields 049, 949, and 090-099.

You should distinguish between full compatibility and strict identity. A fully compatible format is one that can accept pure USMARC records and regenerate them without loss of data or content designation; such a format need not be identical to LC MARC.

Tape Blocking

One aspect of pure LC MARC is tape blocking. The Library of Congress and WLN use a moderately sophisticated method of ar-

---

1 Walt Crawford, "Library Standards for Data Structures and Element Identification: U.S. MARC in Theory and Practice," *Library Trends* 23, no. 4 (Fall 1982): 265-281.

ranging records on tape, which avoids any wasted space due to records of varying length. This special blocked and spanned format, which follows current ANSI and ISO standards, was initiated in 1977 and is used in all MARC Distribution Service tapes.

The LC MARC tape format makes each physical record exactly 2,048 characters long. Each physical record contains one or more record segments. Each record segment begins with a segment control word, which contains the length of the segment and a single numeric control character. The control character assigns one of four possible meanings to the record segment:

- *0:* Complete logical record, beginning and ending within the physical record.
- *1:* Initial segment, beginning in this physical record but continuing to at least one more physical record.
- *2:* Intermediate segment, a physical record that neither begins nor completes a logical record. Each intermediate segment must, by definition, fill a complete physical record.
- *3:* Terminal segment, the conclusion of a logical record that began in an earlier physical record.

An average MARC Distribution Service record will be around 800-1,000 characters for books, somewhat longer for most other formats. Many records will be much shorter, perhaps as short as 250 characters, and some records will be much longer, potentially well over 10,000 characters.

The tape blocking method described above saves input/output processing for shorter records, and can result in more records fitting on a reel of tape. The manner in which five extremely varied records would be written to tape using current LC format follows:

MARC Record A 800 characters
MARC Record B 600 characters
MARC Record C 2000 characters
MARC Record D 5000 characters
MARC Record E 300 characters

LC Tape Format
Physical Record 1
       [00805] Record A
       [00605] Record B
       [10638] Record C (beginning)
Physical Record 2
       [31372] Record C (end)
       [10676] Record D (beginning)
Physical Record 3
       [22048] Record D (continues)
Physical Record 4
       [22048] Record D (continues)
Physical Record 5
       [30248] Record D (end)
       [00305] Record E
...additional data

As of late 1988 OCLC and RLG still produce tapes using the pre-1977 LC MARC format. This format always uses at least one physical block for each logical record, and carries no special control words; multi-block records are recognized by their length, the first five characters of the leader. This "unblocked spanned" format requires more tape and more input/output operations, but does allow simpler software to read the records, and allows systems to add more records to an existing tape. Since OCLC and RLG do not use the LC tape format for most output tapes, neither agency produces pure LC MARC/ USMARC tapes. The same five records would be written as follows using the OCLC/RLG format:

Physical Record 1
          Record A
Physical Record 2
          Record B
Physical Record 3
          Record C
Physical Record 4
          Record D, first 2048 characters
Physical Record 5
          Record D, characters 2049-4096
Physical Record 6
          Record D, characters 4097-5000
Physical Record 7
          Record E

Note that both OCLC and RLG can and do produce tapes using the current LC tape format, at least when writing tapes to go to LC. Continued use of the old format is for the convenience of users and third-party vendors, not for the convenience of OCLC or RLG.

System Compatibility at the Precise LC MARC Level

Precise compatibility poses two different potential problems for a computer system:

- For input data, a system supporting only precisely compatible records and tapes would not be able to handle normal OCLC or RLIN tapes and would not be able to accommodate any added information from those or other tape providers,

- For output data, a system guaranteeing precise compatibility would not be able to communicate any significant local information to another system.

In practice, almost every MARC-based processing system must go beyond precise compatibility to support a variety of extensions and transformations, and almost every system provides some extensions on output.

Beyond Precise Compatibility

Fully compatible formats and systems differ from pure USMARC in two ways: extensions and transforms. Extended formats, generally called simply USMARC in this book, use the pure USMARC structure and incorporate all *UFBD* fields, but add additional information. Thus, a pure USMARC record can be converted to the extended format and restored intact, but some extended records can't be converted to pure USMARC without loss of data.

Transformed formats carry the same information as USMARC, but carry it in a different way. Pure USMARC records can be mechanically converted to the transformed format, and mechanically restored to pure USMARC, again without loss of content or content designation. Extended formats can be processed using standard USMARC software, but transformed formats usually can't. As a result, formats involving transforms are *not* MARClike or USMARC, but may still be MARC-compatible.

Extensions

The most commonly used USMARC formats are actually *supersets* of USMARC, as discussed in chapter 19. That chapter illustrates the most common form of USMARC extension, content designation. At least two other forms of extension are possible: character set extensions and structural extensions.

Character Set Extensions

USMARC uses a much larger character set than is standard for most computers. ANSEL, the American National Standard Extended Latin character set used in USMARC, contains more than 150 printable characters, including the special characters and diacritical symbols needed for most languages that use the roman alphabet. Materials in nonroman languages require other graphic displays; until fairly recently, addition of such graphics constituted an extension to US-MARC.

The New York Public Library began adding Cyrillic and Hebrew characters to MARC records years ago, using their own techniques to identify character strings as nonroman. Those character set extensions were proper supersets. USMARC records containing only ANSEL characters are stored alongside records with additional characters, and the extended records can be transformed to records that do not contain character set extensions.

Since USMARC now provides standard means to store and identify nonroman characters, discussed in chapter 16, character-set extensions are mostly a thing of the past.

Structural Extensions

Database management systems typically store USMARC records in a different structure. That structure may contain elements that assist in processing and that constitute extensions to USMARC. Unlike character set extensions and content designation extensions, structural extensions cannot usually be communicated in USMARC communications format.

One known structural extension uses hierarchical structures for location and copy information, where copy information is contained within location structures. USMARC does not allow for hierarchical structures; an internal system that uses such structures for data entry and storage typically establishes a methodology for representing the structures within the linear format of USMARC, using content designation extensions in order to communicate the internal information.

Transforms

Reversible formats involve one or more transforms that distinguish them from pure USMARC. The four transforms discussed below are samples of possible transforms. All four are actually used in the United States in one way or another. All four types of transforms have two key aspects in common:

- The records can be converted back to pure USMARC by computer, without human intervention and without loss of content or content designation.

- The transforms simplify processing in some manner. Otherwise, the work of doing the transform would be unnecessary overhead.

Character Set Transforms

USMARC uses ANSEL, which is an extended version of ASCII (American Standard Code for Information Interchange). ASCII is simply a standard set of binary representations for characters. Regular ASCII uses seven binary digits for each character. ANSEL uses an eighth binary digit. There are ninety-four printable characters in ASCII; adding another digit doubles the number of printable characters to 188, and ANSEL uses most of the 188 possible character positions.

ASCII is the standard representation for most computer manufacturers in the United States; the one major exception, IBM, bases its large systems (but not its personal computers) on EBCDIC (Extended Binary Coded Decimal Interchange Code). Since IBM computers are widely used in large-scale library automation, many systems use an extended version of EBCDIC to store MARC data. An informal 1981 survey suggests that most very large operations, including OCLC, RLIN, and WLN, use extended EBCDIC internally—for that matter, even the Library of Congress uses extended EBCDIC for internal processing. Whatever character set is used internally, all normal transmission of MARC records on tape is in ANSEL. There are two good reasons for this:

- ANSEL is part of the communications standard,

- There is no single definition for extended EBCDIC; there are at least two distinct versions of extended EBCDIC in common use.

Use of extended EBCDIC for internal processing is generally transparent to the user. If your system can read ANSEL, you needn't be concerned with the character set chosen for internal operations.

Communications Transforms

USMARC was originally designed as a tape communications format, and functions very well in that role. Certain systems may modify the structure of USMARC for online communications without loss of information. One communications transform was used by RLIN for several years to support the "PASS command," in which a record is passed from an RLIN terminal to some other system.

The "PASS command" used a transform for two reasons: the transform reduced the number of characters that must be transmitted; and it was simpler to convert the RLIN internal form into the "PASS" form than into extended MARC form. The "PASS" transform takes the content-carrying elements of the leader and attaches fields, beginning each field with its tag and ending each field with a field terminator. Figure 20.1 shows the record for *Bibliographic Displays in the Online Catalog* using the old "PASS" form.

In this example, the structural transform saves about 20 percent in length. Since this record has only one moderately long field and quite a few short fields, that savings is probably greater than could typically be expected. The "PASS" format was useful only for compressed communications; it lacked the validation capabilities built into USMARC and would be much slower to process, but could be transformed back to USMARC form using a simple program. Note that RLIN now uses MARC to pass records, just as the online transfers in the Linked Systems Project use MARC as it stands.

Offset	Text
0	nam___a_001RLINCRLG86-B27¶005198807281655537.0¶0088
50	61014s1986___nyu_____00110_eng_¶1010_‡a__
100	860153481020__‡a0867291982_(soft)_:‡c$30.00¶1040__‡
150	dCStRLIN¶0500_‡aZ699.3‡b.C69_1986¶0820_‡a025.3/028
200	/5‡219¶10010‡aCrawford,_Walt.¶24510‡aBibliographic
250	_displays_in_the_online_catalog_/‡cby_Walt_Crawfor
300	d,_with_Lennie_Stovel_and_Kathleen_Bales.¶2600_‡aW
350	hite_Plains,_NY_:‡bKnowledge_Industry_Publications
400	,‡cc1986.¶1300__‡avi,_359_p._:‡c_28_cm.¶1440_0‡aProf
450	essional_librarian_series¶1500__‡aIncludes_index.¶65
500	0_0‡aCatalogs,_On-line.¶1650_0‡aOn-line_bibliograp
520	hic_searching.¶1650_0‡aInformation_display_systems‡
600	xLibrary_applications.¶1650_0‡aInformation_display_
650	systems‡xFormatting.¶1650_0‡aMachine-readable_bibli
700	ographic_data.¶70010‡aStovel,_Lennie.¶70010‡aBales
750	,_Kathleen.¶§

Figure 20.1: Structural Transform

Does a PASS-like format represent a "more efficient" or "better" format than full USMARC for telecommunications? The Linked Systems Project designers didn't think so. In those cases where direct transmission of USMARC is sensible, transmission would typically involve small numbers of records at any given time. The 15-20 percent overhead of full MARC appears to be minor in the overall scheme of telecommunications needs. The loss of error-checking and the need to restore full USMARC would appear to counterbalance any efficiency in transmission time.

Storage Transforms

USMARC as a structure is very well suited to sequential processing; it is not as well suited to direct access, as in an online catalog. USMARC as a format was never designed for direct online use and, in fact, was not designed for processing use at all.

Many online implementations transform USMARC data into a different structure that is better suited to direct access. In some cases the data structure must suit the needs of a database management system. As with character set transforms, storage transforms are usually transparent to the user. A system will typically convert US-MARC into its internal storage format when records are read, and convert records back to a USMARC structure for batch processing or communications.

Content Designation Transforms

A system need not store USMARC records with three-digit tags. The BALLOTS II system at Stanford used mnemonics to identify each field, both in data entry and in the database itself. What USMARC calls the 100 field, BALLOTS II called "MEPN" for Main Entry Personal Name. BALLOTS II transformed the content designation of USMARC, reversing the transform when producing tapes.

Quite a few library automation systems, including WLN, use mnemonics for entry and display of MARC variable fields. Even more use mnemonics for entry and display of elements within the leader and variable control fields. Systems can be implemented using mnemonics to define and store elements, or using them as aliases for entry and display. For example, the RLIN database stores fields 007 and 008 as single fields, but displays them as sets of mnemonics and values; OCLC also displays 008 values with mnemonic labels. Another possible transform uses dummy subfield codes to make single-character codes easier to recognize; OCLC uses this technique for field 007.

Mnemonics were more popular in the early years of MARC II, when many analysts felt that numeric MARC tags were too foreign for easy acceptance by librarians. Mnemonics were designed to ease the way into computer-supported systems, although some systems (specifically OCLC) implemented tags for data entry at an early stage.

In the last decade USMARC tags and subfields have become a common language; OCLC's success has contributed to this situation.

The brevity and clarity of tags also helped make them known and used. It is easier to say and write *111* than *Main Entry—Conference or Meeting Name*, and *x11*, when understood, is a particularly brief way of saying *Conference or Meeting Name in any use, including Main Entry, Subject, Series, or Other Added Entry*. Most catalogers dealing with MARC now work directly with tags; the Library of Congress is now converting its systems so that catalogers work directly with tags.

Communications and Processing

USMARC was designed as a *communications* format. Since it was never designed for online use, transformations for such use are natural and proper. USMARC is itself used extensively for batch processing but, here too, some transformation may make sense to make processing work better.

If a processing system uses USMARC for input and output, or uses an output format that is an extended version of USMARC as defined in this chapter, the processing system is fully MARC-compatible and can be considered a MARC-based processing system. The *internal* form in which records are stored is irrelevant, as long as the following is true:

- The internal form is strictly internal, that is, is never used to communicate records,
- The system will properly map all legitimate USMARC records to and from the internal format, both now and in the future.

Testing for MARC Compatibility

Conceivably a standard test suite could be prepared to test a system for MARC compatibility without knowledge of the internal format. Recently some vendors have suggested that such test suites should be available, and that library vendors should be expected to validate their systems against such a suite before asserting MARC compatibility. The late 1980s and early 1990s may see work progress toward such a test suite. To some extent MARC is a moving target; vendors and customers alike may benefit from the ability to determine how closely a system comes to hitting that target.

A useful test suite should test for the limitations discussed in chapter 21. It should also test for widely known extensions to US-MARC, since such extensions appear in most MARC communications. Most likely, relatively few systems would pass a rigorous test suite in its entirety. Ideally, the results of such a suite would enable a vendor to state clearly exactly what limitations its current system had in regard to complete MARC compatibility.

Predictability

If a library could know the limitations, backed up by objective tests, then the library could predict what problems it might have with unusual MARC records. Predictability, in this case, may be as important as compatibility.

There's nothing wrong with being less than 100 percent compatible with every theoretically feasible MARC record. For instance, very few real-world systems could handle a MARC record totaling more than 64,000 characters in length or containing fields more than 9,999 characters long, even though the formats do contain mechanisms that support such extreme lengths. But a system that can handle only 100 fields in a MARC record, while quite adequate for many (perhaps most) purposes, would fail to meet the needs of some archival users in a way that a system limiting records to 64,000 characters would not.

Problems arise because nobody can be quite sure what "almost totally MARC-compatible" means. Some possible meanings appear in chapter 21, but by no means all of them. A standardized test suite, particularly one that could clearly identify the types of failures encountered, would do much to improve predictability and, as a result, to improve communication within the library automation field.

21

Partially Compatible Formats and Systems

Moving beyond the well-defined area of formats and systems fully compatible with USMARC, a great many systems and formats are *partially* compatible. Theoretically, partial compatibility should not be necessary and should be avoided. Realistically, partial compatibility makes sense for some systems and formats.

Unfortunately, there are no clear definitions for partial compatibility—and there have been, and continue to be, cases where partially compatible systems are labeled MARC-compatible. A partially compatible system may be one with some minor limits on the size or complexity of MARC records that can be handled, or it may be one with only the slightest relationship to MARC.

This chapter considers some known and possible varieties of partially compatible formats and systems. The list is far from complete. As in chapter 20, this discussion usually does not distinguish between formats and systems, except where the distinction is critical to a particular point.

Compatible Systems with Minor Restrictions

Many systems can accept, store, and regenerate *almost* all US-MARC records. If the restrictions are known, documented, and stated clearly, and if exceptions are handled gracefully, such systems can be regarded as fully MARC-compatible for most purposes. These systems represent typical real-world limitations on the full variety of USMARC. A few examples of minor restrictions follow.

Record Length Restrictions

Some systems can accept and reconstruct any USMARC record as long as the record does not exceed a certain length. If that *certain length* is high enough for the records actually needed within a system, and if overlength records are truncated intelligently and reported, such systems will work perfectly well.

Records for books typically average less than 1,000 characters (not including local information); probably less than 1 percent of records distributed by LC are over 2,000 characters. Addition of extensions for holdings and other local data can change this dramatically, as can the special nature of some formats. For example, RLIN MARC records average 1,200 characters and about 2 percent are over 2,000 characters; the *average* record length for computer files records in RLIN was over 2,360 characters in mid-1988 (although that length was based primarily on the very long ICPSR records).

Most commercial database systems impose length limitations. For popular library automation systems, this limit can be as low as 3,000 characters. Most bibliographic services have had, or continue to have, length limits. When BALLOTS was still used primarily by Stanford, the tape output program had a length limit of 2,048 characters; RLIN II has a tape limit of 30,000 characters, but a smaller database limit of around 20,000-24,000 characters. Both OCLC and the Library of Congress have length limits on output records, though both limits have increased over the years and are now sufficient to handle almost all records.

A 2,000-character limit may cause problems in most libraries; a 10,000-character limit would rarely cause difficulties except in a collection of archival and manuscript materials. The critical points are that the limit must be known and stated, and that the record-handling software must report when a record has exceeded the limit and take some reasonable action.

Field Length Restrictions

Some systems can handle very long records, but have problems with very long fields. The Library of Congress has distributed USMARC records with contents notes (field 505) in excess of 1,500 characters. Online systems can have problems with such fields, as the single field may run to more than one screen.

A system that limits field length to 1,500 characters will seldom have problems; if it handles those problems automatically there is no real loss of compatibility. A system that limits fields to 500 characters is much less compatible; intervention is required to handle what will be fairly frequent errors. If the length limit is much less than 500 characters, the limit isn't minor. A system with (for example) a 256-character field limit will cause serious ongoing problems and can't be considered to be very MARC-compatible.

Format Restrictions

When USMARC consisted of seven different bibliographic formats for different material types, some systems did not handle all seven formats. That inability—usually arising either because the system's users never intended to deal with certain formats or because the system's designers simply hadn't added format-specific tables—did not limit the system in dealing with other USMARC formats.

Format integration seems likely to eliminate *bibliographic* type-of-material limitations in systems; if a system fully implements one type of material, it will have implemented them all. But authorities and holdings will continue to be special cases. A bibliographic processing system can be fully MARC-compatible for bibliographic records without any ability to read, process, or write authorities or holdings records. Any such system should include, somewhere in its documentation, the restriction to bibliographic records. In practice, at this time, it may be assumed that a system does *not* accommodate the

MARC formats for holdings or authorities unless such support is explicitly stated.

Miscellaneous Restrictions

Some systems may impose other restrictions on USMARC records. As long as the restrictions are well-defined, and do not significantly limit acceptability of USMARC records, the systems may still be highly compatible. A few of the possible restrictions:

- *Character Extensions.* Very few systems or formats are prepared to handle nonroman representations of text such as Chinese, Japanese, Korean, Cyrillic, Hebrew, or Arabic. USMARC now has standard methods for storing such text, and the methods allow systems that can't handle the characters to discard them without damaging the rest of the record. If a system retains nonroman text without displaying it, the system may be considered fully compatible. If the system strips 880 and 066 fields and leading subfield ‡6s when data is loaded, records will be meaningful but some records will lose data. If a system is simply unable to deal with records containing nonroman text, the system is less compatible and, probably, out of date.

- *USMARC Extensions.* Some systems cannot handle the added fields defined in OCLC MARC or RLIN MARC. Such systems may be wholly USMARC-compatible in a technical sense. A system that can't handle format extensions, however, may not be able to play a full role in the emerging national complex of bibliographic interchange.

- *Explicit Record Restrictions.* A system could restrict entry of certain forms of records, such as those not cataloged to *AACR2* standards, or those not showing complete descriptive cataloging. Some systems restrict record entry based on authority control, by deliberate design. It seems likely that any such restriction would be very well known to a system's users, and might well be considered desirable.

- *Explicit Field Restrictions.* A system might have deliberate restrictions on certain obscure fields; if such restrictions do not affect most records, do not affect usefulness, and are well known to users, the system may be considered highly compatible.

- *Complexity Restrictions.* Some systems can handle long fields and long records, but can handle only a certain number of fields per record (or, in some cases, can only *index* a certain number of fields). If the number is high enough—500, for example—the restriction is nearly meaningless, at least outside of the archival community. If the number is small—25, for example—the system will cause serious ongoing problems for its users.

A clear distinction should be made between highly compatible systems as discussed in this section and less compatible systems, discussed in the rest of this chapter. *Most* present-day systems—including RLIN, OCLC, and LC's internal systems—are highly compatible as stated in this section, having some minor restrictions on field or record acceptability. For practical purposes, such systems are MARC-based, MARC-compatible systems. Lower-level systems pose greater problems; generally, any system below this level should be considered partially compatible at best.

Outdated Systems

Many MARC-compatible systems and formats become outdated as USMARC changes to meet new needs. Maintenance of format currency requires significant support from library and computer professionals. If a system is to maintain current compatibility, staff must be assigned to keep the system up to date.

Major shared cataloging systems and library automation vendors typically use the equivalent of at least one full-time highly skilled employee to monitor and maintain USMARC formats. This full-time equivalent might be composed of continuing part-time work by two or more people who are responsible for USMARC updates, augmented by others who prepare and implement actual changes.

If a system is a year out of date, but the system developers are working on upgrades, it may still be workable, and may be restored to a high level of compatibility. If a system is not being maintained at all, it will tend to drift down to lower levels of compatibility and usefulness with time, as more and more records are not handled properly or at all.

Every system falls a little behind at times, but if a system appears to be more than a year behind the published USMARC formats, there should be a good explanation. If it is several years behind—if, for example, a system in 1988 does not properly handle field 773—there is clear evidence that the system is not being maintained and should be considered incompatible with USMARC.

Subsets of USMARC

Some systems and formats retain the content and content designation of USMARC but lose portions of quite a few records. These systems can regenerate a USMARC record that will pass USMARC validity tests, but that may be missing known categories of information from the original record. A proper subset record will contain *at least* the core fields for any USMARC record accepted, retaining all standard ASCII characters and providing ASCII substitutions for extended alphabetic characters. Subset-compatible systems do not maintain reversibility for records that are accepted.

Character Set Subsets

Most USMARC records do not contain diacritics or special characters, and most library processes do not require such characters. Highly compatible systems may store diacritics but suppress them for all displays and products; that suppression does not compromise a system's MARC compatibility. Other systems may discard diacritics and handle special characters in one of two ways:

- Translating special characters to standard ASCII equivalents: Ø becomes *O*, ^{Z} becomes 2, β becomes *beta*. This technique maintains meaningful, useful character strings. Efforts are now under way to establish standard normalizations for indexing and retrieval; such efforts may also result in a standard set of equivalences to use for nonreversible translation of special characters. If so, systems failing to maintain the special characters will at least not necessarily suffer in terms of retrieval power.

- Discarding all characters outside of normal ASCII. If records containing special characters are fed into these systems, the results can be peculiar, as words may be missing letters.

Many highly compatible systems use standard ASCII for display or listing, and most inexpensive display devices are restricted to standard ASCII. For that matter, many displays designed for library use can only display diacritics as separate characters; a proper device for retrieval and use (rather than input and editing) will show the diacritics over and under the following letter, which requires even higher resolution and more sophisticated software.

Libraries must determine how crucial storage of diacritics and special characters is for their future needs. For large research libraries and libraries with extensive non-English holdings, loss of extended characters may well be quite important; for other libraries, the loss may be insignificant.

Field Subsets

Quite a few systems can read USMARC records and regenerate records in USMARC format, but can store only selected fields. If the selected fields constitute reasonably complete bibliographic records, these systems are moderately compatible, reversible with known losses.

Some systems allow a library to make its own decisions regarding completeness. In this case the system itself may be highly compatible; the reduction to moderate compatibility is at the library's option.

Some systems may allow partial record retention for an online database, with full retention offline; such systems can provide short-term efficiencies without reducing a library's long-term flexibility.

One-Way Compatibility

Some systems can accept USMARC records as input but eliminate so much content or content designation that they cannot generate anything that could legitimately be called full USMARC. Such systems offer convertibility from MARC, or unidirectional compatibility.

Conceivably, a system could work the other way around: it could be unable to read USMARC but fully able to generate USMARC output. The uses of such a system seem unclear, except for a system used entirely for original cataloging.

In the past many systems called "MARC-compatible" have actually offered convertibility. Unidirectional compatibility is the fuzziest area of USMARC compatibility, and the area most open to abuse.

Selective Field Retention

Bibliographic records can be compact or lengthy, depending partly on what fields are used. If a circulation system uses only the 1xx, 245‡a, and 260 ‡c, why should the system store all the other fields? If a library never intends to expand its automation, or recognizes that the circulation-system database may be useless for building an online catalog database, brutally selective field retention may be reasonable. Typically, systems that retain very few fields also throw away subfield codes and indicators; if you're abandoning the format, there is little point in halfway measures.

Lack of Output Facilities

Some library systems, particularly systems for small libraries, may not be designed to generate machine-readable records for use by any other system. Such systems could store USMARC records in a manner that would allow regeneration, but be unable to carry out the regeneration.

If a system lacks machine-readable output facilities but stores data in a fully compatible manner, it can be upgraded to full USMARC compatibility with a small development effort. Most systems that lack machine-readable output facilities also change USMARC data on input, for a variety of reasons.

Loss of Internal Content Designation

Systems may retain most content from USMARC records but eliminate indicators and subfield codes as "unnecessary overhead." Such systems retain most of the information needed for searching or display, and may *seem* to be fully compatible.

Problems may arise when libraries attempt to add other functions, because of reduced flexibility of record use and machine manipulation. This reduced flexibility is not matched by a savings in storage. There are savings (typically no more than 5 percent to 10 percent), but they are not sufficient to balance the loss of specificity.

In practice, systems that discard internal content designation are likely to do so for reasons other than storage, such as difficulty in suppressing subfield codes on display. The problem is that the information is lost forever. A well-designed library automation system can suppress subfield codes on display with little trouble; once the subfield codes are gone, they cannot be restored.

Subfield codes and indicators are there for specific reasons: to improve access, support more flexible displays, allow enhanced retrieval and filtering and otherwise make records more useful. A system that discards content designation may be based on a short-sighted view of the library's future needs.

Loss of Field Specificity

The next step after dropping subfield codes is to drop field specificity. A typical record includes author, title, imprint, notes, and subjects: a system could store all this in five fields. Going a bit further, a system could store a record as Headings, Imprint, and Notes: three fields in all.

Such a scheme simplifies data handling, and may well work better with a database management system, but has all the disadvantages noted above, and more. Collapsed fields compromise access as well as flexibility; acceptance of such a system severely limits future use of a database.

Extreme Limitations

Some older and smaller systems limit data in extreme ways. Most such systems are survivors of earlier days in library automation and should be avoided in today's marketplace. Some examples of extreme limitations include the following:

- systems that store information as upper-case letters, numbers, and punctuation;
- systems that limit fields to very short lengths (e.g. fifty characters for authors, forty characters for titles, or even 100 characters for a title field);
- systems that eliminate all content designation and all fields other than a tiny subset.

Incompatible Systems

There have been cases where a system or format was called MARC-compatible even though it could neither accept USMARC records nor generate USMARC records. At best, these systems represent marketing ploys or mistakes.

A system or format is incompatible with USMARC if records in either format cannot be algorithmically converted into the other format in any useful manner. If a system uses MARC tags—or something like MARC tags—but can neither accept USMARC input in machine-readable form nor generate USMARC output in machine-readable form, it may well be "MARClike" in some promoter's eyes, but it is simply not MARC-compatible.

Some library automation systems make no claims for MARC compatibility, although the universe of such systems is probably shrinking. Five years ago it was reasonable to say that such systems might properly meet certain needs for certain libraries, and that total incompatibility with MARC was not necessarily a disabling characteristic.

It may not have been disabling in 1984, but it should be considered a major strike against any system—even a system for very small libraries—in 1989, at least if the system deals with bibliographic data in any meaningful sense. If a system handles any level of bibliographic data and does not maintain MARC compatibility, the burden should be on the vendor to demonstrate that incompatibility is justified. That justification may be difficult.

Microcomputer-based systems can and do handle USMARC records. The additional space required for pure USMARC is relatively minor in most systems; the supposed savings of abandoning content designation or partial content always comes at a price down the road. Any vendor that understands the library market and is seriously interested in serving that market will have learned the complexities of USMARC and established simple, fast routines for handling the records.

There are certainly library-related systems that do not, and should not, involve MARC compatibility—accounting systems, to take an obvious example. But for those systems in some way related to bibliographic data, the days of total ignorance of MARC should be long gone. With CD-ROM sources for MARC information, even very small libraries can build USMARC databases; there is little excuse for any system that requires direct data entry in an incompatible format.

The Case Against Full Compatibility

Complete bibliographic records are longer than they need to be for many applications. Full USMARC records are even longer than complete bibliographic records. Portions of USMARC records would never be displayed for public services or most technical processing, and USMARC content designation carries sophistication that is not needed for many processes.

Long records require more storage than short records; complex records require more sophisticated programming than simple records. Storage costs money, programming costs money, and complex programs sometimes run slower than simple programs.

Money and time are the primary justifications for lower-level compatibility. During the first year of operation, a well-designed system that stores only those data elements needed for the application and eliminates most content designation will almost certainly be cheaper than a similarly well-designed system that maintains full USMARC compatibility.

If a system is being custom-built by programmer/analysts who have not done complex MARC processing, the system will probably be operational sooner if the designers are allowed to reduce US-MARC to a format they are familiar with. Money and time argue against full USMARC compatibility.

Many existing systems were designed when full USMARC compatibility was considered unrealistic. Such systems continue to function; lack of full USMARC compatibility does not make them useless. If a local system maintains full USMARC in offline files, reflecting the current state of the bibliographic records, there is no good reason that a specific online system should carry full USMARC records. The records can always be retrieved from offline storage for any new function or change in needs, while the online system can operate with smaller storage and simpler programs (but see the next chapter).

The Case for Full Compatibility

Library needs change, and the desires and expectations of library users change. Costs of storage and computers also change, and the changes are in different directions. Needs, desires, and expectations almost always rise, while storage and computing costs generally fall at a rapid rate.

The compact record that suited the circulation system of 1978 will restrict access in the online catalog of 1988. The moderately complete record that provides access in the online catalog of 1985 may restrict a library's capacity to offer sophisticated special retrieval or listings in 1995. A short-term savings of lower-level compatibility may be paid for by long-term lack of flexibility. People who deal with full MARC become aware of the two fundamental rules of USMARC compatibility:

- You don't need to process or display all the information just because it's there.
- Once you discard information, don't expect to restore it. When it's gone, it's gone.

22

Library Use for USMARC

So far the discussion has centered on USMARC formats: their structure, how they work, what they include, how they were developed, and what may be meant by "MARC compatible." This chapter works from the other direction: USMARC as a tool to meet library needs.

When a library uses USMARC it needs to consider three major areas, which may involve vendors or other outside agencies:

- *acquiring USMARC records* from the Library of Congress, the major shared cataloging services, agencies that provide US-MARC as a byproduct or directly, or through retrospective conversion;

- *processing USMARC records* to maintain them for later use, and to provide needed services such as catalog cards, union lists, and acquisitions products;

- *using USMARC in local systems*, either turnkey systems provided by an outside agent, locally developed systems, or local extensions to purchased systems.

The final area is outside the scope of this book, although it may now be the most common use of USMARC. USMARC records can be used for any library automation that involves bibliographic materials, and for many that do not. But processing services and local systems do have common aspects in terms of reading and maintaining MARC records, no matter what the source of the records or the purpose of the systems. First, consider the sources of USMARC.

Sources of USMARC

The Library of Congress provides subscriptions to various classes of USMARC records such as books, serials, or films. LC's MARC Distribution Service offers large quantities of original cataloging that conforms to a common set of guidelines, at a low price per record. Records from LC are a major source of cataloging for all the shared cataloging services, most commercial agencies providing cataloging data, and a few large libraries.

Most libraries will *not* find MARC Distribution Service to be the most appropriate source. The tapes include more records than most libraries need, do not include local data, and require a substantial local processing system in order to extract needed records, add local data, and build a library's own database.

OCLC, RLIN, Utlas, and WLN provide millions of MARC records each year to thousands of libraries, providing only the records that libraries have requested. These services support various levels of local data in the records and give libraries access not only to LC cataloging but to contributed cataloging from many other libraries. Records from shared cataloging services cost more per record than MARC Distribution Service subscriptions, but are more likely to meet a library's particular needs. Each shared cataloging service also provides many of the processing services needed by libraries, including catalog cards and various other products.

Several companies (and LC) now sell USMARC databases on CD-ROM. For libraries undertaking major retrospective conversions, such databases may provide one major source of relatively inexpensive MARC data. The CD-ROM databases provide neither the scope nor the currency of the shared cataloging services, but do provide valuable sources of USMARC.

Other agencies including commercial vendors provide USMARC records in various ways. Several book vendors offer to provide cataloging along with the books, in card form or as MARC records; such vendors may be useful for smaller libraries. Some cooperative library agencies, including networks that broker OCLC services, provide additional sources of USMARC records or record processing.

Retrospective Conversion

When a library converts to an online public catalog or any catalog based on machine-readable files, library users and staff may be confronted by a split catalog. Materials cataloged in the last few years are in the online catalog, but older materials are not. Studies of online catalog use show that most people don't go past the first catalog; if something isn't in that catalog, it may as well not be in the library. Consider your own habits in using a library: most of us spend as little time at a card catalog as we possibly can. A split catalog and people's natural tendency to stop after the first lookup result in loss of access to much of a library's collection, including most serious literature and older works in the humanities. If weeding takes place based on use studies, valuable material may be discarded because lack of access has resulted in low circulation.

The solution to this problem is retrospective conversion—converting older (retrospective) manual records to machine-readable form. Retrospective conversion can yield a complete online catalog, but is neither simple nor inexpensive, and no single method is ideal for every library. Common methods include the following:

- *Online conversion* using large source databases, usually one of the shared cataloging services. Library staff take catalog cards and look for records that match, adding local holdings and call numbers when records are found. If no match is found, material will be converted to machine-readable form, possibly working to a lower-than-usual standard, since the material is usually not in hand. In some cases libraries will enter unmatched records directly into their local system rather than entering them into the major bibliographic service.

- *Batch conversion using unique keys* matched by a commercial agency, a library network, or a shared cataloging service. The library submits lists of keys on diskette, on tape, or in paper form; the service matches those lists against its database, returning matched records. In some cases local holdings are submitted along with the keys and added to the retrieved records. OCLC, WLN, and RLIN all support microcomputer-based batch retrospective conversion. Unique keys can include LC Card Number, ISBN, ISSN, or numbers assigned by an agency. Microcomputers have made batch conversion more feasible by making it easy and cheap for libraries to enter keys in machine-readable form. Unique-key batch conversion is typically done in combination with the next method, used where unique keys are not available.

- *Batch conversion using title or other search*, supported by almost every agency that provides unique-key batch conversion services. This method is used where no unique key is available or the key is ambiguous. This method requires more keyboard work and may be more error prone, but does not require the additional searching in other sources that may be needed for unique-key conversion (in those cases where the catalog cards do not contain unique keys). Contemporary microcomputer-based systems intermix unique-key and search techniques.

- *Contract keying or conversion.* The library photoreproduces its catalog cards and ships the film to an agency; that agency does searches or keys the cards into machine-readable form.

- *Full local record entry* in MARC form. If retrospective conversion is for brief-record entry only, full local entry may be useful for small and medium-sized libraries; if libraries are looking toward more extensive local systems requiring more extensive records, full local entry is likely to be too labor-intensive to be justified. As with contract keying, local record entry made more sense when OCLC, RLIN, and WLN databases were smaller. It may still make sense for very specialized collections, where the likely percentage of found records will be small.

Many libraries use some mix of techniques for various portions of total conversion. For example, a library might use batch conversion for a first pass, moving to online conversion for those records that did not yield single matches during batch conversion.

A library must have experienced MARC users—preferably cata-logers—available to evaluate the quality of retrospective conversion. A library must also establish its minimum standards and determine how much post-conversion editing it can afford to do. Retrospective conversion contracts are usually made on the basis of price, but the price of a conversion is not the cost of the conversion. If records are incomplete or scrambled, the cost of conversion in terms of required editing or lost information may be much higher than the direct price. A trial conversion may be the only way to evaluate the quality of an agency's work.

Processing and Local Use

Once USMARC record sources are identified, the records must be processed and used. Vendors and processing agencies provide a number of processing services, including the following:

- *Tape checking and maintenance:* OCLC MARC subscriptions and RLIN transaction tapes need to be checked promptly, and need to be refreshed periodically to be sure no deterioration has occurred. Some vendors provide such services, possibly combined with elimination of duplicates, for libraries that are building toward local systems;

- *File maintenance and authority control:* Vendors that check and maintain tapes may also maintain MARC files. This involves sorting the records on the tapes into some predetermined order, then replacing records with newer versions as they appear. Some vendors also apply authority control to existing records, validating and updating bibliographic headings based on authority files,

- *Conversion to other formats:* Some vendors convert USMARC tapes into formats required for local circulation systems or other systems when those systems can't accept USMARC directly,

- *Product generation:* A number of vendors prepare printed or microform products from databases made up of MARC tapes submitted by a library. Such products can include full catalogs, lists of new holdings, and specialized access lists,

- *Union list generation:* Vendors can combine tapes for several libraries into unified databases and products, including union lists on paper, fiche, or CD-ROM.

Problems with USMARC Tapes

Any supplier of USMARC records, whether commercial, bibliographic service, or the Library of Congress, will occasionally supply a bad tape. Tape problems fall into a number of distinct categories:

- *Incorrect or blank tapes.* No agency can guarantee that every tape will be labeled and shipped correctly. All tapes, whether from LC, shared cataloging services, or other vendors, should receive an initial reading and check immediately after receipt. Some agencies may (quite reasonably) be unable or unwilling to replace a defective tape after a stated period has elapsed.

- *Tapes with defective records.* Magnetic tape is a somewhat imperfect medium; flaws in the creation, shipping, or reading process can render one or more records unreadable.

- *Incorrect records.* The chance of invalid MARC structure from LC or the shared cataloging services is very small; any such case would probably be caused by physical tape defects. Newer vendors may have problems that have not been identified or resolved, but such problems can usually be straightened out once they are apparent. Records from any source may sometimes have incorrect content designation or contents.

- *Misunderstandings.* Agencies receiving MARC Distribution Service tapes may expect that LC will implement all MARC format changes exactly on schedule, and that any current tape will contain cataloging that follows current interpretations. Neither expectation is based on LC assertion or on reality. LC's distribution of MARC format changes is based on the wider needs of the library community as well as its own needs.

Misunderstandings may also arise with bibliographic services when changes are made in tape format or content. It is the bibliographic service's responsibility to document its practices and identify the date when practices change, but it is the library's responsibility to read that documentation and pass it on to processing agencies. Misunderstandings with other vendors may arise through documentation problems, contractual problems, simple communication problems or failure to perform. In every case careful attention to the promises made and services actually received should avoid some problems and resolve others.

Reading MARC Records

Whether you do your own processing or a vendor does it for you, the first step is to read the tapes. Even if a vendor is archiving tapes for you until you're ready to use them, the vendor must read the records to assure proper maintenance of the tapes.

Physical Structure

The physical structure of a MARC tape includes the number of tracks, the density of information expressed in bits per inch (BPI), the labeling, and the character set. Most USMARC tapes are nine-track.

though some suppliers may offer seven-track tapes as an alternative. Three tape densities are widely used: 800 BPI, 1600 BPI, and 6250 BPI. Some USMARC suppliers offer libraries a choice of 800 BPI or 1600 BPI; others offer 1600 BPI or 6250 BPI and some may offer all three. Higher densities are generally preferable, if processing vendors can handle them. A density of 6250 BPI puts almost four times as much data on a reel of tape as 1600 BPI, and tapes written at 6250 BPI tend to be more reliable than those written at 1600 BPI. Some processing agencies, however, may not be able to read 6250 BPI tapes.

All standard MARC tapes use standard reel computer tape and all standard MARC tapes have standard internal ANSI labels and are written in ANSEL (or a minor variation from ANSEL). Other tapes represent alternative transmissions, but may well be used in certain cases. Alternative labeling schemes include unlabeled tapes, IBM OS labels, and IBM DOS labels; the only alternative character set in wide use is EBCDIC. Any tape that doesn't have ANSI labels and isn't written in ANSEL or an agreed variant isn't a standard MARC tape. Tapes with no internal labels may be rejected by processing centers, as they pose serious handling problems.

Logical Structure

Standard USMARC tapes come in two different logical structures. Some vendors may be unaware that two structures exist, and others may have a cloudy picture of what the two structures are. Computer processing agencies that have not previously handled MARC data will almost certainly not recognize either structure. The two structures were discussed in chapter 20.

Tape Checking and Reporting

You need to know what your vendor or processing center will do to make sure a MARC tape is valid and correct, particularly if the vendor is handling tapes for a library with no current local capabilities. Tapes do get mislabeled and can be damaged in shipping; without prompt checking it may be difficult or impossible to replace a bad tape.

Vendors should be willing to describe their checking procedures. At the very least, the tape should be read and records should be counted, with the final count compared to a count provided along with the tape. While such a process will show that the records are readable, and having the right number of records generally suggests that the correct tape is in hand, this process may not turn up minor tape problems.

A vendor may provide more thorough tape checking and analysis. Such analysis could include counts by type of material, consistency checks for the leader and directory, tests for library identifiers in appropriate locations, validity checks comparing the directory with the actual data, and possibly other tests. Libraries should be alerted to any anomalies found in such testing.

Handling MARC Extensions

You probably won't provide a vendor with pure USMARC tapes. Most USMARC tapes for individual libraries contain extensions to MARC, defined by shared cataloging services, vendors, or the libraries themselves. Can the vendor handle the tapes you provide? If you change sources for records, will the vendor be able to handle the change?

Keeping Up with USMARC Changes

Changes in MARC affect a vendor's ability to read and process records. Will a vendor keep up with changes in USMARC? Will the vendor actively pursue such changes, or handle them passively as client libraries request them?

Tape maintenance programs and simple processing systems may go for years without requiring change. Agencies may be using programs written elsewhere, or written by programmers no longer available to do maintenance. Vendors may not have staff with the library and computer background needed to analyze changes in USMARC. If a vendor has internal MARC expertise, you can probably get the name of at least one staff expert. If there is some doubt as to a vendor's actual knowledge, a brief discussion with that expert should resolve your questions.

Processing Limitations

You're satisfied that the vendor or agency can read the records you send, and that the vendor's view of USMARC will be kept up to date. If you're paying for processing in addition to tape maintenance, you need to know more about MARC handling. Reading USMARC is less complicated than processing USMARC. The vendor may be able to read all your records but may have some limits on processing. Chapters 20 and 21 show some of the limits that may be present. Ask vendors about their limitations. Every known system (including WLN, RLIN, and OCLC) has limitations, and vendors should be able and willing to specify what their limitations are.

Record Length and Complexity

How many access points can a single record generate? Archival and manuscripts control records may contain more than a hundred added entries; some sound recordings and other records may generate fifty or more entries. Can a system handle that many index points for a single record? Can it generate proper displays, with needed page breaks? Can it even store long records? Will the system be able to handle MARC holdings, including compression and expansion?

Other Limits

A new vendor or agency, particularly a college computer center or city data processing department, may have problems with the subfield delimiter and field terminator and with the extended characters. Any vendor that has successfully processed any MARC records will have resolved the delimiter and terminator problems, and most will have addressed the extended character situation.

Every known vendor, including the shared cataloging services, has some presentation limits. The most common presentation limit involves extended characters and nonroman characters. If a vendor translates extended characters in such a way that the product is meaningful, a limited character set may be acceptable and possibly even preferable. If a vendor simply ignores characters that cannot be printed, you will lose important information in many non-English records and a few English language items as well. Understand the vendor's limits, and consider them in light of your needs, comparative pricing, and alternative sources.

Unrecognized and Unused Data

A vendor that is building a database from your records may not include everything that's in the records. Acquisitions information isn't relevant for a union list, and coded fields are rarely relevant for a batch product of any sort. You may also provide data that the vendor can't deal with, either because it is outside the vendor's scope or because your record supplier has added elements that the vendor doesn't know about yet. What does the vendor do with such data? Is it all stored and maintained, is it listed out as error reports, or is it just thrown away? If you're satisfied with your current processing, you may not care; if you expect to add new functions later on, you'll want to be able to use the data. You should always remember: once data is lost, it is expensive or impossible to replace.

Maintenance

Every vendor that accepts your MARC tapes is doing some form of record maintenance. Tape maintenance vendors do so directly; other processing agencies maintain records indirectly. You may be assuming more maintenance than a vendor expects to provide; if so, you may have problems when your library adds new functions or integrates old ones.

"Maintenance" here means safeguarding records as received: records sent to a vendor in 1989 should be useful in 1994 when you bring up a different online catalog. Vendors may take a more active role, eliminating duplicate records or even upgrading records through authority control, but maintenance of existing data is a fundamental requirement.

Will a vendor retain all the data you supply? More to the point, will the vendor retain all the data in the most current version of each record? When a vendor is creating a fiche catalog, the vendor may not be retaining data irrelevant to that catalog. You should never assume that a vendor is providing full data maintenance: any such requirement should be explicitly stated in writing. You need full retention if you're planning for the future. USMARC is a foundation for successful library automation; the integrated systems of the future will rely even more heavily on the versatility of USMARC.

If your full records are only on tape, as is usually the case, you should know how often the tapes are checked or rewritten. Tape is a useful but imperfect medium. Tape does age, both physically and electrically; very old tapes that have never been refreshed are likely to be useless. The simple act of mounting a tape and winding it at high speed helps to maintain the tape's usefulness. Your archival tapes should probably be refreshed—which usually means copying to another tape—at least twice a year; quarterly refreshing is even better.

Is the vendor building a database on disk? If so, how often is the disk backed up to tape? Has the vendor attempted to restore a disk from the tape backup? Magnetic disks are extremely reliable, but do fail; such failures can be catastrophic. Disks can be backed up in two ways: on duplicate disk or on tape. A full set of duplicate disks can be maintained; this is the best, but most expensive, form of backup. Agencies that use this form are also likely to use tape backup. Tape backup copies all or portions of the database to magnetic tape on a regular basis, typically weekly; daily transactions are also backed up so that a faulty disk can be recreated from some combination of tapes. Backup methods need testing: there have been cases, not necessarily in library automation, where backups were done regularly but files could not be recovered from the backups.

Security involves two other issues. Is the library's data protected against electronic intrusion and destruction? A careful vendor will always have copies of your data in a form not accessible by telecommunications and may well have backup copies in remote storage, to protect against physical disasters. A more sensitive security issue is business failure. What happens to your data if the vendor goes out of business? Do you have written safeguards to assure that your data, and the information necessary to process that data, will be available to you in case of bankruptcy or default? This last issue has nothing to do with USMARC as such, but is an extreme example of the need to be sure that your data is there when you need it.

Times To Avoid USMARC

Should a library always use USMARC for every computer-based bibliographic system? No, not necessarily. In addition to the situations mentioned above where briefer, simpler records are used online but linked to full MARC on disk or tape, there are cases where USMARC represents unnecessary complexity and expense.

The most obvious cases are the small projects taken on by small libraries to gain some measure of control over a collection. If your library has no database of any sort, just acquired a microcomputer, and desperately needs a list of its 500 current periodicals, MARC is *not* the answer. What you need is a simple database (possibly even a word processing file) that will allow you to key in the titles and other relevant information, sort them, and print them out. Almost any simple database program should do: Reflex, pfs:File, Q&A, Notebook II, PC-File +, and many others.

If your library maintains an Information and Referral file and also has an online catalog based on USMARC, you may find it useful to define pseudo-MARC records for your I&R records, thus making them available in your online system. But if you just need to put your I&R records on a computer and don't have an online catalog, you can define a simpler and more appropriate format with a few hours of work.

Beyond the small library and the simple system, USMARC makes more and more sense. While a simple record format with two or three elements might work best for a one-shot list of 500 serial titles, a MARC-based system will almost certainly serve you better if you need to maintain control of 5,000 or 50,000 serials. It won't all be MARC, at least not today: serials checkin will probably use linked records in some entirely different format. But when you have 5,000 serials, you need the kind of bibliographic detail and flexibility that USMARC offers.

Using USMARC

The measures suggested earlier are designed to assure that your records are ready for use when your library is ready to use them. In most cases, whether you use a turnkey computer system, do your own programming, or some mixture of the two, your future library automation plans should be based on USMARC.

USMARC provides a common reference, a standard, a vocabulary. The data communications format allows for fast and flexible processing, while the common content designators allow you to use cataloging done by others and modify the records to serve your own needs. USMARC is not ideal for online storage and full USMARC is overkill for many library operations. Maintenance of full USMARC as a background activity preserves your options. Computers and storage are getting faster and cheaper, and users are becoming more sophisticated and more demanding. Relatively few of yesterday's library systems took full advantage of the richness of USMARC. Today, many systems make the most of MARC, and we may suppose that almost all of the next generation of systems will do so.

Even if you never actually see a tape reel of USMARC records, your library is likely to benefit from USMARC, now and in the future. Your awareness of the format and its implications helps you to work with that future.

Appendix A

USMARC: *Underlying Principles*

O n October 29, 1982, MARBI and the USMARC advisory group approved *The USMARC Formats: Underlying Principles*. While these principles changed nothing in the formats, they establish a framework for considering change and explain some principles used in building USMARC. The document appears here in full, interspersed with annotations (which appear as indented italic text).

Some changes and refinements in the principles have taken place since 1982, and significant changes are implied by adoption of format integration. Because the principles were never included in *MARC Formats for Bibliographic Data* or *USMARC Format for Bibliographic Data*, they have not been well-maintained. At the end of the numbered principles appear additional principles adopted as part of format integration.

Underlying Principles: Preface

T he following statement of underlying principles for content designation in the USMARC formats was approved on October 29, 1982, by the American Library Association's RTSD/LITA/RASD Committee on the Representation in Machine-Readable Form of Bibliographic Information (MARBI), in consultation with representatives from the national libraries and bibliographic networks. This statement is intended to reflect those principles which account for the current state of the USMARC formats and to constitute a provisional set of working principles for further format development. The statement will be included as prefatory material in *MARC Formats for Bibliographic Data* and *Authorities: A MARC Format* and will be revised as necessary in the future.

> *The key statement in the preface is "provisional set of working principles for further format development." This means that the Underlying Principles can serve as a filter for proposed changes. Those changes which do not follow the existing principles can be identified. If there is sufficient reason to violate the existing principles, the principles must be revised. For the first time, a written set of guidelines is available to use in considering format revision.*

Section 1. Introduction

1.1. The USMARC Formats are standards for the representation of bibliographic and authority information in machine-readable form.

1.2 A MARC record involves three elements: (1) the record structure, (2) the content designation, and (3) the data content of the record.

1.2.1. The structure of USMARC records is an implementation of the *American National Standard for Information Interchange on Magnetic Tape* (ANSI Z39.2-1979) and of *Documentation—Format for Bibliographic Information Interchange on Magnetic Tape* (ISO 2709-1981).

1.2.2. Content designation—the codes and conventions established explicitly to identify and further characterize the data elements within a record and to support the manipulation of that data—is defined in the USMARC Formats.

1.2.3. The content of those data elements which comprise a traditional catalog record is defined by standards outside the formats—such as the *Anglo-American Cataloguing Rules* or the *National Library of Medicine Classification*. The content of other data elements—

coded data (see Section 9. below)—is defined in the USMARC Formats.

1.3. A MARC format is a set of codes and content designators defined for encoding a particular type of machine-readable record.

1.3.1. At present, USMARC formats have been defined for two distinct types of records. *MARC Formats for Bibliographic Data* contains format specifications for encoding data elements needed to describe, retrieve, and control various types of bibliographic material. *Authorities: A MARC Format* contains format specifications for encoding data elements which identify or control the content and content designation of those portions of a bibliographic record which may be subject to authority control.

1.3.2. The *MARC Formats for Bibliographic Data* are a family of formats defined for the identification and description of different types of bibliographic material. USMARC Bibliographic formats have been defined for Books, Films, Machine-Readable Data Files, Manuscripts, Maps, Music, and Serials.

1.3.3. The USMARC Formats have attempted to preserve consistency of content designation across formats where this is appropriate. As the formats proliferated and became more complex, however, definitions and usages have diverged. While complete consistency has not been achieved, a continuing effort is being made to promote consistent definition and usage across formats.

The introduction neatly separates content designation from content. USMARC deals with content definition, but only for coded elements and other elements outside the scope of traditional cataloging. A USMARC record contains the contents of a cataloging record, but USMARC itself does not define those contents.

The final paragraph attempts to strike a balance between theory and practice. This is always an uneasy balance in USMARC, and has grown more sensitive as use of USMARC has flourished. If a change to the formats will increase consistency but would require that OCLC change 100,000 records or that RLIN change 50,000 records, there are strong reasons to oppose the change. Those who work on the formats are frequently engaged in compromise between theoretical consistency and the value of existing records.

Section 2. General Considerations

2.1. The USMARC Formats are communications formats, primarily designed to provide specifications for the exchange of records between systems. The communications formats do not mandate the internal formats to be used by individual systems, either for storage or display.

2.2. The USMARC Formats were designed to facilitate the exchange of information on magnetic tape. In addition, they have been widely adapted for use in a variety of exchange and processing environments.

These sections establish two important things: that USMARC does not mandate processing formats, and that USMARC is widely used for processing. The last sentence of the second paragraph is a key recognition of USMARC as a processing format, the first such recognition to appear in the published formats. Most online systems do not use USMARC structure, though they may use USMARC content designation. Many batch systems use all of USMARC, content designation and structure.

2.3. The USMARC Formats are designed for use within the United States. An attempt has been made to preserve compatibility with other national formats. Lack of international agreement on cataloging codes and practices has made complete compatibility impossible, however.

2.4. The USMARC Formats serve as a vehicle for bibliographic and authority data of all types, from all agencies. Historically and practically, the formats have always had a close relationship to the needs and the practices of the library community. In particular, the formats reflect the various cataloging codes applied by American libraries.

The first paragraph simply recognizes the impossibility of maintaining international compatibility within a national format. The second states, correctly, that the formats reflect library cataloging rules, but also explicitly says that the formats can serve to carry bibliographic data of all types, from all agencies. USMARC has been moving away from a strict mirroring of a single set of cataloging rules.

2.5. Historically, the USMARC Formats were developed to enable the Library of Congress to communicate its catalog records to other institutions. National agencies in the United States and Canada...are still given special emphasis in the formats, as sources of authoritative cataloging and as agencies responsible for certain data elements.

This paragraph says, in effect, that there is a legitimate historical basis for institutional bias (sometimes called "LC-centrism"). While institutional bias is generally disappearing from USMARC, the second sentence explicitly recognizes the continuing validity of special status for national agencies such as the Library of Congress and National Library of Medicine.

2.6. The institutions responsible for the content, content designation and transcription accuracy of data within a USMARC record are identified at the record level, in field 008, byte 39, and in field 040. This responsibility may be evaluated in terms of the following rule.

The Responsible Parties Rule

2.6.1. Responsible Parties Rule.

(a) Unmodified records: The institution identified as the transcribing institution (field 040 ‡c) should be considered responsible for content designation and transcription accuracy for all data. Except for agency-assigned data (see section 2.6.2.1 below), the institution identified as the cataloging institution (field 040 ‡a) should be considered responsible for content.

(b) Modified records: Institutions identified as transcribing or modifying institutions (field 040 ‡c,d) should be considered collectively responsible for content designation and transcription accuracy. Except for agency-assigned and authoritative-agency data (see section 2.6.2 below), institutions identified as modifying or cataloging institutions (field 040 ‡a,d) should be considered collectively responsible for content.

2.6.2. Exceptions.

2.6.2.1. Certain data elements are defined in the USMARC formats as being exclusively assigned by particular agencies (for example, International Standard Serial Number, Library of Congress Card Number). The content of such *agency-assigned elements* is always the responsibility of the agency.

2.6.2.2. Certain data elements have been defined in the USMARC Formats in relation to one or more *authoritative agencies* which maintain the lists or rules upon which the data is based. Where it is possible for other agencies to create similar or identical values for these data elements, content designation is provided to distinguish between values actually assigned by the authoritative agency and values assigned by other agencies. In the former case, responsibility for content rests with the authoritative agency. In the latter case, the Responsible Parties Rule applies, and no further identification of source of data is provided. Authoritative-agency fields are:

050   Library of Congress Call Number
060   National Library of Medicine Call Number
082   Dewey Decimal Classification Number
[DDC is maintained by the Library of Congress]

> Section 2.6 is perhaps the most important new principle in the Underlying Principles. More than any other statement, the Responsible Parties Rule moved the formats from LC MARC to USMARC. It came after various proposals to show the source of each data element at the field level, or otherwise make it easier for a library to tell who was responsible for a record's contents. MARBI was generally opposed to the idea of field- level source identification; the bibliographic services, which would have to support the record-keeping, were (in general) vehemently opposed. Some statement was required, which would identify those responsible for a record without overloading the record itself. Such a statement would be intended as a limit to source identification, with any exceptions specifically treated as such.
>
> The Responsible Parties Rule fills this need succinctly and thoroughly. It also indirectly addresses another need: opening the MARC Formats for general use. Through 1982, and even into 1983, only a national agency could create a complete MARC record. Only a national agency could create a

classification number, and only a national agency could assign subject head-ings (other than local headings). The two largest bibliographic services had users that skirted the latter rule; both were aware of the situation. Both services supported moves to open subject headings for general use; since both services rely on shared cataloging as a basis of operations, this is only natural.

2.7. In general, the USMARC Formats provide content designation only for data which is applicable to all copies of the bibliographic entity described.

2.7.1. Information which applies only to some copies (or even to a single copy) of a title may nevertheless be of interest beyond the institutions holding such copies. The USMARC Formats provide limited content designation for the encoding of such information and for identifying the holding institutions (see, for example, subfield ‡5 in the 7XX fields).

2.7.2. Information which does not apply to all copies of a title, and is not of interest to other institutions, is coded in local fields (such as field 590).

Aspects of the archival and manuscripts control format make section 2.7.1 somewhat questionable. The holdings format makes 2.7.1 even more questionable, and suggests that a different categorization of data elements is needed.

2.8. Although a MARC record is usually autonomous, data elements have been provided which may be used to link related records. These linkages may be implicit, through identical access points in each record, or explicit, through a linking field. Linking fields (76X-78X) may contain either selected data elements which identify the related item or a control number which identifies the related record. An explicit code in the Leader identifies a record which is linked to another record through a control number.

Section 3. Structural Features

3.1. The USMARC Formats are an implementation of the *American National Standard for Information Interchange on Magnetic Tape* (ANSI Z39.2-1979). They also incorporate other relevant ANSI standards, such as *Magnetic Tape Labels and File Structure for Information Interchange* (ANSI X3.27-1978).

3.2. All information in a MARC record is stored in character form. USMARC communication records are coded in Extended ASCII, as defined in Appendix III.B of *MARC Formats for Bibliographic Data*.

> *Only Extended ASCII characters are valid for communication of US-MARC, but no such requirement exists for "MARC records" as a generic term. Character-form storage is a more fundamental requirement than is Extended ASCII. Most of the major processing systems using USMARC formats for processing use extended versions of IBM's EBCDIC (Extended Binary Coded Decimal Interchange Code); all, however, translate to Extended ASCII for communication. USMARC records also communicate nonroman scripts, as discussed in chapter 16, but such scripts are always carried as ASCII characters using escape sequences.*

3.3. The length of each variable field can be determined either from the "length of field" element in the directory entry or from the occurrence of the "field terminator" character [1E hex, 8-bit; 36 octal, 6-bit]. Likewise, the length of a record can be determined either from the "logical record length" element in the Leader or from the occurrence of the "record terminator" character [1D hex, 8-bit; 35 octal, 6-bit]. (In the past, the field terminator of the last field was omitted, and the record terminator identified the end of that field.) The location of each variable field is explicitly stated in the "starting character position" element in its directory entry.

Section 4. Content Designation

4.1. The goal of content designation is to identify and characterize the data elements which comprise a MARC record with sufficient precision to support manipulation for a variety of functions.

4.2. For example, MARC content designation is designed to support such functions as:

(1)Display—the formatting of data for display on a CRT, for printing on 3x5 cards or in book catalogs, for production of COM catalogs, or for other visual presentation of the data.

(2)Information retrieval—the identification, categorization, and retrieval of any identifiable data element in a record.

4.3. Some fields serve multiple functions. For example, field 245 serves both as the bibliographic transcription of the title and statement of responsibility and as the access point for the title.

Early use of LC MARC went further in this direction: an indicator in the 1XX (main entry) field could specify that the main entry was also a subject—and, thus, should be traced and have a subject entry. This usage is now rare and obsolete.

4.4. The USMARC Formats provide for display constants (text which implicitly accompanies particular content designators). For example, subfield ‡x in field 490 (and in some other fields) implies the display constant "ISSN", and the combination of tag 780 and second indicator value "3" implies the display constant "Superseded in part by:". Such display constants are not carried in the data, but may be supplied for display by the processing system.

The provision of, and definition of, display constants makes USMARC a relatively compact format in some cases. Quite a few fields have display constants, controlled in some cases by indicators. A specific processing system can define its own additional display constants or alternative display constants, but those defined in MFBD are most commonly used.

4.5. The USMARC Formats support the sorting of data only to a limited extent. In general, sorting must be accomplished through the application of external algorithms to the data.

Section 5. Organization of the Record

5.1. A MARC record consists of three main sections: (1) the Leader, (2) the Directory, and (3) the Variable Fields.

5.2. The Leader consists of data elements which contain coded values and are identified by relative character position. Data elements in the Leader define parameters for processing the record. The Leader is fixed in length (24 characters) and occurs at the beginning of each MARC record.

5.3. The Directory contains the field identifier ("tag"), starting location and length of each field within the record. Directory entries for variable control fields appear first, in tag order. Entries for variable data fields follow, arranged in ascending order according to the first character of the tag. The order of fields in the record does not necessarily correspond to the order of directory entries. Duplicate tags are distinguished only by location of the respective fields within the record. The length of the directory entry is defined in the Entry Map elements in the Leader. In the USMARC Formats, the length of the directory entry is 12 characters. The Directory ends with a "field terminator" character.

5.4. The data content of a record is divided into *Variable Fields*. The USMARC Formats distinguish two types of variable fields: *Variable Control Fields* and *Variable Data Fields*. Control and data fields are distinguished only by structure (see section 7.2 below). [The term "fixed fields" is occasionally used in MARC documentation, referring either to control fields generally or only to coded-data fields such as 007 or 008.]

Section 6. Variable Fields and Tags

6.1. The data in a MARC record is organized into fields, each identified by a three-character tag.

6.2. According to ANSI Z39.2-1979, the tag must consist of alphabetic or numeric basic characters (such as decimal integers 0-9 or lower-case characters a-z). To date, the USMARC Formats have used only numeric tags.

> *While USMARC has included only numeric tags, some local extensions to USMARC have used alphabetic tags. Designers of such extensions have made the reasonable assumption that USMARC will not use tags beginning with alphabetic characters.*

6.3. The tag is stored in the directory entry for the field, not in the field itself.

6.4. Variable fields are grouped into blocks according to the first character of the tag, which identifies the function of the data within a traditional catalog record (such as main entry, added entry, subject entry). The type of information in the field (such as personal name, corporate name, title) is identified by the remainder of the tag.

6.4.1. For bibliographic records, the blocks are:

0XX = Variable control fields, identification and classification numbers, etc.
1XX = Main entry
2XX = Titles and title paragraph (title, edition, imprint)
3XX = Physical description
4XX = Series statements
5XX = Notes
6XX = Subject added entries
7XX = Added entries other than subject, series
8XX = Series added entries
9XX = Reserved for local implementation

6.4.2. For authority records, the blocks are:

0XX = Variable control fields, identification and classification numbers, etc.
1XX = Heading
2XX = General see references
3XX = General see also references
4XX = See from tracings
5XX = See also from tracings
6XX = Treatment decisions, notes, cataloger-generated references
7XX = Not defined
8XX = Not defined
9XX = Reserved for local implementation

> *The blocks are not always quite as neat as they appear. For 7xx and 8xx, the "blocks" cover only up to 740 and 840, respectively. Higher 7xx and 8xx tags have been used for very different purposes. 76X-78X have now been reserved for linking entries, and 88X is now reserved for links within a record. The proposed holdings format will use a group of tags from 851 through 866. Since USMARC has never used alphabetic tags, blocks aXX-zXX are not mentioned.*

6.5. Certain blocks contain data which may be subject to authority control (1XX, 4XX, 6XX, 7XX, 8XX for bibliographic records; 1XX, 4XX, 5XX for authority records).

6.5.1. In these blocks, certain parallels of content designation are preserved. The following meanings are generally given to the final two characters of the tag:

X00 = Personal name
X10 = Corporate name
X11 = Conference name
X30 = Uniform title heading
X40 = Bibliographic title
X50 = Topical subject heading
X51 = Geographic name

Further content designation (indicators and subfield codes) for data elements subject to authority control are consistently defined across the bibliographic formats and in the authorities format. These guidelines apply only to the main range of fields in each block, not to secondary ranges such as the linking fields in 760-787 or the 87X fields. [Numerous exceptions to this principle presently exist in the formats.]

6.5.2. Within fields subject to authority control, data elements may exist which are not subject to authority control and which may vary from record to record containing the same heading (for example, subfield ‡e, Relator). Such data elements are not appropriate for inclusion in the 1XX field in the authorities format.

6.5.3. In fields not subject to authority control, each tag is defined independently. Parallel meanings have been preserved whenever possible, however.

> *Section 6.5 was suggested by Walter Grutchfield of The New York Public Library at an open hearing on the Underlying Principles. It explicitly relates bibliographic and authority tags. Consistent definition of content designation makes it possible to carry out authority control by computer. USMARC shows more consistency in the fields mentioned above than in most other fields. Most tags in the 2XX, 3XX, and 5XX ranges are defined as needed, since parallels are rarely available. Parallels at the subfield level are much more frequent.*

6.6. Certain tags have been reserved for local implementation. Except as noted below, the USMARC Formats specify no structure or meaning for local fields. Communication of such fields between systems is governed by mutual agreements on the content and content designation of the fields communicated.

6.6.1. The 9XX block is reserved for local implementation.

6.6.2. In general, any tag containing the character "9" is reserved for local implementation within the block structure (see section 6.4 above).

6.6.3. The historical development of the USMARC Formats has left the following exceptions to this general principle:

009 Physical description fixed field for archival collections
039 Level of bibliographic control and coding detail

359   Rental price
490 Series untraced or traced differently

> *Section 6.6 reserves areas for local implementation; this explicit inclusion (and another in 8.4.2.3, below) represent a recognition within USMARC of the need for local extensions.*

> *Each of the exceptions in section 6.6.3 represents a different historical situation. Fields 009, 039, and 359 are now obsolete.*

> *Field 490 is the major exception to the "9s rule," and is a heavily used field. Definition of field 490 using a "9" took place before the "9s rule" was enunciated, at a time when "local data" was less important than it currently is.*

> *The major bibliographic services do define "local" fields, and they also define their use; see chapter 19 for examples of such definitions.*

6.7. Theoretically, all fields (except 001 and 005) may be repeated. The nature of the data often precludes repetition, however. For example, a bibliographic record may contain only one title (field 245) and an authority record, only one entry (1XX fields). The repeatability/nonrepeatability of each field is defined in the USMARC Formats.

Section 7. Variable Control Fields

7.1. 00X fields in the USMARC Formats are variable control fields.

7.2. Variable control fields consist of data and a field terminator. They do not contain either indicators or subfield codes (see section 8.1 below).

7.3. Variable control fields contain either a single data element or a series of fixed-length data elements identified by relative character position.

> *Control fields are not always fixed-length fields. Field 001 is variable-length, and different versions of field 007 vary in length. If a control field contains more than one element, all elements (except the last) must be fixed-length: otherwise, identifying elements by relative character position would not work.*

Section 8. Variable Data Fields

8.1. Three levels of content designation are provided for variable fields in ANSI Z39.2-1979:

(1) a three-character tag, stored in the directory entry;

(2) indicators stored at the beginning of each variable data field, the number of indicators being reflected in the Leader, byte 10; and

(3) subfield codes preceding each data element, the length of the code being reflected in the Leader, byte 11.

8.2. All fields except 00X are variable data fields.

This section does place one restriction on local extensions to USMARC: any field, local or national, that begins with characters other than "00" must contain two indicator positions and at least one subfield code.

8.3. Indicators

8.3.1. Indicators contain codes conveying information which interprets or supplements the data found in the field.

8.3.2. The USMARC Formats specify two indicator positions at the beginning of each variable data field.

8.3.3. Indicators are independently defined for each field. Parallel meanings are preserved whenever possible, however.

8.3.4. Indicator values are interpreted independently—that is, meaning is not ascribed to the two indicators taken together.

8.3.5. Indicators may be any lower-case alphabetic or numeric character or the blank. Numeric values are assigned first. A blank is used in an undefined indicator position, or to mean "no information supplied" in a defined indicator position.

This section explicitly chooses two as the number of indicator positions. It also adds twenty-six more values to the range of indicators possible in USMARC. No alphabetic indicators have ever been assigned in USMARC; section 8.3.5. explicitly opens the way for such assignment, if needed in the future.

8.4. Subfield Codes

8.4.1. Subfield codes distinguish data elements within a field which do (or might) require separate manipulation.

8.4.2. Subfield codes in the USMARC Formats consist of two characters—a delimiter [1F hex, 8-bit; 37 octal, 6-bit] followed by a data element identifier. Identifiers defined in the USMARC communications formats may be any lowercase alphabetic or numeric character.

8.4.2.1. In general, numeric identifiers are defined for parametric data used to process the field, or coded data needed to interpret the field. (Note that not all numeric identifiers defined in the past have in fact identified parametric data.)

8.4.2.2. Alphabetic identifiers are defined for the separate elements which constitute the data content of the field.

8.4.2.3. The character "9" and the following graphic symbols are reserved for local definition as subfield identifiers: 9 ! " # $ % & ' ( ) * + , - . / : ; = ?

> Most numeric subfields (but not all) can be suppressed in displaying or printing a field; some of them provide information useful in processing the field. Most alphabetic subfields (but not all) contain text that should be displayed as part of a field.

> Adoption of the Underlying Principles recognized the possibility of adding local subfields to nationally defined fields, by explicitly reserving twenty-two symbols as locally defined subfield identifiers.

8.4.3. Subfield codes are defined independently for each field. Parallel meanings are preserved whenever possible, however.

8.4.4. Subfield codes are defined for purposes of identification, not arrangement. The order of subfields is specified by content standards, such as the cataloging rules. In some cases, such specifications may be incorporated in the format documentation.

8.4.5. Theoretically, all data elements may be repeated. The nature of the data often precludes repetition, however. The repeatability

/ nonrepeatability of each subfield code is defined in the USMARC Formats.

UFBD normally lists subfields in alphabetic order for convenience; there is no implication that subfields should be keyed in that order. A common misconception is that every variable data field begins with a ǂa subfield, which always appears first: this has never been true, is not implied by the formats, and is clearly wrong in certain cases. Field 040 (Cataloging source) frequently lacks subfield ǂa; subfield ǂp (Introductory phrase) in field 534 (Original version note) is always entered as the first subfield of the field, before subfield ǂa.

Section 9. Coded Data

9.1. In addition to content designation, the USMARC Formats include specifications for the content of certain data elements, particularly those which provide for the representation of coded values.

9.2. Coded values consist of fixed-length character strings. Individual elements within a coded-data field or subfield are identified by relative character position.

9.3. Although coded data occurs most frequently in the Leader, Directory, and Variable Control Fields, any field or subfield may be defined for coded-data elements.

9.4. Certain common values have been defined:

_ (blank) = Undefined
n = Not applicable
u = Unknown
z = Other
| = Fill character [i.e. No information provided]

Historical exceptions do occur in the formats. In particular, the blank (_) has often been defined as "not applicable," or has been assigned a meaning.

Since discussion of the Underlying Principles began, changes in coded values have consistently worked toward more consistent use of these values.

The values contain some small but important distinctions. The fill character "|" indicates that the cataloger has chosen not to provide information. The "n" means that the coded data is simply not applicable to the item, while the "u" means that the cataloger intended to supply a value but was unable to determine one. The blank indicates nothing: no information is given.

The special meaning of blank is crucial to the maintenance of the formats. When an indicator has not been defined, it is always blank; when it is later defined, existing records must still be valid. The blank is also more broadly used to mean "no information"—not "no information provided" or "information not applicable," but simply "no information."

Additional Principles, 1988

A specific 5xx note field is needed when at least one of the following is true:

1) Categorical indexing or retrieval is required on the data defined for the note. The note is used for structured access purposes but does not have the nature of a controlled 6xx-8xx access point.

2) Special manipulation of that specific category of data is a routine requirement. Such manipulation includes special print / display formatting or selection / suppression from display or printed product.

3) Specialized structuring of information for reasons other than those given in 1) or 2).

Changing Principles

The Underlying Principles reflect fourteen years of MARC format development. They reflect an evolving body of working principles, and make those principles available for broader use. New principles may be needed as the formats continue to evolve. Existing principles may require expansion or modification. There are two crucial principles that are not stated in the Underlying Principles but play a major role in all USMARC change.

Whatever changes there are in the Underlying Principles, these two continue to be important:

Preservation of Existing Data

While "the future is longer than the past," it is also based on that past. Literally tens of millions of USMARC bibliographic records are in use, representing an enormous investment of money and cataloging skills. Future changes in USMARC will assure that those records continue to be useful.

Conservation of Maintenance Energy

"If it isn't broken, don't fix it." Those working on USMARC maintenance are interested in theoretical elegance, but not at the expense of proven workability. They also recognize the cost of keeping up with format changes (updating documentation and software); only changes that are justified by practical advantages should be approved.

Glossary

Terms are defined as used in this book; these definitions may not be universally applicable.

AACR2 *Anglo-American Cataloguing Rules* 2nd Edition.

ACRL Association of College and Research Libraries. A division of the American Library Association.

ADABAS A commercial database management system used as the basis for the Western Library Network, BLIS, and the University of California's MELVYL.

AFR Automatic Format Recognition; computer techniques to assign MARC tags and subfield codes to bibliographic descriptions stored as text. AFR was thought to be an efficient method for retrospective conversion in the late 1960s and early 1970s. The technique can be fairly successful, but has never demonstrably produced comprehensive, fully content-designated records.

Agency-Assigned Elements Data elements that can be assigned only by a particular agency. The ISSN (assigned by various national serials agencies) and LCCN (assigned by the Library of Congress) are examples. Content of agency-assigned elements is always the responsibility of the agency, though accuracy of transcription is the responsibility of the library that transcribes the information.

ALA The American Library Association.

Alternate Graphic Representation Field 880 in USMARC. This field always contains the content of some other field in a record, but at least some portion of that content is in some nonroman representation.

Analytics Bibliographic records that describe part or parts of a larger item. An analytic record might describe an article in a journal, an illustration in a book, or an individual piece of music on a sound recording. *See also* Component Part.

ANSEL American National Standard Extended Latin character set, codified in *American National Standard for Latin Alphabet Coded Character Set for Bibliographic Use, ANSI Z39.47-1985*. ANSEL is the base character set used in USMARC records when no alternate character set is explicitly stated.

ANSI American National Standards Institute; the overall organization for voluntary standards in the United States and the U.S. member of ISO (the International Organization for Standardization). ANSI does not create standards; it certifies standards organizations, reviews the process used to approve standards, and in some cases publishes and distributes standards. ANSI standards relating to libraries generally come from the National Information Standards Organization (NISO).

ARL The Association of Research Libraries.

ASCII American Standard Code for Information Interchange. Computers store characters as combinations of bits (binary digits). ASCII assigns standard meanings to those combinations so that information can be interchanged. For example, any computer that uses ASCII will treat the pattern "01000010" as the letter "B."

Authoritative Agency Agency that maintains lists or rules upon which a USMARC element is based. The Library of Congress is the authoritative agency for field 050 (Library of Congress Call Number) and 082 (Dewey Decimal Classification Number); while other agencies may create such numbers, they must follow the rules or lists created by the authoritative agency.

Authority Control Maintenance of established headings, both within an authority file and within bibliographic files including card catalogs. Authority control can be done manually (using card files or online authority files) or through direct computer-based control

Authority Record A record of an established heading or of a variant form with reference to one or more established headings.

Automatic Format Recognition *See* AFR.

BALLOTS Bibliographic Automation of Large Library Operations using a Time-sharing System. A project begun at Stanford University in 1967 that eventually led to an online shared cataloging system. BALLOTS was adopted by the Research Libraries Group and transformed into RLIN.

Base Address Bytes 12-16 of the USMARC leader, the offset at which the first data character (the first character of field 001) will be found.

Bibliographic Level Byte 7 of the USMARC leader, the second character in the Legend. Typical values are *m* (Monograph) and *s* (Serial). Other values include *a* (Component part, monographic), *b* (Component part, serial), *c* (Collection), and *d* (Subunit).

Bibliographic Utilities Common term for OCLC, RLG/RLIN, WLN, and Utlas, the four major shared technical processing systems.

Binary Data Technically, all information used in a modern computer is binary data. More commonly, the term signifies data stored in ways other than as strings of characters. USMARC explicitly forbids use of pure binary data within records.

Binary Digit The smallest element of computer data. Equivalent to Bit *(which see)*.

Bit Short for *Binary digit*, the smallest element of computer data. A bit has two possible values: on or off, usually interpreted as one or zero.

BPI Bits Per Inch. A measure of tape writing density. For nine-track tapes, such as are typically used for USMARC, BPI equals characters per inch. The most common values are 1600 BPI and 6250 BPI; some systems use 800 BPI.

Byte A group of bits treated as a single character in computer processing. In most modern computers, a byte is eight bits. "Byte" and "character" are usually synonymous.

Cataloging Code Any codified set of practices for descriptive or subject cataloging. The best known cataloging code is *AACR2*, but a number of special disciplines have other well-established cataloging codes. USMARC supports *AACR2* but is deliberately not limited to *AACR2*.

Cataloging Source Source of cataloging information, represented in a USMARC record by field 008, position 39 (for a few coded values) and field 040, which gives NUC codes for the cataloging agency, transcribing agency, and any agencies that modify the record.

CDS Cataloging Distribution Service, the agency within the Library of Congress that distributes tapes of LC cataloging (and other catalog-related products).

Character Code In computer usage, a defined set of bit string equivalences for graphic characters. For example, in the EBCDIC character code, the character 2 is represented by the machine value "hexadecimal F2," whereas 2 is represented by "hexadecimal 32" in the ASCII character code.

Character Set An organized set of character codes and their graphic equivalences. ANSEL represents one character set; the Cyrillic character set defined for bibliographic use represents another.

Characters In MARC usage, those elements that can be portrayed as graphics (letters, numbers, punctuation, diacritics) and the four special characters used in USMARC (fill, subfield delimiter, field terminator, and record terminator).

Chronology For holdings, the date information provided for individual issues, such as year, month, and week.

CIP Cataloging In Publication, a program of the Library of Congress to make partial cataloging information available for items before they are published. CIP records are distributed as MARC records; the data also frequently appears on the verso of title pages.

CJK Chinese, Japanese, and Korean. The brief name for RLG's project to enable cataloging of such items in the original graphic representation found on the item. *CJK* is a trademark of RLG.

CLR Council on Library Resources, Inc. A funding agency for a variety of projects in the library field.

Coded Data Elements stored in coded rather than free-text form. Codes must be represented in some list in order to be useful. Most such lists for USMARC are contained within *USMARC Format for Bibliographic Data* or related USMARC publications. Well-known examples are Country of Publication and Language.

Collection A group of items treated together for convenience in cataloging and control, or treated as a single unit because of the nature or significance of the collection itself.

Component Part Something that is physically part of a larger item (called the host item); that which can be described by an analytic entry. A chapter is a component part of a book.

CONSER Conversion of Serials. A nationwide cooperative retrospective and prospective conversion project, based on OCLC and managed by OCLC for most of its life, building a large database of serials records and, more recently, adding abstracting and indexing information to those records.

Content Designation "The codes and conventions established explicitly to identify and further characterize the data elements within a record and to support the manipulation of that data" (*Underlying Principles*, Section 1.2.2). USMARC designates content through tags, indicators, and subfield codes. Theoretically, catalog cards designate content elements through ISBD punctuation.

Control Fields *see* Variable Control Fields.

Control Number A distinctive number used by a system to identify something. USMARC requires a control number in field 001. Fields 010 and 035 also store control numbers.

Copy-Specific Information Information that pertains only to a single copy of an item, as opposed to *bibliographic data* (normally applicable to all copies of an edition).

Data Element Identifier The character that follows a subfield delimiter ‡ and precedes the text of the subfield. The data element identifier may be a lower-case alphabetic character, a digit, or one of twenty-one symbols. The numeral *9* and punctuation symbols are reserved for locally defined subfields.

DBMS Database Management System, a set of programs designed to build and maintain databases. Examples include ADABAS (used by WLN) and SPIRES (used by RLIN).

Delimiter A special character used to set off parts of a MARC record. USMARC uses three delimiters: the subfield delimiter preceding each data element identifier; the field terminator at the end of each field; and the record terminator at the end of each record.

Directory A series of fixed-length entries following the leader. The directory defines the contents of the record. Each directory entry in a USMARC record is twelve characters long, and is made up of a three-character tag, a four-digit length-of-field portion, and a five-digit starting-character-position portion.

Display Constant Text string expected to precede a USMARC field or subfield when it is displayed or printed, but not entered into the USMARC record. Display constants can be as short as "In " or as long as "Superseded in part by: ".

EBCDIC Extended Binary Coded Decimal Interchange Code. Character code used in most IBM mainframes and compatibles (but not microcomputers), relating characters and controls to bit strings. EBCDIC serves the same function as ASCII. It should never be used to communicate USMARC records on tape.

Entry Map Bytes 20 through 23 of a leader in any record following ANSI Z39.2, including USMARC records. The entry map defines the directory except for the tag. It consists of four single-digit numbers giving the length of each possible portion of a directory entry: length of field, starting character position, implementation-defined portion, and an undefined position. USMARC records always contain *4500* in the entry map.

Enumeration Numbering, as in serial volume and issue numbering.

Escape Sequence A sequence of three characters, beginning with the Escape control character, that signals a change of character set. The second and third characters indicate the character set being escaped to. (USMARC also includes some nonstandard two-character escape sequences to support superscript and subscript numbers and three Greek letters not defined in ANSEL itself.)

Extensions Additions to USMARC as defined in *UFBD*. Extensions include subfields, indicator values, fields, and even graphic representations.

Field A string of characters defined by a directory entry, identified by a tag, beginning at the starting character position and ending with a field terminator, having a total length defined by length of field. The tag is not part of the field itself. Indicators, subfield codes, and the field terminator are part of the field.

Fill Character A special character (usually printed as a solid or broken vertical bar |) used in some coded positions to indicate that no attempt has been made to provide information. This is a subtly different meaning than blank, which indicates only that no information is provided.

Format Integration A set of changes, primarily defined by MARBI Proposal 88-1, that aligns the individual bibliographic formats and combines them into a single USMARC format for bibliographic data.

GPO Government Printing Office.

Hexadecimal A notation system frequently used for computer codes. Each digit can have 16 values, from 0 to 9 and A to F. Decimal 15 is hexadecimal (or *hex*) F; decimal 255 is hexadecimal FF. A single character has one of 256 different values; hexadecimal notation states all such values as two-digit strings, from 00 to FF.

Host Item An item that contains component parts.

Identifier Equivalent to Subfield Code *(which see)*. ANSI Z39.2 uses "Identifier" throughout; USMARC documentation consistently uses "Subfield code."

Identifier Length A single-digit number stored in Byte 11 of MARC leaders. For USMARC records, the identifier length is always 2. An identifier length of 2 means that subfield codes are two characters long (the delimiter and the data element identifier).

IFLA International Federation of Library Associations.

Implementation-Defined Byte 22 of the MARC leader is a single-digit number giving the length of a fourth portion of each directory entry, the "implementation-defined portion." USMARC carries *0* in Byte 22, since USMARC has never defined an implementation-defined portion.

Indicator A character at the beginning of a variable data field containing codes that convey information to interpret or supplement the data found in the field. Each USMARC variable data field contains two indicators.

Indicator Count A single digit carried in Byte 10 of any MARC leader, specifying the number of indicators carried in each variable data field. The indicator count in USMARC records is always 2, since each field other than 00x fields begins with two indicators.

Interchange Format Any agreed format for interchange of information. The ALA Interlibrary Loan Request form is a manual interchange format. USMARC is a computerized interchange format.

ISBD International Standard Bibliographic Description. Best known in terms of ISBD punctuation, the distinctive and sometimes arcane punctuation pattern used in almost all American cataloging since 1974.

ISBN International Standard Book Number, carried in field 020 (which also carries binding and, sometimes, price information).

ISO International Organization for Standardization (or, more commonly, International Standards Organization). The international body for voluntary technical standards, with representatives from national standards organizations such as ANSI.

ISSN International Standard Serial Number. Carried in field 022 in USMARC records, also in subfield ‡x of 76x-78x fields and some other fields.

ITAL *Information Technology and Libraries*. Official journal of the Library and Information Technology Association, a division of ALA. Continues *Journal of Library Automation*.

JOLA The *Journal of Library Automation*. Official journal of the Information Science and Automation Division of ALA, and of the renamed Library and Information Technology Association until 1982, when it was continued by *Information Technology and Libraries*. Many significant articles on the early progress of MARC appeared in *JOLA*.

LC The Library of Congress.

LC MARC Another name for MARC II, sometimes written as LC/MARC. All LC MARC records are USMARC records, but most USMARC records are not LC MARC: that is, RLIN MARC, OCLC MARC, and other USMARC records outnumber MARC records generated by LC.

LCCN Library of Congress Control Number. On LC MARC distribution tapes, the LCCN appears as field 001; on other US-

MARC tapes (such as those generated by RLIN or OCLC) LCCN appears in field 010.

LCSH Library of Congress Subject Headings.

Leader The first twenty-five characters of a MARC record. The leader contains elements that allow a program to process the remainder of the record.

Legend Bytes 6 through 9 of the MARC leader. Byte 6 is type of record; byte 7 is bibliographic level. Bytes 8 and 9 have not been defined. The legend must be used to interpret field 008 correctly; prior to format integration, it also defined the format of a record.

Length of Field Four digits in each USMARC directory entry, immediately following the tag, giving the length of the field (including field terminator).

Linked Record Code Position 19 of the USMARC leader. Usually blank. An *r* in this position means that a linking entry field in the record contains a record number for another record, and lacks descriptive information for the related record. The other record is, therefore, required in order to process this record completely.

Linking Entry Any field with a tag between 760 and 789. Linking entries establish some form of relationship between the record containing them and some other bibliographic entity (not necessarily another USMARC record). Examples of linking entry fields include 780, Preceding Item, and 773, Host Item.

LITA Library and Information Technology Association, a division of the American Library Association. Formerly ISAD (Information Science and Automation Division). One of the divisions represented on MARBI.

Logical Record Length The length of a logical record—that is, a self-contained MARC record. The "logical record" distinction arises because MARC records are communicated in a manner that separates *physical records* (what the computer or communications medium treats as a record) from *logical records* (what the program treats as a record).

MARBI The committee that reviews proposed changes to US-MARC, in cooperation with LC and liaisons from other interested parties. The full name is "ALA RTSD/LITA/RASD Committee on the Representation in Machine-Readable Form of Bibliographic Information." MARBI advises LC, but does not itself determine the content of USMARC.

MARC *Machine-Readable Cataloging*. The term was coined in 1966, at the time of MARC I and the MARC Pilot Project. MARC is a general term covering many different formats in many countries.

MARC I The initial machine-readable cataloging format used by LC for the MARC Pilot Project (1966-1968).

MARC II The record structure designed by LC in 1968. The term applied to all of the MARC formats until 1983, when it was succeeded by USMARC.

MARC-Compatible A format or system that can accept any pure USMARC record and, as needed, regenerate the same USMARC record without loss of content, content designation or structure. A fully MARC-compatible system must also maintain any editing in such a way that a proper USMARC record, including the changes, can be generated.

MFBD The *MARC Formats for Bibliographic Data*, predecessor to *UFBD (which see)*.

MUDG MARC Users Discussion Group, a group within ISAD that met to discuss various MARC issues, including early uses of the format. The group merged with the Library Automation Discussion Group (LADG, formerly COLA, the Committee on Library Automation) in the late 1970s, to form the Library and Information Technology Discussion Group. That group dissolved a few years later.

Network Within the library world, any formal organization of libraries. There are dozens of library networks within the United States. While the four major shared cataloging services (OCLC,

RLIN, Utlas, and WLN) may be some of the largest networks, there are many other networks of varying size and type.

NISO National Information Standards Organization, formerly American National Standards Committee Z39. The accredited voluntary technical standards organization concerned with libraries, publishing, and information science.

NLBR National Level Bibliographic Record. A series of documents establishing standards for bibliographic records. NLBR requirements have been merged into *UFBD*.

NUC National Union Catalog; also used to refer to NUC Codes *(which see)*.

NUC Code Code identifying a library in the National Union Catalog and, later, in MARC records. The NUC code is used in field 040 and in other places as a distinct identifying string for a library. NUCs are geographically based, vary in length from two to eight (or more) characters, and (at least in the past) are case-sensitive: that is, uppercase and lowercase letters have distinct meanings within an NUC code.

OCLC Online Computer Library Center, the largest shared cataloging service in the United States. A complex of people, computers, and data providing shared cataloging (and other services) for several thousand libraries. Formerly OCLC, Inc.; originally Ohio College Library Center.

OCLC MARC USMARC with OCLC extensions, as defined and generated by OCLC.

Offset Relative position from the beginning. The first position is offset 0. The second position is offset 1.

RASD Reference and Adult Services Division of ALA. One of the divisions represented on MARBI.

REACC The RLIN East Asian Character Code, created by The Research Libraries Group, Inc.; later published as the *USMARC Character Set, Chinese, Japanese, Korean* and adopted as American National Standard Z39.64, *American National Standard for Information Science—East Asian Character Code for Bibliographic Use.*

Record Length *see* Logical Record Length.

Record Status A single-character code carried in Position 5 of MARC leaders. The most commonly used values are *n* (New record), *c* (Changed record), and *d* (Deleted record).

Record Terminator The single character, hexadecimal 1D, that ends every MARC record.

Repeatability Whether or not a field or subfield can be repeated. Theoretically, all fields and subfields are repeatable. In practice, some fields and subfields are regarded as non-repeatable. *UFBD* specifies repeatability.

RLG The Research Libraries Group, Inc. A consortium of research institutions and libraries created to pursue common aims in library and scholarly fields. Operates the Research Libraries Information Network (RLIN), a large online shared cataloging system.

RLIN The Research Libraries Information Network. The computer support for RLG and a large shared cataloging service, with more than thirty million bibliographic records and more than 1,100 terminals.

RLIN MARC USMARC with RLIN extensions, as defined and generated by RLG.

RTSD Resources and Technical Services Division of ALA. One of the three ALA divisions represented on MARBI.

Sequence Control Number Subfield ‡6 in the USMARC Holdings Format, containing a number that can be used to sort fields 853-855 into proper order and to sort fields 863-865 and relate them to specific 853-855 fields.

Starting Character Position Five digits in each directory entry, following the Length of Field. The starting character position is the offset of the first character of a field from the first character in the first field. The starting character position for field 001 is always *00000*. The actual position of a field is the starting character position plus the base address.

Subfield Portion of a USMARC field that begins with a subfield code and is terminated by either subfield delimiter or a field terminator.

Subfield Delimiter A single character, hexadecimal 1F, that is followed by a data element identifier. The two in combination make up a subfield code. The subfield delimiter is normally displayed as a double dagger ‡ or dollar sign $.

Superset A format is a superset of another format if all elements of the second format are included in the first, but not the reverse. OCLC MARC and RLIN MARC are both supersets of USMARC; neither format is a superset of the other.

Tag Each variable field in a USMARC record is identified by a three-character tag, stored in the directory. Tags are the level of content designation used to define independent elements of a record.

Type of Record Byte 6 of a MARC leader, the first character of the legend. This code distinguishes between bibliographic, authority and holdings records; before format integration, it also played some part in determining the bibliographic format of a record.

UFBD The *USMARC Format for Bibliographic Data*, published by the Library of Congress as a looseleaf publication with occasional updates. The data dictionary for USMARC.

USMARC The machine-readable cataloging format used in the United States. Formerly known as LC MARC, LC/MARC, MARC II, and just MARC.

Utlas The largest shared cataloging service in Canada; now a division of a private corporation, but formerly the University of Toronto Library Automation System.

Utlas MARC USMARC or CAN/MARC with Utlas extensions, as defined and generated by Utlas.

Variable Control Fields USMARC tags 001-009 and potentially 00a-00z. Control fields do not have indicators or tags and can be composed of one or more data elements. Every element except the last one in a variable control field must be fixed-length, since elements are identified only by their position in the field.

Vernacular Data   Bibliographic data carried in a graphic representation other than the roman alphabet.

WLN   The Western Library Network, formerly the Washington Library Network. A regional shared cataloging service in the Pacific Northwest; also a set of software used by a number of agencies in several countries.

Selected Bibliography

T he first edition of *MARC for Library Use* included a lengthy bibliography covering everything consulted in any way while preparing that book as well as everything cited within the book. Many of the items were out of print or had never been publicly available; many more are now obsolete and out of print.

This brief list does not include most of the books and papers cited in footnotes, and most certainly does not include everything consulted while preparing the two editions. Instead, it is a short list of a few noteworthy articles and books dealing with certain aspects of USMARC. Most or all of these should be readily available in any substantial library-related collection. Some inclusions represent early reports on shared cataloging services or interesting uses of USMARC; others represent statistical overviews of MARC. They are primarily items that I think people interested in USMARC might want to read. Documentation from the Library of Congress and other agencies is not included.

Allison, Anne Marie, and Ann G. Alan, eds. *OCLC, A National Library Network.* Short Hills, NJ: Enslow, 1979. Includes an extensive bibliography.

Attig, John C. "The Concept of a MARC Format." *Information Technology and Libraries* 2, no. 1 (March 1983): 7-17.

Avram, Henriette D. *MARC, Its History and Implications.* Washington, DC: Library of Congress, 1975.

Baker, Barry B., ed. *The USMARC Format for Holdings and Locations: Development, Implementation, and Use.* New York: Haworth Press, 1988. Series of papers on early uses of the holdings format.

Bierman, Kenneth John, and Betty Jean Blue. "A MARC Based SDI Service." *Journal of Library Automation* 3, no. 4 (December 1970): 304-319. Early batch MARC-based service of a type rarely found in recent years.

Bowden, Virginia M., and Ruby B. Miller. "MARCIVE: A Cooperative Automated Library System." *Journal of Library Automation* 7, no. 3 (September 1974): 183-200. Early report on an early, continuing system.

Butler, Brett. "Automatic Format Recognition of MARC Bibliographic Elements: A Review and Projection." *Journal of Library Automation* 7, no. 1 (March 1974): 27-42. Early discussion of AFR, which has not progressed much since 1974.

Crawford, Walt, Lennie Stovel, and Kathleen Bales. *Bibliographic Displays in the Online Catalog.* White Plains, NY: Knowledge Industry Publications, 1986. (Now available from G.K. Hall.) Includes extensive field occurrence tables based on 1986 activity within RLIN.

Crawford, Walt. "The RLIN Reports System: A Tool for MARC Selection and Listing." *Information Technology and Libraries* 3, no. 1 (March 1984): 3-14. Straightforward use of control-table-driven software for bibliography and list production and record selection, working from pure USMARC.

Epstein, A.H., and Allen B. Veaner. "A User's View of BALLOTS." *Proceedings of the 1972 Clinic on Library Applications of Data Processing.* Urbana: U. of Illinois, 1972. Early notes on BALLOTS, precursor to RLIN.

Epstein, Hank. "MITINET/Retro: Retrospective Conversion on an Apple." *Information Technology and Libraries* 2, no. 2 (June 1983): 166-73. Early microcomputer-based system for building MARC records.

Furlong, Elizabeth J. "Index Access to On-line Records: An Operational View." *Journal of Library Automation* 11, no. 3 (September 1978): 223-38. A description of NOTIS, Northwestern's Online Total Integrated System, MARC-based from the beginning.

Gapen, D. Kaye. "MARC Format Simplification." *Journal of Library Automation* 14, no. 4 (December 1981): 286-92. Brief version of an important report on the desirability and feasibility of simplifying MARC.

Godwin, Ruta Pempe, and Susan H. Vita. "Management Information for the CIP Program Using SAS." *Information Technology and Libraries* 7, no. 2 (June 1988): 154-65. Good example of a MARC analysis system that, quite properly, does not store intermediate information in MARC format, since the intermediate information is purely for statistical purposes.

Hagler, Ronald. *The Bibliographic Record and Information Technology.* Chicago: American Library Association, 1982. Includes a detailed description of CAN/MARC.

Hickey, Thomas B. *Research Report on Field, Subfield and Indicator Statistics in OCLC Bibliographic Records.* Dublin, OH: OCLC, 1981. Tables of figures based on a 1 percent sample of OCLC's database. Compare the (more recent) figures in Crawford's *Bibliographic Displays in the Online Catalog* and in this book.

Hirshon, Arnold. "Considerations in the Creation of a Holdings Record Structure for an Online Catalog." *Library Resources & Technical Services* 28, no. 1 (January 1984): 25-40. One seminal paper in the history of the USMARC holdings format.

"In-Depth: University of California MELVYL." *Information Technology and Libraries* 1, no. 4 and 2, no. 1 (December 1982, March 1983): 350-80, 58-115. Extensive discussion of a large modern MARC-based online catalog.

Jarvis, William E., and Victoria E. Dow. "Integrating Subject Pathfinders into a GEAC ILS: A MARC-Formatted Record Approach." *Information Technology and Libraries* 5, no. 3 (September 1986): 213-27. Example of creative local extension of MARC, defining a special MARC-tagged format for pathfinder records so that they can be retrieved together with bibliographic citations.

Kilgour, Frederick G., et al. "The Shared Cataloging System of the Ohio College Library Center." *Journal of Library Automation* 5, no. 3 (September 1972): 157-83. Important early discussion of OCLC as an online MARC-based system.

Malinconico, S. Michael, et al. "Vernacular Scripts in the NYPL Automated Bibliographic Control System." *Journal of Library Automation* 10, no. 3 (September 1977): 205-25. Early system for handling Cyrillic and Hebrew in MARC records; very different from system finally adopted.

Martin, Susan K. *Library Networks, 1986-87: Libraries in Partnership.* White Plains, NY: Knowledge Industry Publications. Thorough discussion of the current state of shared cataloging services and regional library networks.

McCallum, Sally H, and James L. Godwin. "Statistics on Headings in the MARC File." *Journal of Library Automation* 14, no. 3 (September 1981): 194-201. Another statistical report, this one on LC's own master file.

Reed, Mary Jane Pobst. "The Washington Library Network's Computerized Bibliographic System." *Journal of Library Automation* 8, no. 3 (September 1975): 174-99. Fairly early discussion of WLN, now the Western Library Network.

Renaud, Robert. "Resolving Conflicts in MARC Exchange: The Structure and Impact of Local Options." *Information Technology and Libraries* 3, no. 3 (September 1984): 255-61. Discusses the problems that arise when a MARC-based system adds local extensions that do *not* include a "9" in the tag—and the same tag is later added to USMARC.

Reynolds, Dennis. "Entry of Local Data on OCLC: The Options and Their Impact on the Processing of Archival Tapes." *Information Technology and Libraries* 1, no. 1 (March 1982): 5-14. Discusses use of OCLC MARC extensions.

Williams, Martha E., et al. "Summary Statistics for Five Years of the MARC Data Base." *Journal of Library Automation* 12, no. 4 (December 1979): 314-37. Fairly extensive reporting on the statistical makeup of LC MARC records for the late 1970s.

Index

A

AACR2, 2, 29, 99, 111 - 112, 118, 123, 173, 265, 309
Abbreviated title (210), 74
ACRL, 135
Acquisitions, 262
Actions (583), 137 - 138, 175
Added entry—personal name (700), 18
Agency-assigned elements, 312
ALA, 135, 207 - 208
ALA Extended ASCII, 188
Alternate graphic representation (880), 188 - 192
AMC, 112, 115, 133 - 145, 161
American Library Association. *See* ALA
American National Standard for Bibliographic Information Interchange. *See* Z39.2
American National Standards Institute. *See* ANSI
Analytics, 38, 176 - 185
Anglo-American Cataloguing Rules, 2nd edition. *See* AACR2
ANSEL, 190, 270 - 271, 298
ANSI, 31, 251, 266, 298, 308

ANSI Z39.2. *See* Z39.2
Archival and manuscripts control. *See* AMC
Archival control, 136
Archives, Personal Papers,and Manuscripts, 134 - 135
Argonne National Laboratory, 205
ARL Committee on Automation, 204
ASCII, 271
Association of College and Research Libraries, 135
Attig, John, 214, 225
Authoritative agencies, 311
Authorities, 147 - 159, 309
  History, 148 - 150
  Kinds of records, 151 - 153
Authorities: A MARC Format, 148, 150
Authority control, 296
  Bibliographic fields, 23
Avram, Henriette, 203 - 204, 206 - 207, 219

B

Bales, Kathleen, 226
BALLOTS, 209, 274, 278
Base address (Leader/12), 37

Bearman, David, 135
Becker & Hays, Inc., 210
BIBLIST, 206
Bibliographic formats, 3 - 4
Bibliographic level (Leader/07), 36
Bilingual records, 257 - 260
Books, 57 - 65
British Library, 257
Brown, Barbara, 135
Bruns, Phyllis, 112
Burroughs Corporation, 168

C

California State Library, 205
Call numbers
    OCLC MARC, 246 - 247
    RLIN MARC, 251 - 252
    Utlas MARC, 256
CAN/MARC, 2, 249, 255, 257
Cartographic materials. *See* Maps
Case file characteristics note (565),
    128
Catalog Distribution Service
    (CDS), 216
Cataloging source (040), 15
CD-ROM, 293
Character restrictions, 280
Character sets present (066), 188 -
    189
Character subsets, 283 - 284
Chinese, Japanese, and Korean.
    See CJK
Circulation, 262
CJK, 187 - 197
CLR, 149, 203 - 204, 213
Coded data, 323 - 324
Coded mathematical data (034), 79
    - 80
CODEN, 164

College Bibliocentre, 210
Communications, 275
Compatibility, 263 - 289
    Extensions, 269 - 270
    One-way, 284 - 286
    Partial, 277 - 289
    Precise, 264 - 268
    Testing, 275 - 276
    Transforms, 270 - 275
Complexity restrictions, 281
Computer files, 123 - 132
CONSER, 67, 71, 75, 173, 213, 239,
    249, 253
Constant angular velocity, 118
Content designation, 8, 285, 308,
    315-316
Control number (001), 12
Cornell University Library, 205
Country of producer code (044),
    114
Country of producing entity
    (257), 114
Crawford, Walt, 226, 265
Creation/production credits note
    (508), 115
Criterion videodiscs, 118
Current publication frequency
    (310), 73
Cyrillic, 197, 199 - 201, 270

D

Date and time of latest transaction
    (005), 12 - 13
Date/time and place of event code
    (033), 101
Date/time and place of event note
    (518), 101 - 102
Delimiters, 43
    See also subfield delimiter, field

terminator, and record terminator
Descriptive cataloging form
(Leader/18), 38
Dewey Decimal call number (082),
16
Directory, 33, 39 - 41, 316
Sequence, 39 - 40
Uses, 40 - 41
Display constant, 48 - 49, 315
Dodd, Sue, 123

E

EBCDIC, 271
Ekstrom, Ann, 150
Emory University, 162
Encoding level (Leader/17), 38
Entry map (Leader/20), 33, 39, 316
Escape sequences, 188
Extensions, 243 - 262, 269 - 270
Character set, 269 - 270
Structural, 270

F

Faxon, 169
Field length restrictions, 279
Field terminator, 43, 316
Fields, 8, 317-321
Blocks, 317-318
Common, 22 - 25
Commonly used for AMC, 138 -
140
Commonly used for books, 58 -
61
Commonly used for computer
files, 125 - 127
Commonly used for maps, 78 -
79
Commonly used for scores, 88 -
89

Commonly used for serials, 68 - 71
Commonly used for sound
recordings, 98 - 99
Commonly used for visual
materials, 113 - 114
Deleted, 238 - 239
Obsolete, 236 - 237
Subject to authority control, 23
Subsets, 283 - 284
Variable control, 12 - 14, 24, 39, 41 -
42
Variable data, 14 - 18, 42 - 43
Films. *See* Visual materials
Films: A MARC Format, 111
Fixed length data elements (006),
232
Books, 57 - 58
Computer files, 125
Maps, 77 - 78
Music, 87 - 88
Serials, 67 - 68
Visual materials, 112 - 1133
Fixed length data elements (008),
13 - 14
Books, 57 - 58
Computer files, 125
Maps, 77 - 78
Music, 87 - 88
Serials, 67 - 68
Visual materials, 112 - 113
Florida State University, 162
Form of composition (047), 94, 109
*Form Terms for Archival and
Manuscripts Control*, 121
Format integration, 6, 88, 132, 214,
221 - 241
Details, 230 - 241
Fixed length data elements, 231 -
232

History, 222 - 230
Format restrictions, 279 -280
Formatted contents note (505), 177
Freitag, Ruth, 204
Funding information note (536), 127

G

Geac, 62
General note (500), 17
Geographic area code (043), 62
Geographical classification code (052), 84
Georgia Institute of Technology, 205
Government Printing Office. *See* GPO
GPO, 216
Graphic Materials: Rules for Describing Original Items and Historical Collections, 112
Grutchfield, Walter, 319
Guiles, Kay, 204

H

Harvard, 169, 205
Hebrew, 197 - 201, 270
Henson, Steven L., 134 - 135
Holdings, 161 - 170
  Enumeration and chronology, 165 - 167
  Experimentation with format, 168 - 169
  History of format, 162
  Link to bibliographic record, 163 - 164
  OCLC MARC, 245 - 246
  RLIN MARC, 251 - 252
  Serial, 161

Serials control, 169
Standards problem, 170
USMARC extensions, 262
Utlas MARC, 256 - 257
Host item entry (773), 180 - 185

I

IBM, 271, 298
ICPSR, 126, 278
Illinois State Library, 205
Immediate source of acquisition note (541), 136
Imprint. *See* Publication, distribution, etc.
In (773), 38 - 39
Incompatible systems, 286 - 288
Index term—function (657), 140
Index term—genre/form (655), 121, 140
Index term—occupation (656), 140
Indiana University, 205
Indicator count (Leader/10), 36
Indicators, 8, 45 - 50, 321
Information Science and Automation Division (ALA ISAD), 207
Inter-university consortium for political and social research. *See* ICPSR
InterMARC, 2
International Organization for Standardization. *See* ISO
International Serials Data System. *See* ISDS
International Standard Book Number. *See* ISBN
ISAD, 211
ISBD, 265
ISBN (020), 15, 40, 164

ISDS, 74
ISO, 197, 199, 266
ISO 4-1972, 74
ISO 2709, 209, 308
ISSN, 75

K
Key title (222), 75
Kilgour, Frederick, 203
Kind of cutting (007/11), 29
Knapp, John F., 207

L
Lambda, 168 - 169
Language code (041), 92
LC, 2, 5 - 6, 8, 15, 17, 21, 28 - 29, 35,
    88, 102, 111, 121, 133 - 135, 148 -
    150, 157, 162, 170 - 171, 179, 188,
    195, 200, 204 - 205, 208, 210 - 211,
    213, 215, 218, 221, 223, 226, 228,
    230, 236, 243, 249, 265, 271, 278 -
    279, 292
    Practice notes, 29
LC control number. *See* LCCN
LC MARC, 2, 6, 203, 265, 267
LC-centrism, 311
LCCN (010), 14
LCF. *See* Utlas MARC
LCSH, 17, 158
Leader, 34 - 39, 316
Legend (Leader/06), 35 - 36
Library Journal, 75 - 76
Library of Congress. *See* LC
Library of Congress call number
    (050), 15
*Library of Congress Subject
    Headings. See* LCSH
Linked record code (Leader/19),
    38 - 39

Linked Systems Project. *See* LSP
Linking, 171 - 186
    Analytics, 176 - 185
    Collocation, 171
    Host item entry (773), 180 - 185
    In analytics, 180 - 185
    Inter-record, 176 - 185
    Intra-record, 172 - 176
    Linking entry fields (76x-78x),
        56, 178
    Materials specified (‡3), 174 - 176
    Subrecords, 172, 178 - 180
Linking entry complexity note
    (580), 73
LITA, 211
LITA Newsletter, 73 - 75, 168
Local data, 319
Local use, 295 - 296
Logical record length (Leader/00),
    34 - 35
LSP, 149 - 150, 157 - 158

M
Machine readable data files. *See*
    Computer files
Map & Geography Round Table,
    217
Main entry—personal name (100),
    16
Manuscripts format, 133
Maps, 77 - 85
MARBI, 8, 123, 135, 170, 174, 188,
    211 - 218, 221, 223, 228, 236, 308
MARC
    Definition, 2
    See also USMARC
MARC compatibility, 263 - 289
MARC Distribution Service, 2, 292
MARC Editorial Office, 2

MARC for Library Use, 140
MARC Formats for Bibliographic Data. See MFBD
MARC Institutes, 207
MARC, Its History and Implications, 219 - 220
MARC I, 205 - 206
MARC Pilot Project, 204 - 206, 210
MARC XX, 215
MARC II, 2, 21, 203, 205 - 210
    Distribution, 208
    History, 206 - 210
MARC Users' Discussion Group, 208
Maruyama, Lenore, 123, 148
MARVEL, 169
Mathematical data area (255), 80 - 81
McCone, Gary, 170
MFBD, 21, 26, 28, 112, 223, 265, 307, 309
Microforms, 64
MicroLinx, 169
Mnemonics, 274
Montgomery County Public Schools, 205
Motion picture presentation format (007/04), 119
MRDF. *See* Computer files
Music. *See* Scores and Sound recordings
Music Library Association, 8
Musical presentation statement (254), 90

N

NACO, 157 - 158
Name Authority Cooperative Project, 157 - 158

Name Authority File, 157 - 158
Nassau (County) Library System, 205
National Agricultural Library, 8, 205, 217
National Coordinated Cataloging Operation, 157 - 158
National Information Standards Organization. *See* NISO
National Information Systems Task Force, 135
National Level Bibliographic Record. *See* NLBR
National Library of Canada, 8, 239, 249
National Library of Medicine, 8, 217, 309, 311
National Serials Data Program, 75
New York Public Library, 270, 319
NISO, 31, 170, 195, 199
NISTF, 135
NLBR, 213
Nonfiling characters, 47
Nonroman text, 187 - 201
Northwestern University, 169
Notes and added entries control, 47 - 48
NOTIS, 169
NUC, 62, 251
Number of instruments or voices code (048), 90, 94, 109

O

OCLC, 1, 3, 8, 62, 88, 123, 149, 157, 168 - 169, 179, 194 - 195, 203, 209 - 210, 212 - 213, 218, 226, 228, 250 - 251, 253, 262, 265, 267, 271, 274, 278, 292, 294 - 295
OCLC MARC, 2, 244 - 249, 255

Call numbers, 246 - 247
Field extensions, 245 - 249
Holdings, 245 - 246
Subfield extensions, 244 - 245
Old Church Slavonic, 197
Online Audiovisual Catalogers, 217
Online Computer Library Center. *See* OCLC
Open Systems Interconnection (OSI), 157
OS, 298
Outdated systems, 281 - 282

P
Partial record updates, 149 - 150
Participant or performer note (511), 101
Patterson, Margaret, 150
Pennsylvania State University, 214
Physical description (300), 17, 118
Physical description fixed field (007)
Maps, 83 - 84
Microform, 64
Motion pictures, 119
Nonprojected graphics, 120 - 121
Sound recordings, 102
Videocassettes, 117 - 118
Playing time (306), 101
PRECIS, 257
Preservation, 137 - 138, 218
Printed and manuscript music. *See* Scores
Processing, 295
Publication, distribution, etc. (260), 17

Publisher number for music (028), 92
Pulsifer, Josephine S., 150, 210

R
Rare Books and Manuscripts Section, 135
RASD, 211
Rather, Lucia J., 207
RBMS, 135
REACC, 194 - 195
Record length restrictions, 278 - 279
Record status (Leader/05), 35
Record terminator, 43
Recordings. *See* Sound recordings
Redstone Scientific Information Center, 205
Regularity (008/19), 72
Repeatability, 320
Reproduction note (533), 64
Research Libraries Group. *See* RLG
Research Libraries Information Network. *See* RLIN
Responsible parties rule, 311 - 313
Restrictions on access (506), 115
Retrospective conversion, 218, 293 - 295
Rice University, 205
Richard Abel & Company, 210
RLG, 15, 28, 121, 135, 149, 157, 180, 187 - 188, 195, 199 - 200, 223, 226, 228, 249, 267
RLIN, 1, 3, 8, 15, 67, 88, 125, 133, 138, 140, 157, 169, 175, 187 - 201, 209, 218, 262, 271 - 272, 292, 294 - 295
RLIN East Asian Character Code. *See* REACC

RLIN MARC, 2, 199, 249 - 255, 278
   Acquisitions data, 253 - 254
   Field extensions, 250 - 254
   Subfield extensions, 250
RLIN PASS command, 272
RTSD, 211
RTSD CC:DA, 8

S

SAA, 8, 135, 217
Scale note (507), 79
Scores, 87 - 95
Serial holdings, 251
Seriality, 221 - 222
Serials, 67 - 76
Series statement/added entry—
   title (440), 17
Shared cataloging services. *See*
   OCLC, RLIN, Utlas and WLN
SKED, 206
Society of American Archivists, 8,
   135, 217
SOLINET, 168 - 169
Sony, 111
Sorting, 316
Sound recordings, 97 - 110
Source of information, 49
Southeastern ARL Libraries
   Cooperative Serials Project, 162
Standard recording number (024),
   100
Stanford University, 209, 274, 278
Subfield
   ‡2 (Source), 55
   ‡3 (Materials specified), 46, 56
   ‡4 (Relator code), 56
   ‡5 (Institution to which field
      applies), 56
   ‡6 (Linkage), 46, 188 - 190

   ‡7 (Control subfield), 56
   ‡w (Control number), 56
Subfield code count (Leader/11), 36
Subfield codes, 5, 322 - 323
Subfield delimiter, 43
Subfields, 8, 45 - 46, 50 - 56
   Basic aspects, 51 - 55
   Consistently defined, 55 - 56
   Patterns, 53 - 55
Subject added entry—topical term
   (650), 17 - 18
Subject Authority File (SAF), 158 -
   159
Successive/latest entry indicator
   (008/34), 72
SUNY Albany, 62
SUNY Biomedical
   Communications Network, 205
System control number (035), 62,
   218
System details access to computer
   files (753), 128

T

Tags, 5, 8, 42 - 43, 45
Tape format, 265 - 268
Tape labels, 298
Target audience (521), 115
Time period of content (045), 92, 95
Title statement (245), 16
Transforms, 270 - 275
   Character set, 271 - 272
   Communications, 272 - 273
   Content designation, 274 - 275
   Storage, 273 - 274
Transliteration, 187, 197
Tucker, Alan, 135
Type of contents, 50

Type of musical composition code
(047), 90
Type of record (Leader/06), 35 - 36

U

U-matic, 111
UFBD, 1, 3, 21 - 30, 42, 138, 221, 243
- 244, 265, 269, 307
UKMARC, 2, 172, 257
Underlying Principles, 2, 154, 214,
224 - 225, 307 - 325
Union lists, 296
Universal Product Code, 100
University of California Institute
of Library Research (Los
Angeles), 205
University of Chicago, 205
University of Florida, 162, 169, 205
University of Georgia, 162, 169
University of Kansas, 169
University of Miami, 162
University of Missouri, 205
University of Tennessee, 162
University of Toronto, 205, 209
UPC, 100
USMARC, 31 - 44
Changes, 6 - 7
Coded values, 28 - 29
Compatibility, 263 - 289
Definition, 2 - 3
Extensions, 2
History, 21 - 22, 203 - 220
Library uses, 291 - 305
Maintenance, 215 - 218
Record organization, 316
Sources of records, 292 - 293
Structure, 31 - 44
Tape problems, 296 - 299
Tape structure, 297 - 298

Transmission form, 44
USMARC advisory group, 8, 111,
123, 135, 162, 170, 211, 225
USMARC Code List for Countries, 30
*USMARC Code List for Geographic
Areas*, 30
USMARC Code List for Languages,
30
*USMARC Code List for Relators,
Sources, Description Conventions*, 30
USMARC Extensions, 243 - 262,
280
*USMARC Format for Authority
Data*, 1, 3, 150
*USMARC Format for Bibliographic
Data. See* UFBD
USMARC Format for Holdings Data,
1
*USMARC Formats: Underlying
Principles. See* Underlying
Principles
*USMARC Specifications for Record
Structure, Character Sets, Tapes*, 30
USMARC subsets, 282 - 284
Utlas, 1, 3, 8, 123, 209, 226, 262, 292
Utlas MARC, 255 - 261
Field extensions, 255 - 261
Fields for bilingual information,
257 - 260
Fixed-field extensions, 255
PRECIS, 257

V

Variable control fields, 320
Variable data fields, 321
Variant access title (212), 74
Variant name (87x), 173
Varying form of title (246), 75
Vernacular text. *See* Nonroman text

Virginia Polytechnic Institute and State University, 162
Visual materials, 111 - 122
  History, 111 - 112
VTLS, Inc., 169

W

Washington Library Network. *See* WLN
Washington State Library, 205, 209
Weisbrod, David, 224
Western Library Network. *See* WLN
WLN, 1, 3, 8, 133, 149, 168, 209, 226, 228, 266, 271, 274, 292, 294 - 295
Woods, Elaine W., 224

Y

Yale University, 157, 205, 224
Yiddish, 197, 199 - 200

Z

Z39, 31
Z39.2 (MARC), 3, 31 - 34, 178, 209, 308, 314
Z39.42 (summary holdings), 170
Z39.44 (serial holdings), 162, 170
Z39.57 (nonserial holdings), 170
Z39.64 (CJK character set) 195

About the Author

Walt Crawford is principal analyst for special projects at The Research Libraries Group, Inc. (RLG). He served as a liaison from RLG to the USMARC advisory group from 1981 to 1987 and as a MARBI member from 1985 to 1987. Mr. Crawford is active in the Library and Information Technology Association (LITA) of the American Library Association (ALA), serving on the LITA Board from 1988 to 1991 and as editor of the *LITA Newsletter* from 1985 to 1991. Mr. Crawford also edits *Information Standards Quarterly*, a publication of the National Information Standards Organization (NISO) that began in 1989. Mr. Crawford has written several books in the Professional Librarian series.

This book is set in Zapf Calligraphic, a type family created for Bitstream, Inc. by Hermann Zapf. Zapf Calligraphic is one of a series of Bitstream typefaces optimized for digital typography. Zapf based the design on his own classic Palatino, a type family designed with an eye toward the early Renaissance. With the exception of certain figures in chapter 2 and chapter 16, the book was prepared in its entirety using Ventura Publisher and a Hewlett-Packard LaserJet Series II printer.